"I'd recommend *Pitchers of Beer* highly to anyone who wants a well-written, well-documented history of what still stands for many as the true Golden Age of Seattle baseball." —Arne Christensen, Seamheads.com

"This book is entertaining, informative, and well researched. It's a minor-league *Ball Four*, from an era in which ballplayers' warts were invariably ignored in print. Even those who lived in Rainiers-era Seattle will be surprised to learn some of the things going on behind the scenes." —Dwight Perry, *Seattle Times* sports columnist

"For those who love the game of baseball for the game and the characters that have played throughout its history, this book will be a delight. If readers have fond memories of hometown teams, this book may cause them to walk down memory lane themselves." —Leslie Heaphy, *Arete*

"I've worn the Rainiers (Mariners throwback) uniforms. Readers will love Dan Raley's book." —Ken Griffey Jr.

"[A] wonderful tribute to Rainier lore." —John Vorperian, Southern New England Chapter SABR

"While I was first reading Dan Raley's wonderful history of the Seattle Rainiers, I thought it must rank as one of my two all-time favorite baseball books. Now, for the life of me, I can't seem to recall the title of the other one." —J Michael Kenyon, first *Seattle Post-Intelligencer* Mariners beat writer and talk radio host

PITCHERS

THE STORY OF THE SEATTLE RAINIERS

OF BEER

Dan Raley | PHOTOGRAPHS FROM THE DAVID ESKENAZI COLLECTION

UNIVERSITY OF NEBRASKA PRESS | LINCOLN AND LONDON

© 2011 by the Board of Regents
of the University of Nebraska

All rights reserved
Manufactured in the
United States of America
♾
Library of Congress
Cataloging-in-Publication Data

Raley, Dan.
Pitchers of beer : the story of the Seattle
Rainiers / Dan Raley, photographs from
the David Eskenazi Collection.
    p.   cm.
Includes bibliographical references.
ISBN 978-0-8032-2847-4 (cloth: alk. paper)
ISBN 978-0-8032-4085-8 (paper: alk. paper)
1. Seattle Rainiers (Baseball team)—History.
2. Pacific Coast League—History. I. Title.
GV875.S39R35 2011
796.357′6409797772—dc22
2010027932

Set in Quadraat by Bob Reitz.
Designed by Ray Boeche.

Contents

Preface   vii

1. Civic Duty   1
2. Sick and the Needy   15
3. Hutch, a Teen Idol   34
4. Turning Tigers Loose   58
5. The Babe   78
6. Balls and (Air) Strikes   90
7. Kewpie Dick   120
8. TV, Rajah, and Jungle Jim   135
9. Hutch Returns   167
10. The Secret Stairs   190
11. Man behind the Microphone   204
12. Major Intrusion   219
13. Joltin' Joe   245
14. Last At-Bat   270

Acknowledgments   293
Appendix: All-Time Roster   295
Bibliographical Essay   321

Preface

Dave Eskenazi and I were kids, five years apart, when we were drawn to Sicks' Stadium from opposing directions in Seattle. He resided in the south end; I lived in the northern part of the city. Independently, we both stepped inside this magical stadium for the first time in 1964, the final season for Emil Sick's Seattle Rainiers.

Eskenazi's interest in the local baseball team was given to him by his grandfather, Albert Alhadeff, and uncle, Leon Alhadeff. Albert Alhadeff operated a shoe repair business across the street from Seattle's Ambassador Hotel, a place frequented by Rainiers and visiting ballplayers, many of whom he befriended. Leon Alhadeff was simply a huge fan. Memories were handed down, generation to generation.

A young Eskenazi soaked up the lore and shared in his family's love for this team. In time, Eskenazi established his own Seattle business, providing financial services not all that far from where his grandfather had cobbled shoes. On the side, Dave built a unique collection of sporting memorabilia, artifacts, and heirlooms.

He filled his home with uniforms, photos, championship rings, and various keepsakes derived from all sorts of West Coast teams from all kinds of sports, with a notable emphasis on the Rainiers and Northwest baseball. His collection would spill into his office, ballpark museums, websites, and publications.

Years after the fact, Eskenazi became acquainted with the very same men his grandfather and uncle had discussed over dinner or in a moment of reflection, now personally hearing these players describe their swings and the way they used to throw a baseball.

The Rainiers entered my life at the same time my father left it. In 1963 I was nine when Bill Raley, who was commissioner of the Olympic National Park, an appointed judge, took me and the rest of my family to a Cheney Studs–Rainiers exhibition game in Port Angeles, my home at the time. My dad died the next day in a spectacular car accident. My last memories of him are at an Olympic Peninsula ballpark.

We moved back to Seattle, and one of my ways of coping with the loss of the most important man in my life was to head for Sicks' Stadium. I was never sad there. After the Rainiers had long disappeared, I played a high school game there. After it was torn down, I would become a *Seattle Post-Intelligencer* sportswriter and find myself seated at the ballparks that came next, the Kingdome and Safeco Field, covering the Seattle Mariners and some of the game's greatest players, in a sense getting called up to the big leagues. My dad would have been proud.

The book that follows is a five-year, collaborative effort

between Dave Eskenazi and myself. It has taken us to restaurants, taverns, and funerals. It sent my friend digging deep into his collection for valuable resource materials. It kept me prowling through newspaper archives and put me on the phone with dozens of former players as old as ninety-five.

We delighted over each new story that was uncovered and the manner in which it emerged, such as when the late Buddy Hancken bravely supplied details of the 1938 Fred Hutchinson trade that involved him while Hurricane Katrina bore down on his Texas home; relatives were on the way to evacuate him. We suffered together over the death of each Rainiers figure that took place during the process; when we called to request interviews with club executive Ralph Allen and pitcher Art Fowler, for example, their relatives tearfully informed us that they were in grave condition. Sadly, a dozen former players who were interviewed for this book have passed away without seeing the end result.

Telling the story of the Rainiers is our way of preserving an athletic civic treasure, something that meant as much to thousands of people in Seattle as it did to us. The words are mine. The photos are Eskenazi's. The team is yours to adopt or reclaim.

1. Civic Duty

On a Sunday afternoon in the middle of Seattle, a half-dozen federal agents piled out of cars and conducted a raid. Banking on the element of surprise, these men had told no other government agency what they were doing. That would explain why these dour, serious-minded law-enforcement types came face to face with a squadron of uniformed Washington State Patrolmen riding up on motorcycles, sirens blaring, moments later at the same address.

Both groups, unbeknownst to each other, had shown up with a similar purpose in mind: administer justice as swiftly and efficiently as possible. The ensuing scene was hectic, if not hilarious, with so many badge-carrying people scrambling around and aimlessly bumping into each other they could have held a cop convention. Certainly a dangerous criminal ring had to be the target of these competing operations: Counterfeiters? Gun runners? With the world turning more anxious each day, with war approaching, maybe it was foreign spies?

It was September 19, 1937, on an overcast day in the Northwest, when federal treasury agents briskly strode through the gates of the dilapidated Civic Stadium at the foot of Queen Anne Hill. They entered a well-worn baseball stadium, having determined that the Seattle Indians minor-league team was the one threatening the peace, putting everyone on high alert, and necessitating the swift police action.

The Indians were an unhappy, cash-strapped outfit, which, in compiling an 81-96 record and a fifth-place finish in the Pacific Coast League, hadn't seen this many eager and excited people together in the grandstands all season. Employees working the ticket windows were confronted between games of a season-ending doubleheader against the visiting Sacramento Solons. The feds demanded that outstanding admission taxes be handed over from the accumulated game receipts. They barely had time to identify themselves when the uniformed state patrol officers rode up in more pronounced fashion on behalf of the state tax commission. It seems the Indians were in arrears in paying all of their bills, and people representing different entities were trying to confiscate what they could.

"The feds beat us to it," one patrolman was overheard saying after rifling through an empty till. "Let's grab the bleacher gates." Ticket sellers at the Republican Street windows were approached next, and all of their cash was seized. It might have been the first legalized holdup staged in the city.

Sensing that the quest for available finances was quickly turning into a free-for-all, a member of a third public agency got involved. William "Wee" Coyle, a Civic Stadium administrator and a former University of Washington football quarterback, stuck his hand in a drawer and pulled out $190 for the city. This would pay off most of the team's outstanding stadium lighting tab. "Now you fellows can fight for the rest," Coyle teased the deputized bill collectors.

While much of the crowd of five thousand fans was oblivious to this frantic money grab, others wanted their designated cut. "Hey, what's going on here?" Sacramento manager Bill Killefer yelled from the field. "How about the 40 percent that belongs to us?" Getting no response, Killefer climbed into the stands in search of a lawyer to help the visiting team obtain its rightful portion of the suddenly dwindling gate intake, but his efforts were futile.

The three agencies retrieved what they thought were all of the available funds, but an Indians official had stuffed several bills into the uniform pockets of the team's first-base coach, hiding money in a place the others would never think to look for it—on the field. While all this haggling was going on over the stadium cash, there also was a heated attempt in the home clubhouse to cut team expenses.

Seattle pitcher Dick Barrett was in line for a $250 bonus if he won twenty games. The round-faced player had entered the season-ending doubleheader with eighteen victories, a commendable total that had brought him an earlier $250 stipend. In this time of rubber-armed pitchers, Barrett was set to throw both games, the second contest scheduled for seven innings following a regulation nine, in an attempt to achieve the maximum performance bonus.

Beleaguered Indians owner Bill Klepper, the man having all of the trouble settling up with his various creditors, ordered field manager Johnny Bassler not to use Barrett again after a 4–1 victory over the Solons in the first game. Money was the

•

Owner Bill Klepper's mismanagement of the Seattle Indians led to the creation of the Seattle Rainiers.

only reason for this decision, and the club officials came close to blows before Bassler shoved the angry Klepper out the door and proceeded to get his team ready for the second contest. The Indians' starting pitcher for the next game would remain the same, as would the outcome.

Winning 11–2 in the nightcap, Barrett had his twenty victories and collected his incentive money, which he eventually handed over to the supportive Bassler out of gratitude. Bassler was fired that night over the incident, but was likely out of a baseball job even if he had submitted and used different pitchers. Klepper emerged the next day with a black eye, compliments of an unnamed baseball player away from the park.

Rugger Ardizoia, a San Francisco Mission Reds pitcher who would play for Seattle more than a decade later, wasn't surprised when he heard about Klepper's last-day shiner. The Indians owner was known for reneging on his financial commitments to players or for paying them late. On an earlier trip to Seattle during that 1937 season, Ardizoia had seen irrefutable proof of this: "We went into the Gowman Hotel on Stewart Street, where we were staying, and a guy named [Bill] Thomas, a pitcher, was chasing Klepper around," he recounted. "Klepper was hanging onto a light fixture, yelling, 'Thomas is trying to kill me!' All Thomas wanted was his paycheck."

The law-enforcement raids at the ballpark were preceded by warrants filed by the state tax commission a week earlier for the collection of $5,395 in unpaid business and admission taxes, and were reported the following morning in a bold, banner headline stripped across the top of the *Seattle Post-Intelligencer* that declared: "G-Men Seize Ball Game Cash." Momentarily overshadowed was front-page news of a planned visit to Seattle, Bremerton Naval

Shipyard, and Bonneville Dam by President Franklin Roosevelt, who was on a speech-making crusade, pushing for his social reform, or what was described in wire-service stories as "his fight for liberal interpretation of the constitution." What was happening here was a baseball team going on welfare while the nation's leader was trying to pull the rest of the country off it.

As the authorities filed out of the ballpark with whatever loot they could find, bringing the 1937 season to a comical close, professional baseball in Seattle was listing badly. The local team was bankrupt, facing threatened eviction from Civic Stadium. The makeshift ballpark was a grassless field more suited for football, if not mud wrestling, and hardly something to fight over. Baseball was on life support.

The process by which Seattle reached this depressing stage, in which professional baseball had to fight for its survival, was predictable. The game had existed in the Puget Sound port for a half-century, surviving Washington's progress to statehood, a skyline-altering fire, World War I, Prohibition, and the Depression to field teams and stake an athletic foothold. There were several different versions of the team, among them the Chinooks, Giants, Purple Sox, Seattles, Siwashes, and Turks. These clubs won championships and built loyal followings, only to stumble financially and then disappear.

On May 24, 1890, the city's first pro baseball game was held in a newly assembled ballpark in Madison Park overlooking Lake Washington. A midafternoon encounter attracted 1,200 curious fans, with the hometown Seattles defeating Spokane 11–8. Many of the uniformed participants once had been big-league players, brought in from Chicago and other cities to provide high-level

Dan Dugdale, right, franchise owner and stadium builder, was an early proponent of pro baseball in Seattle.

competition for Seattle's pro sporting debut. However, the team, and the Pacific Northwest League it played in, folded within two years, providing nothing more than a starting point.

There were a few more aborted attempts to establish the game in the city before Daniel E. Dugdale arrived in 1898. A huge man, he was a former big-league player and a turn-of-the-century opportunist. He rearranged the Seattle baseball landscape to his liking. His teams had success, winning minor-league pennants in 1898, 1909, 1912, 1915, and 1918, yet his departure was as abrupt as anyone's.

His crowning moment was building Dugdale Park on Rainier Avenue. His most agonizing moment was having Dugdale Park, which he no longer owned at the time, disappear in flames. The handsome wooden stadium had opened in 1913 and catered to Seattle's baseball needs for more than two decades. With its double-decker grandstand, Dugdale Park was unique; nothing on the West Coast resembled it. And in the fire, nothing vanished quite as quickly as this place, either.

On July 4, 1932, the south Seattle baseball facility was reduced to ashes overnight. Dugdale Park went up in flames after the holiday doubleheader, and the plumes of its destruction could be seen for miles throughout the city. Fireworks hadn't done this damage. Three years later, serial arsonist Robert Driscoll would admit that he had torched the stadium, counting it among 115 fires he had set throughout the city. "I came home on an old streetcar and noticed all these black pieces of paper wafting around in the air, and it was the old ballpark burning down, just over the hill," said Vince O'Keefe, a Beacon Hill resident and later a sportswriter for Seattle's two largest newspapers.

Dugdale wasn't around to hear Driscoll's confession. On March 9, 1934, the baseball executive stepped off a curb in Seattle while heading to his parked car, hesitated for some reason, and was struck by a Seattle City Light truck. He was knocked to the ground at the intersection of Atlantic Street and Fourth Avenue South. He was sixty-nine when he died three hours later at Providence Hospital.

Seattle Indians slugger Mike Hunt liked Civic Stadium
so much he was married there.

Without Dugdale's shining baseball fortress, the sport began
to struggle for survival in the city. Games now had to be played
at Civic Stadium, a multipurpose athletic facility that rewarded
only the dead-pull hitter to left field. It was just 265 feet down
the line to hit one out, a mere pop-up away. Indians slugger
Art "Mike" Hunt—whose nickname, when used in conjunction
with his surname, resulted in an obscene baseball joke that
was also used to identify countless other players with the same

surname—took full advantage of the Civic short porch. He led or shared the team lead in homers each year from 1934 to 1937, crunching a career-high and league-best thirty-nine during the latter season. Hunt liked the stadium so much he got married at home plate before a 1937 game, with his baseball-themed wedding well publicized and well attended and turned into a Seattle social event.

Civic Stadium had little charm to it otherwise. Seats were nothing more than splintered old boards. Few offered backing. Lighting poles erected for football games were located just inside the left-field foul line, giving outfielders fielding obstacles they encountered nowhere else. When it wasn't muddy, the field was hard and unpleasant, full of rocks, and not the least bit conducive to baseball.

"If a horse got stranded out there, he would have starved to death," quipped Edo Vanni, a neighborhood kid who would become a regular inside the gates, first as a clubhouse attendant and then as a player.

Nothing worked right at Civic Stadium, at least in terms of baseball. Even Ted Williams, one of the game's greatest left-handed batters, made almost no contact at the place. Before becoming a Hall of Fame player for the Boston Red Sox, he was an outfielder for the 1937 San Diego Padres and suffered through two virtually hitless visits to the Seattle ballpark that season, collecting just three singles in twenty-five at-bats (.104) and one run batted in.

Baseball was struggling mightily in Seattle. Night games and radio coverage had given the professional sport a boost elsewhere around the country, but not in this faraway northwest city, which was slowly bouncing back from the double whammy of the Depression and Prohibition. It was enough to drive local fans to drink—or find a baseball owner who could cater to that urge.

As the 1937 season played out in a dismal manner, Klepper, the Indians' owner, announced two days before the end of the season that his besieged franchise was up for sale. "I have decided to accept a reasonable offer and retire to the grandstand where I can watch a game in comfort," he told reporters. Criticism of Klepper's baseball leadership had mounted around town after it was reported there had been season-long dissension on the team. In addition to the conflict over payment of players witnessed by Ardizoia in which Klepper was left hanging from a chandelier, the owner had, earlier in the season, fired the manager Spencer Abbott, before turning the team over to Bassler and then firing him after the final pitch.

On the day the 1937 season ended, Shirley Parker, owner of the Yakima and Spokane baseball teams in the lower-level Western International League, was singled out in the local newspapers as the most likely candidate to purchase the Indians. Yet when interviewed, Parker, who kept homes in Yakima and Seattle, was coy about a possible takeover. "Sure, I love baseball and I think somebody could make Seattle the best ball team in the minor leagues," he said. "But I already own a team, and it's a good one. I don't know whether the Seattle proposition would interest me."

Behind the scenes, Parker made an offer for the franchise but withdrew it when the stubborn Klepper turned martyr, waffling over giving up total interest. Lawsuits were filed against the ballclub, including one by Edward Gerrick and Herbert Pollock, who claimed they were owed $964 for unpaid construction work. The Seattle City Council voted to ban the baseball team from playing in the stadium the following season. Nothing more happened regarding the Seattle franchise ownership until early November, when the Pacific Coast League's winter meeting was held in San Diego. The first line of business was a stunner: Klepper was publicly ousted as owner, a move ordered by baseball commissioner Judge Kenesaw Mountain Landis and minor-league baseball president W. G. Bramham.

In a letter read to other PCL owners, Bramham charged Klepper with mismanaging the Seattle team. The league was prepared to take control of the franchise until new ownership was secured, with hints dropped of an unnamed buyer waiting in the wings, someone apparently willing to assume the $80,000 in debt besides offering a purchase price. The identity of this possible buyer was at that point a well-guarded secret. A day later, a contrite Klepper announced he had resigned as owner, citing health reasons, though his financial health was probably the more likely cause. The franchise would remain rudderless until two weeks before Christmas, when Seattle baseball fans finally learned the identity of the aforementioned mystery man.

In early December, brewery mogul Emil Sick stepped forward and revealed himself as the Indians' next owner. Sick was no stranger to Seattle, with his beer and surname practically synonymous. Powerful union leader Dave Beck and hometown gadfly Roscoe "Torchy" Torrance had encouraged Sick to get involved, as had the beer man's good friend, Col. Jacob Ruppert, the New York Yankees owner and a fellow beer producer. Sick was one of the few in his hometown who could afford a baseball team. While the rest of Seattle remained in economic recovery from the Depression, with unemployment topping out at 26 percent and a large "Hooverville" slum area still sprawling next to the downtown business corridor, the brewer had accumulated great sums of money by taking over the family business and expanding it into Canada. He sold the one thing everyone had to have during these still lean and difficult times—booze.

Sick's new acquisition was hardly on sound footing, but this was America's sporting passion, even in an isolated outpost such as Seattle, and someone had to rescue it. Besides, with the right guy running it, the franchise could hold promise. The Indians were a steady member of the eight-team Pacific Coast League, which had been in existence in some form since 1903. This was minor-league baseball, Class AA ball, the best the game had to offer to this largely undeveloped half of the United States, still an untapped sporting marketplace. None of the Major League teams in operation—eight in the American League, eight in the National League—were located west of St. Louis. The PCL mostly was a collection of California teams, with franchises in Los Angeles, San Francisco, San Diego, Hollywood, Sacramento, and Oakland, supplemented by Pacific Northwest entries in Seattle and Portland. Plenty of people in this region were willing to be entertained; they just needed something to get excited about.

Sick would set out to do what the Seattle Mariners pulled off nearly six decades later when the modern-day team took up residence in $550 million Safeco Field near the waterfront and trotted out such unforgettable players as Ken Griffey Jr. and Ichiro Suzuki: change ownership, build a new-age ballpark with all the amenities available, and put talented, fan-pleasing characters in uniform. Sick had resisted when approached in previous years to bail out the Indians, but now the situation had turned so dire the brewer felt compelled to get involved.

"The field was without grass and was certainly hard on the players' feet," Sick said. "We were in rather desperate times and in 1937 the club hit its lowest point. It was heavily burdened with debt. The city was being urged to put the club out of [Civic Stadium]. Of course, the club was in no financial condition to build a new park. I decided to do something about the situation."

The new owner's energy came at the city like a 100-mph fastball. He had no particular love for baseball, but he had money and was willing to spend it to address a pressing civic responsibility. He was a tough businessman who aimed high: he pursued and offered jobs to two of baseball's biggest names, Rogers Hornsby and Babe Ruth, hired one of them, and then eventually turned both of them away. He secured the reputation of Seattle as a serious baseball town, pointing it in the direction of the big leagues, though he didn't share in that eventuality. He took over a sporting entity that would mirror the growth and stagnant times of the city for nearly three decades, creating one of the nation's most successful and popular minor-league franchises, one that remains a huge part of his Seattle legacy.

Yet had Sick shaken one of his bottles of beer and sprayed it all over everyone as the calendar was set to leave 1937 behind, he couldn't have created more of a mess than the one he was entrusted with cleaning up. "When Mr. Sick bought that team, baseball was at rock bottom," said Vanni, who turned up on the Rainiers' payroll for much of the franchise's existence. "He was the savior of baseball in Seattle."

2. Sick and the Needy

After his 1937 franchise takeover, Seattle's new baseball proprietor turned up at a Pacific Coast League (PCL) meeting held in Sacramento, California, and introduced himself to one of his peers with a handshake and the words, "Sick here." To which the other man responded in wise-guy fashion: "I'm not feeling too well myself." Some easily could have questioned Emil Sick's sanity, if not his future health, for deciding to involve himself in Seattle's complicated baseball affairs.

Those who knew him understood. Sick enjoyed nothing better than taking a calculated risk. As a student at Stanford University in Palo Alto, California, he didn't always show up for class, and in the evenings he preferred to go gambling with friends rather than study for upcoming tests. The following day, the Tacoma native made the obligatory classroom appearance and aced those exams with ease. His scores were so high it was suggested to Sick that he become a chemist. To some degree, by later mixing

Beer brewer Emil Sick saved baseball in Seattle out of a sense of civic duty.

barley and hops together, he did. "He was brilliant, well to the point of genius, but a strong neurotic," said Diana Ingman, one of Sick's five children. "Nobody that brilliant is normal."

Sick, who didn't graduate from Stanford, could exhibit plenty of backbone, too. With the Nazis coming into power in the 1930s, he wanted a firsthand look at the turmoil boiling in his family's native Germany, and he impulsively boarded a steamship to Europe. Once there, he questioned the obvious mistreatment of Jewish citizens in a defiant manner. He spoke German and had no problem engaging anyone in heated discussion. Locals finally pulled him aside and suggested his outspoken ways had put him in considerable danger, with Hitler coming to power and squashing anyone else's opinion. He heeded this advice and toured elsewhere before returning home.

Sick had a zest for adventure and certain fearlessness. Whether it was in brewery business dealings or world affairs or baseball, he was a confident man, always in control. He was comfortable, if not driven, in building a more visible public profile. Privately, he had a nasty temper and could be unbending in negotiations, intimidating even to family members. In their nastiest confrontation, one that nearly drove a wedge between them, Sick and his father, Fritz, argued over the older man's subscription to *German American Bund*, a white supremacist and anti-Semitic magazine, before it was cancelled, to avoid business and social backlash.

"He was very demanding," said Sean Sheehan, one of Sick's grandsons and later a Seattle assistant city attorney. "He wanted his children and grandchildren to dress right. If not, he'd tell you that you looked like a bum. He was an old-fashioned guy. Emil was quite a formidable presence. When he was in a heavy brood, there was a palpable black air."

Ten days before Christmas in 1937, Sick demonstrated only his best qualities to a rapt audience of local newspaper reporters bent on quizzing him about his recent baseball acquisition for the first time. He was well organized and charming while fielding questions from all directions. The forty-three-year-old man promised a vibrant, generous leadership. He vowed to build a new ballpark with all of the latest conveniences. He planned to hire an accomplished field manager and acquire half a dozen new players, even prying some of his best ones from Seattle's neighborhoods.

Sick announced his team would be called "Rainiers." He would name it after his beer, which was named after the mountain, which was christened after a British explorer. He would not be the first to use this moniker, either for the team or for his beer: in 1919 and 1920, other Seattle baseball teams had called themselves Rainiers, and Rainier beer had been around since the 1800s. Sick's alcohol-inspired team also answered to an obvious pet nickname used by various newspaper headline writers: "The Suds." He made everyone in Seattle want a taste of whatever he was selling, by bottling and distributing baseball like no one before in the area.

All of this happened with the pledged support of his long-term brewery buddy Col. Jacob Ruppert, who doubled as owner of the New York Yankees. The two had become close friends in 1936 while serving on a brewery industry committee. Ruppert urged Sick to mix beer with baseball, telling him there was great fun to be had in this sporting venture, though not much money. The Yankees owner had attracted nationwide attention following his highly publicized contract haggling with one Babe Ruth. Ruppert suggested to his fellow brewer in the Northwest that their respective teams enter into a player-working agreement to assist Sick in stockpiling baseball talent. "My friend Jake Ruppert may help us, but I don't expect he'll let me have Joe DiMaggio," Sick wisecracked to reporters.

Money was of no concern to a man who had followed his

German-born and Canadian-raised father into the brewery business, and who preferred scotch over beer because it was the boardroom drink. He would occasionally sip his product, but only over lunch. By 1944, Sick had eleven plants under his direction, six in the United States and five in Canada, making him the world leader in this industry while producing more than a million barrels and $20 million in revenues per year. He was an aloof and aggressive businessman, much like the modern-day Bill Gates, similarly attempting to monopolize an industry with a product, created in Seattle, that was in great demand, and occasionally feeling compelled to push the law to do so. In 1941 Sick was the biggest name among dozens of people in the alcohol, tobacco, and fish trades who were lumped together in a federal grand jury indictment accusing them of price-fixing, a wartime issue later settled when President Franklin Roosevelt introduced price-ceiling laws.

"He was a capitalist, that's what he was, and he didn't apologize for it one bit," Sheehan said. "He was a financier and a businessman. Emil was not a fundamental brewer. He was a money guy."

Sick exhibited no fear when he assumed control of a Seattle baseball team riddled with debt. The Indians had attracted only 144,866 fans for the entire 1937 season and were on the verge of becoming homeless with the Civic Stadium eviction looming. Sick provided $200,000 up front, setting aside $25,000 to be used as working capital with the rest going toward unpaid bills. He came up with another $200,000 for a new stadium, handing over $40,000 to George Vanderveer, landowner of the Rainier Avenue site that once housed Dugdale Park, after briefly considering locations at the south end of Lake Union and in

Sicks' Stadium, shown in the mid-1940s, after name change from
"Sick's Stadium" to include the owner's entire family.

north Seattle near busy Aurora Avenue, or what was also known
as Highway 99. Sick's total franchise investment, according to
his memoir, was $650,000.

Most of the city's population base was centered in the north
end, but Sick's chief reason for building a baseball centerpiece
in Rainier Valley was for fan comfort. Temperatures at this site,
favored by local farmers because it was naturally shielded, would
be five to ten degrees warmer than in the north, with no Puget
Sound breeze swirling through stadium seats. The stadium was
built next to a tomato patch, and farms and gardens tended by
Italian immigrants filled the low-income neighborhood, which
was nicknamed "Garlic Gulch." Modest single-family homes were
interspersed among the sprawling agricultural activity, and baseball was something to break up the monotony, though the rural
setting quickly began turning to pavement soon after the addition
of Sick's ballpark on one end of the valley and the 1940 completion
of the Lake Washington floating bridge on the other.

On the front entrance of the finished product, everyone would know who built and owned the place: large lettering across the top of the ballpark announced the arrival of "Sick's Seattle Stadium." This name was later altered to "Sicks' Seattle Stadium" to recognize the entire Sick family, though the brewer could have called the facility anything he wanted. If it made money, he was interested. Sick transferred $1.5 million to a San Francisco brewery to reclaim the brewery naming rights to "Rainier," which previously had been a Seattle brand. This team had answered to "Indians" for seventeen seasons, so this rechristening took a little getting used to. Some fans welcomed the beer-related moniker, some didn't.

In a letter to the editor in the *Seattle Post-Intelligencer*, baseball fan James Campbell wrote, "Everybody is delighted with the new owners but I think the general public patronizes baseball because they love it and are not interested in seeing the Seattle club a walking advertisement for one of Mr. Sick's products. Jake Ruppert, the famous eastern brewer, didn't change the name of the New York Yankees. The Seattle team has been called Indians for fifteen years, and we fans don't think 'Rainiers' is any improvement." Responding to this indignant reader in one of his columns, *Post-Intelligencer* sports editor Royal Brougham said, "I don't care what they are called, as long as the team isn't so far behind that we have to call them bums by next July."

Under Sick's leadership, baseball in Seattle would come off the ventilator in no time. He made a succession of calculated hires, naming Jack Lelivelt, a man who had previously won multiple PCL pennants for the Los Angeles Angels, as his field manager; Bill Mulligan, a respected figure throughout the Oregon horse racing industry, as his business manager; and for vice president

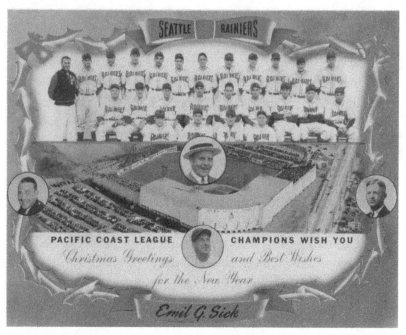

The Seattle Rainiers' 1940 Christmas card showed a championship team, ballpark, and front office staff.

choosing Torchy Torrance, a likeable little guy who stuck his nose in everything happening around town, particularly at his alma mater, the University of Washington. All were former baseball players who knew the game on an intimate level.

Sick put experienced people on the payroll and essentially got out of their way. He rarely visited the clubhouse. Players used to joke that he didn't know the difference between baseball and football. He often was spotted sitting in his box seat, cigar or cigarette in hand, reading a newspaper, hardly paying attention to the activity on the field and often leaving early for home.

Initially, not everything fell into place as smoothly as Seattle's new baseball leader wanted. Even with an accelerated winter construction plan drawn up by a Canadian company, the eagerly awaited Sicks' Stadium wasn't ready for use as promised when the 1938 season began. Another two months of work was needed to complete the mammoth job, so the Rainiers reluctantly headed back to hardscrabble Civic Stadium for their first two home stands. Considering that the new baseball owner had a surplus of money and was liberally spending it and paying bills, the city council offered no objections.

Early on, some local newspaper sportswriters still stubbornly insisted on calling the team "Indians" in print, unwilling to embrace change. The state liquor board registered its own concerns. Conscious of the alcohol connection Sick's ownership brought to baseball and its possible effect on impressionable young fans, the agency initially prevented Sick from placing a large, scripted "R" from his Rainier beer logo onto the flannel team uniforms. Early on, it was in block letters only across the front. That was okay with Sick. He had to be careful himself. He was hiring kids to do a man's job.

The new owner's earliest player moves were designed to encourage an emotional response from the city. In late January in 1938, the Rainiers signed pitcher Fred Hutchinson and outfielder Edo Vanni, close friends who had played the previous spring at Seattle high schools, Franklin and Queen Anne, respectively. They were both eighteen. They each briefly attended the University of Washington (UW). Vanni already had been a ballpark fixture, a neighborhood kid working as Civic Stadium clubhouse help. Top local prospects rarely stuck around to play pro ball in their hometown Seattle, but these two were bound to Rainiers contracts within a forty-eight-hour period.

Considered a can't-miss player, Hutchinson accepted a $2,500 bonus and the promise of 20 percent of the sale price over $10,000 from any future Rainiers transaction sending him to a Major League team. He put his initial money toward a college education, specifically a business degree. He rejected solid offers from the Cleveland Indians and Detroit Tigers to start his pro baseball career in his hometown. The New York Yankees had rejected his father's request for a $5,000 signing bonus for his son. Detroit's best offer was $4,000 and a scholarship allocation to attend the UW, but the Hutchinson family said no thanks.

Vanni received more money from the Rainiers, though he was the lesser talent of the two. In his Italian immigrant family, the situation was stickier: his mother wanted him to stay in school and his father had suffered a stroke, and the kid needed extra incentives to sign. An impressive gathering of the city's sporting literati, summoned by the baseball team and the university, filed into the offices of Western Printing at 2100 5th Avenue in downtown Seattle to discuss the prospect, with half bent on facilitating a deal and the other intent on squelching one. In attendance were Vanni, accompanied by Bobby Morris, a respected sports referee and family friend who was designated as Vanni's legal guardian; Sick, who was joined by Mulligan, his general manager; Jim Phelan, the University of Washington's veteran football coach; and Torrance, who had competing interests, given that he doubled as a Rainiers club executive and an enthusiastic UW football supporter. As the Western Printing owner, Torrance facilitated the meeting.

Vanni had enjoyed a successful UW freshman football season as a quarterback and kicker for a 6-0 team. In a scrimmage against the varsity, he had impressed Phelan with an improvised thirty-yard touchdown run, turning a fumbled snap on a field-goal attempt into an instant score. He had converted ninety-seven of one hundred extra-point kicks in a recent football practice. The coach envisioned the player's broken-field runs and fiery leadership taking the Huskies to a Rose Bowl or two.

Sick wanted this competitive, 5-foot-8, 163-pound athlete from Queen Anne for Seattle's minor-league baseball team. He identified Vanni as an automatic fan attraction as he reorganized the ballclub. The tug-of-war began in earnest. The Rainiers offered Vanni $400 per month and a $5,000 bonus to sign. The Huskies were paying him $185 per month as a scholarship football and baseball player. With everything laid out before him, Vanni addressed his questions to the baseball people.

"Let me ask you this," the resourceful athlete said to Sick. "The club was in last place the year before, and if we win the pennant, can I get an extra $300?

"If I hit .300, can I get $300?

"If I score 100 runs, can I get $300?

"If I play in 175 games, can I get $300?"

The baseball men momentarily were taken aback, but they agreed on everything Vanni had proposed. Yet more negotiations were needed. Morris inquired about further sweetening the deal on the versatile athlete's behalf, and the referee and Sick retired to another room. In their private exchange, it was agreed that Vanni would receive one thousand shares of Rainier beer stock for every year he played for the team.

Vanni still needed to sleep on the offer. The Huskies were the number one game in town at the time, and walking away from them would not be easy. Aware of this, the UW football coaches were confident that Vanni wouldn't leave them behind. But after mulling his prospects at the Doghouse Restaurant in downtown

Edo Vanni was a personable player from Seattle
who was an obvious gate attraction.

Seattle that night, and hearing his mother sob at the prospect
of him leaving college early, he did just that. He called everyone
and told them of his immediate plans to become a professional
baseball player. "Phelan was really pissed off," Vanni said.

The longest-running baseball relationship in Seattle was now
firmly cemented. Vanni, the one-time clubhouse attendant,
would become a Rainiers right fielder, and later a first-base
coach, publicist, field manager, and then general manager for
Seattle's various minor-league franchises. He would also help
usher in big-league baseball while installed in a front-office
marketing job with the Seattle Pilots three decades later. The
first set of high-stakes negotiations involving one of the city's
sporting heroes had just played out, and baseball had won.
Vanni was a slap hitter similar to Ichiro Suzuki, the right fielder

for the Mariners in the early twenty-first century, only he came to the ballpark each day with more of an edge to him than the reticent Japanese player, and he spoke Italian. He was a randy brawler as a player and was repeatedly ejected from games as a manager. He knew how to get on the nerves of opposing crowds or incite his followers, by pulling out a red flag and waving it in their direction.

Vanni's aggressive style had its drawbacks, though. He irritated people, always chirping away and trying to get under someone's skin. He was famous for starting a fight and letting others settle it. Understood was the unwritten rule that the last guy joining a ballpark fracas had to buy everyone beer later. Once, a fight broke out while he was urinating in the clubhouse, causing the late-arriving Vanni, pants zipper down, to trip a teammate on purpose so he could avoid paying the alcohol tab.

Vanni also was prone to injuries, beaned so severely as a rookie by an infield throw from San Diego pitcher Manuel Salvo that he spent four days in a California hospital. He was hit in the head while running between first and second base in the fourteenth inning, but kept on going and scored the tying run before collapsing at home plate. There was no indication that Salvo had thrown with malicious intent, but it wouldn't have surprised anyone if he had. Eighteen years later, when Vanni was a first-base coach for the Rainiers, another opposing player's throw beaned him in the head; maybe an unfortunate coincidence, maybe not.

"Edo was in there with a lot of mouth," said catcher Bob Stagg, who would know: he was a teammate with Vanni when playing for the Rainiers and Queen Anne High, although the two were never buddies.

"He could be a huge pest," confirmed Rod Belcher, an early Rainiers fan and later the team's play-by-play radio and TV broadcaster.

Vanni was so feisty as a baseball player that his wife, Margaret, joked he could start a fight in an empty room. However, he was just what Sicks' Stadium needed, because things weren't going to be boring with him on the field, and he was one of the reasons the new ballpark wouldn't be empty when it opened. More than anyone, he would serve as the face of the franchise for the next seven decades, well after it had disappeared. The new owner would never regret handing over all those closed-door incentives to little Edo Vanni.

Everything Sick had promised as the new leader of the franchise came together at midseason on June 15, 1938: The stadium was unveiled to rave reviews, with more than thirteen thousand curious fans showing up for a 2:30 p.m. game against the Portland Beavers. Another three thousand sat on a ridge outside the left-field fence and watched for free, able to see everything except balls hit to the outfielder directly below them, enjoying a bargain vantage point that would become known as "Tightwad Hill" or "Cheapskate Hill."

Everyone was struck how airy and cheerful the ballpark was. On the field, a police band played and speeches were made. Vanni did his own christening: he picked up the first hit, stolen base, and run recorded in the new digs, creating history, though it wasn't enough to affect the outcome that day. The Rainiers lost, 3–1. "This park is a dream," gushed John Rosen, a man seated in a front-row seat for the historic opener. Fans sat closer to the action than at most ballparks. The new place was both tempting and impossible for the average hitter, measuring 335 feet down each foul line and 415 to the deepest part. The field was immaculately groomed, with countless players describing it as the best surface any of them had encountered in pro ball, including the big leagues. Everything was so shiny and positive that the Rainiers immediately built a huge following, achieving attendance numbers that would reverberate nationwide.

The team would become a needed part of the city's social fabric, a unifying force for an isolated baseball town in an unknown part of the country. People everywhere in the city tuned into the game on warm summer nights: whether in Ravenna or West Seattle, no one would miss a pitch. Popular Rainiers radio broadcaster Leo Lassen, a holdover from the Indians and not nearly as noticeable before, somehow was inside nearly every house now, his distinctive voice echoing through open windows and out onto the street, the sound of it becoming synonymous with baseball success. If you stopped at a stoplight, chances were that your car radio had the game on, as did the car behind yours, and the one behind that. If you entered any downtown restaurant or tavern, a healthy serving of Lassen and the Rainiers would be delivered alongside whatever else you had ordered, since descriptions of the ballpark activity continually echoed through most night spots. Practically overnight, Rainiers baseball had woken up a depressed, slumbering town.

The experience of Addis Gutmann's family was typical of those endearing times. His parents and another family shared four box seats at the new ballpark, and Gutmann, a strident Rainiers fan and later a civic leader and a popular Seattle youth league baseball coach, attended perhaps sixty-five games per year. His girlfriend and eventual wife, Leatrice DeLeon, sat in another set of box seats with her family. If Gutmann couldn't sit in his seats, he sat in hers. "People accused me of that's why we were dating," he said.

Many fans rode a city bus, the "7 Rainier," to the ballpark, taking a mesmerizing, meandering route through the heart of this suddenly baseball-crazed city. The bus started in north Seattle, rolled down Third Avenue, made a left turn on Jackson Street, zigzagged through the International District, and took a right turn on Rainier Avenue, which fed into Sicks' Stadium. Kids who showed up without a parent in tow, and there were many of these liberated young fans, had to campaign a little harder to get inside. You had to approach another adult cold, a stranger at that, and ask him or her to accompany you through the turnstiles, which wasn't a difficult task, or even a scary thing to do, in this safe, festive environment.

Bob Moliter, even at the young age of ten, was one of the 7 Rainier regulars during the war years. With his mother's permission, he caught the bus with his boyhood chums at the intersection of Northeast Fifty-fifth Street and Twenty-fifth Avenue Northeast in Seattle's Ravenna district. Moliter and his north-end friends would purchase the least-expensive bleacher tickets sold and hand them over at the turnstile, skirt across the cement concourse of Sicks' Stadium, eyeball the players' photos hanging on the walls, smell the ballpark aromas of hotdogs and popcorn, and then scramble up the stairway and into a baseball wonderland. "I would stare blankly at the most beautiful sight my young eyes had ever seen," Moliter said.

Before him was a lush green baseball field, a frenzy of concession hawker activity with their auctioneer pitches competing for business, and a glistening Mount Rainier propped up as a snow-covered backstop beyond the outfield walls. "There are not many places you can look out at the center-field fence and see a mountain," observed Merlin Nippert, a Rainiers pitcher in 1962–64 and Oklahoma flatlands native. The sounds were as memorable as the scenery, with fans craning their necks whenever a particular heavyset Italian vendor would shuffle past, calling out, "Ladies and gentlemen, get the beer that made Emil Sick!" or when one of his cohorts cradling another bin would chortle, "Hotdogs thick and greasy, go down easy!" Cowbells clanged throughout the stands.

Rainiers baseball became a weeklong adventure, a seven-game series against one opponent. Monday was an off day. Tuesday was the opener. Saturday was a huge draw. Sunday was the closing afternoon doubleheader. The team usually was home for two weeks and then gone for two. It was so detached from the eastern baseball front, the Pacific Coast League tried to pass itself off as a third Major League, but there was a difference. The Seattle ballclub and its competing franchises were built around career minor leaguers, players either on their way up or down, who wouldn't stay long in the Majors. These familiar faces would remain with Rainiers teams for years, creating natural rivalries, long-term fan clubs and a cross-generational interest in the game.

"Entire families were raised on baseball, and there would be a half a mile of people trying to get in," Vanni said. "You'd walk around those people and they would know you, and it would make you feel good."

"They were like movie stars to us," said Leatrice Gutmann, the other half of that romantic liaison enhanced by Rainiers season tickets.

After three hours of sacred activity between the lines, the lights were turned down and satisfied people filed out of Sicks' Stadium, listening to a recorded version of "God Bless America" sung by Kate Smith, the music echoing through the ballpark over the public-address system and out into the city.

A night at the ballpark was now great fun for everyone. Sick had made it entertaining and provided summertime heroes for everyone to latch onto. As Seattle took an increasing interest in Sick's team, the fans grew attached to a long list of creatively christened players. Among their favorites, by name alone, were Dick "The Needle" Gyselman, "Coffee Joe" Coscarart, Bill Schuster "the Rooster" (also known as "Broadway Bill" Schuster), Alan "Inky" Strange, Paul "Pops" Gregory, Bill "High Pockets" Lawrence, "Farmer" Hal Turpin, and, best of all, the man in the middle of the Seattle Indians' last-ditch cost-cutting efforts, Tracey "Kewpie Dick" Barrett.

Most who filled out Rainiers uniforms were big-league rejects and well-traveled players. Mike Hunt, the man renamed for poetic reasons, played for six different teams during the 1933 season alone. Among them were the big-league Boston Braves, and the Bay Area–based Missions, Oakland, Atlanta, Harrisburg, and San Francisco in the minors. In his unique way of thinking, the slugger never got a real chance to stick in the Majors with the Braves due to wardrobe restraints: "Because the pants they gave me were too tight and small, I was afraid to extend myself," Hunt explained in his Seattle media guide biography.

No one roaming the ballpark seemed to notice the talent differential between the Rainiers and the faraway big-league teams, least of all Dan Evans, who, as a youngster, was a Sicks' Stadium devotee during that first season, and later grew up to be the governor of the state of Washington. "When Sick came along, that was like the Major Leagues," Evans said. "That was a real jump in Seattle's growth. He sold a lot of beer, but it created a lot of kids who suddenly said, 'We're winners.'"

The new owner gave his fans, young and old, one player to worship more than any other, a Rainiers pitcher who was one of them, born and raised in Seattle. He was briefly called "The Iceman," a nickname that he barely acknowledged and one that didn't stick. Everyone else knew him as Hutch.

3. Hutch, a Teen Idol

Growing up as a doctor's kid during the Depression years, Fred Hutchinson should have leaned to the soft side. He should have acted as if he were someone of absolute privilege. He should been able to snap his fingers and get anything he wanted. Instead, on the baseball field Hutch came at you as if he hadn't eaten in a week, as if his father hadn't worked in six months. He always appeared hungry and angry. On cue, Hutch was the mistreated one, serving up a message pitch.

"If any batter walked into the batter's box and dug a hole for his right foot, for better leverage, the first pitch would probably be under the batter's chin," said J. B. Parker, Hutchinson's first catcher at Seattle's Franklin High School in 1935. "He never allowed anyone to dig in against him. I would give him a signal. I would snap my fingers together."

Hutchinson played baseball in a simmering rage. He did everything that way when a winner and loser were to be determined.

No one ever felt comfortable stepping in to hit against him. The right-hander, the least educated man in his family but quite possibly the most determined, wouldn't permit it under any circumstance.

"He was tough, hard-nosed tough; he was known for being mean tough," said Walt Milroy, a 1937 all-city first baseman and a frequent opponent from crosstown rival Roosevelt High School. "You hated him when you played against him."

Hutchinson never said anything on the mound. He just glared, trying to intimidate people. The only real gauge of his mental state was his face. When his intensity level went up, his small mouth would pucker up, breaking into all sorts of contortions.

"Off the field, Hutch was pretty well under control, a nice fellow, sociable as hell," said Len Tran, a Franklin High batboy and later a Rainiers utility player. "When he got on the baseball field, he was really different. He was almost growling at hitters when they came up."

With powerful shoulders and a small waist, Hutch filled out a Franklin jersey that had a huge green crest stitched on the front and the letter F in the middle, but no number across the back. He pitched his teams to a pair of city championships. He threw a no-hitter against Ballard High and helped the Quakers crush Broadway 32–4. Twice singled out as an all-city pitcher, he had this competitive thing down.

Hutchinson's emotions swung wildly, his mood moving from insufferable to enjoyable and back, always turning on and off. The pitcher was an accomplished prankster who took his jokes to the extreme, always determined to get a big laugh. After his Seattle-based Palace Fish Company team lost the championship game of the 1934 American Legion national tournament in Topeka, Kansas, Hutchinson entertained J. B. Parker and the rest of his teammates back at the hotel by impishly dropping water-filled balloons out a window, aiming for people walking on the street below. That night, he also stole a straw hat that belonged to his coach, Ralph "Pop" Reed, and fed it into a circulating fan, shredding it. He was someone who, in a crowd, would boldly reach around a friend and pinch a woman on her backside then watch with great delight when his unfairly accused buddy was slapped.

Family ties and friendships were tested if the persons concerned ever showed up on the other side of the diamond from Hutchinson. No one wearing a different uniform was cut any slack. Competitive lines were always drawn. After joining a Yakima semipro team, Hutchinson went up against a Renton ballclub that had his brother Jack and good buddy Edo Vanni in the lineup. Vanni was knocked to the ground with Hutch's first pitch, but he reached base with a single. Jack Hutchinson hit the dirt with the first pitch he saw, but he singled off his brother, too, scoring Vanni. The game ended 1–0, leaving a silent, brooding Fred Hutchinson. "In the car, Fred never said a word to us on the way home," Vanni said.

The Rainiers had to have this confident kid with the hound-dog profile and the fierce Doberman bite. They signed him six months after he graduated from Franklin High School. Big-league teams were after him, too. It helped that the local baseball club and the newly constructed Sicks' Stadium were stationed just six miles from the pitcher's family home in Rainier Beach.

For what he did over the next six months, Hutchinson became

As a rookie pitcher for the Rainiers in 1938, Fred Hutchinson was forced to wear an old Seattle Indians uniform during spring training.

a Seattle legend and a permanent part of the city's sporting folk-lore. His name and image now appear in more places than those of any other local athlete or coach: prominently on a modern-day cancer facility, subtly on the end of each row of seats at modern-day Safeco Field, and nearly forgotten on a south-end playfield.

He was sensational throughout the summer of 1938, with the notable exception of his disastrous professional debut in San Diego on the second day of the season.

On April 3, 1938, Hutch was pulled after facing just six batters and registering a solitary out, protected by his wise handlers. Nerves had got the best of this otherwise steely personality. He was just eighteen, trying to act tough, but making a big transition, too. He returned to the mound two days later and fared much better, throwing three-hit ball over seven innings at Oakland, though he didn't figure in the decision. He was now on a roll that would mesmerize his hometown and the league throughout the summer.

Overnight, Hutchinson became a Seattle sensation, with people anxiously staring and pointing at him wherever he wandered away from the ballpark. He had pinpoint control and that tough-guy attitude rather than a smoking fastball or overpowering stuff. Piling up victory after victory, Hutch's scheduled outings, at home and on the road, became must-see events, circled on the calendar by both big-league scouts and curious fans. He put all of his well-rounded baseball talents on display in his sixth and final Civic Stadium appearance. On May 27, he pushed his pitching record to 7-3 and singled, doubled, and homered in a 19–4 rout of the San Francisco Seals.

"When Hutch was pitching, we'd go to every game we could," said Keith Sherlie, then a University of Washington student from Snohomish and a serious baseball fan who had grown up a few blocks from Hall of Fame player Earl Averill but now had a new hero. "We'd get into a car caravan just to watch him pitch."

Hutchinson could turn gunslinger when pressed, adding to his growing baseball allure. In the first game of a June 6 doubleheader in Portland, with Cleveland Indians scout Cy Slapnicka taking copious notes on him in the stands, the youngster suddenly walked off the mound. He had found himself in trouble against the Beavers in the eighth inning. To calm himself, Hutchinson pulled a big-league move, nonchalantly calling for a timeout and striding to the Seattle dugout. A concerned Rainiers manager Jack Lelivelt approached him in a hurry and asked if there was anything wrong. "I'm thirsty," Hutch replied sternly. "I want a drink of water." There was more to it than that. Hutchinson was composing himself the only way he knew how. The rookie pitcher took a sip, swished it around his mouth, and spit it out, all along measuring his dilemma and considering his options. Then, he headed back to the mound, got out of the jam that had permitted two runs to score, and finished off a 7–3 victory over the Beavers.

"He had tensed up and he was trying to decide which pitch to make," recounted Vanni, who played in right field during both games of the doubleheader. "He had to take some time before making the next pitch, and he didn't have time out there. He didn't just throw it out there."

Hutchinson and Sicks' Stadium were made for each other. On June 16, the initial night game in the ballpark, the rookie took to the new mound for the first time and beat Portland, 7–0, picking up his tenth pitching victory with a six-hitter. On July 1, ten thousand people turned out in Rainier Valley to watch the teenager earn his twelfth victory in seventeen decisions, beating the Hollywood Stars, 5–4, in ten innings.

Six days later in San Diego, Hutchinson used his arm and bat to defeat the San Diego Padres, 2–1, in the second game of a doubleheader, throwing a six-hitter and doubling home the

Cover of the Rainiers program sold on the night of August 12, 1938, when Fred Hutchinson secured his nineteenth pitching victory on his nineteenth birthday.

winning run in the seventh and final inning. He won his four-teenth game in a 15–3 rout at Hollywood, at one point opposing Stars rookie reliever Ralph Hutchinson, who was no relation. People had to see Seattle's unstoppable pitcher. A crowd of thirteen thousand filled the seats in Sicks' Stadium to watch Hutchinson collect win number fifteen, an 8–3 decision over the Oakland Acorns, leaving him with a 5-0 record in July.

On August 2, Hutchinson lost for the first time in five weeks, 5–2, to the Portland Beavers, before a hometown gathering of 12,657. He threw a shutout for the first five innings, but was touched for four runs in the sixth, when future Rainiers manager Bill Sweeney rapped out a two-run single to ignite the scoring. Getting a second chance against the Beavers at home a few days later, Hutch earned win number eighteen with a 7–5 victory in the opening game of a fight-filled doubleheader.

None of Hutchinson's trips to the mound in Seattle was more memorable than his August 12 outing, which happened to fall on his birthday, a coincidence that was widely publicized because of the matching numbers involved: fans were invited to come see Hutch turn nineteen and win his nineteenth game. He held off the San Francisco Seals, 3–2, and everyone in town wanted to blow out the candles. A bustling crowd of 16,354—the largest of the season, and one that held up as the Rainiers' all-time attendance best for a single game—squeezed into the 14,600-seat ballpark for the fun-filled occasion. A pregame skit, dignitary introductions, a table filled with gifts, a ballpark serenading of the player, and a home-plate cake presented by two batboys made the teenager blush preceding the nerve-wracking nine innings. It also was publicized that a pair of scouts, Jack Doyle of the Chicago Cubs and Harold Ireland of the Cleveland Indians, would be in the stands for the game, which wouldn't start until 8:30 p.m.

Dan Evans, the future governor, was among those left spellbound by the ballpark birthday celebration. Just twelve years old at the time, Evans sat in center field with his father and two brothers—and their seats actually were in center field. With so many fans intent on attending the special game and Rainiers management wanting to accommodate every last customer and rake in as much pay as possible, the outfield was roped off and the field temporarily shortened. This gesture later was repeated for other must-see Rainiers games. No fan would be turned away, the club promised, and Evans and others occupied grass seats, watching the game from makeshift rows that went four deep, with any balls hit into the crowd designated as ground-rule doubles.

With all of this attention directed his way, Hutchinson was noticeably nervous while opposing the veteran Lou Koupal, a former Seattle Indians pitcher. His jittery state caused his father, Dr. Joseph Hutchinson, to remark afterward, "I almost thought Freddie wasn't going to make it." Of course, that drinking fountain was never far away if the pitcher needed it.

Five days after his ballpark birthday bash, young Hutchinson beat the Sacramento Solons at home, 9–0, logging his twentieth victory and fifth shutout in his most complete performance of the season. He struck out twelve and induced eleven batters to fly out, allowing just three hits and a walk. That was only half of it. Always a good hitter swinging from the left side, he went 3-for-3 with a walk, furnishing a home run, four runs batted in, and three runs scored. In the next morning's edition, the *Post-Intelligencer* reported the following: "Fred Hutchinson 9, Sacramento 0."

In his next start, Hutch hurt the Solons from both ends again. In the first game of a doubleheader, he collected pitching victory number twenty-one by allowing six hits and striking out eight in an 8–2 decision. At bat, he went 3-for-3, driving in three runs and doubling twice, making him 6-for-6 with seven RBI for the week. More scouts were eyeballing him that night, including Jack Fournier of the St. Louis Browns, Ernie Johnson of the Boston Red Sox, and Cleveland's Ireland. Fournier previously had played for a Seattle baseball team in the Northwestern League, while Johnson was a former manager of the Seattle Indians.

Johnson told reporters that he had tried hard to sign the kid straight out of Franklin High School but couldn't make a breakthrough. "You fellows are laughing because [you think] we Major League scouts passed up on Hutch, but you're wrong," the Red Sox scout said, setting the record straight. "I wore out a new pair of shoes trying to sign the kid. But his dad was too tough for me. I couldn't close a deal."

Now that Hutchinson was in a Rainiers uniform, a midseason debate centered on whether he should strive to be a pitcher or, considering his obvious bat prowess, an everyday player. San Francisco Seals manager Lefty O'Doul, a two-time National League batting champion and later a Rainiers manager, noted that Hutch was one of the more natural hitters he had encountered in the Pacific Coast League. It also was mentioned by others that Babe Ruth had started out as a successful pitcher before wisely deciding to concentrate on hitting and making a comfortable living. Either way, Seattle's 6-foot-2, 220-pound teen idol was on a fast track to the big leagues. His fastball still wasn't overpowering, but he threw hard enough, had pinpoint control, and again took great pains to protect the plate.

Hutch roomed with Vanni, which was a good thing, as it allowed two intensely competitive guys to push each other nonstop. They'd go over opposing batters on days that Hutchinson pitched, sharing insights. They'd watch each other's back on the field, sharing in insults. "He was so tough," said Vanni, who missed the first month of his rookie season with a torn thigh muscle but batted .301 when he came back. "They used to knock me down and he'd say, 'Wait until that sonofabitch's best hitter comes up and I'll knock him down for you.'" After losing to San Francisco one night, Hutchinson took out his frustration on the covered ramp to the clubhouse. He broke every light in the tunnel. His path of destruction didn't stop there: "We couldn't find the way to the clubhouse," Vanni said, humored by the memory. "Inside the clubhouse, all the bats were on the floor."

As August pulled to a close, Hutchinson had become a full-blown curiosity up and down the coast. In San Francisco, eighteen thousand people—the league's largest crowd of the season—turned out on a Friday night at Seals Stadium to see the pitcher pick up his twenty-second victory. There were plenty of distractions during the game, including what was described in a newspaper report as "a near riot" when a hometown player, Harley Boss, was called out in a close fifth-inning play at first base. Hutch was not at his best against these guys, but he toughed it out, went the distance, and got credit for a 7–6 win.

The Seattle ace picked up his twenty-third win at Hollywood, prevailing 9–2 in the first game of a doubleheader. A week later on September 4, he collected his twenty-fourth victory in a 6–1 decision at Sicks' Stadium against the same Stars in the opener of another two-game set. There were thirteen thousand fans in the seats, including New York Yankees scout Joe Devine, who had managed an earlier Seattle minor-league team and years later would apply for the Rainiers' top dugout job again. Devine said he was impressed by the kid pitcher, especially his increasing popularity. "He looks awfully good to me and what a drawing card," the Yankees talent scout remarked to the press gathering. "Why, the fellow is as great a turnstile attraction as Babe Ruth, comparatively speaking."

On September 11, Hutchinson picked up number twenty-five—his eighth consecutive pitching victory and final one of the glorious summer—in a 7–2 decision over Hollywood. A crowd of 15,710 people jammed into Sicks' Stadium to see him beat the Stars for the third time in eleven days, all in doubleheader openers. On a warm Sunday afternoon, fans lined both foul poles and, in a scene more resembling a picnic gathering than a baseball game, again were seated in rows four and five deep in a roped-off outfield. Contributing to the team's expanding profile, the twin-bill sweep allowed the Rainiers to pull within two games of the first-place Los Angeles Angels.

Unfortunately, Hutchinson was beaten in his final regular-season outing, a surprising outcome for the 14,498 fans that congregated at the Seattle ballpark. They had come to expect dominance. It was September 16, and he lost 6–1 to San Diego, serving up four ninth-inning runs in what had been a closely contested outing but one that got away from him late. The regular-season statistical line was stunning for the teenager: a 25-7 record, 2.48 earned run average, 145 strikeouts, and 99 walks. Behind Hutch's lead, the Rainiers did everything except win the Pacific Coast League pennant that first season. They compiled a 100-75 record, leaving them three and a half games behind the pennant-clinching Los Angeles in the final standings, likely just another bat shy from winning it all.

In the President's Cup series that followed, Hutch opened the four-team postseason playoffs against third-place San Francisco, and the outcome was equally disconcerting to Rainiers loyalists. He lost again, 4–2, to the Seals. It was the first time all season he had dropped consecutive outings, and it was the first time in four decisions that he had come up a loser to San Francisco. No one was saying it, but the teenager's arm might have been weary. Counting his President's Cup starts, he would surpass three hundred innings in that first pro season. Hutch's magical run ended on yet another sour note when he lost the next time out, too, falling 5–4 to the Seals in the Bay Area. The second-place Rainiers had been eliminated from the playoffs in five games.

The late-season slump, however, did nothing to diminish the high regard for Hutchinson. He completed thirty-one of thirty-seven pitching starts. He was named Pacific Coast League and *The Sporting News* minor-league players of the year, and his services now were available to the highest bidder. He was widely regarded as baseball's most desirable young prospect, and everyone inquired about him and measured his possibilities. Throughout the season, he constantly had been compared to Bob Feller, another nineteen-year-old pitcher who threw harder and already was playing in the big leagues for the Cleveland Indians. To settle the intrigue on that point, an October exhibition game featuring the two strong-armed and fresh-faced pitchers was arranged in Seattle. It settled nothing. It was more carnival than competition. In front of a crowd of six thousand at Sick's Stadium, Hutchinson gave up six runs, Feller five, in a sloppily played game won by Hutch's side, 9–8.

Pacific Coast League players claimed that Hutchinson's unique windup distracted them as much as anything. They referred to his motion as a double hitch or a double pump, if not a convulsive move. Illusion seemed to be as important as location for his plate offerings. "He would go down, come up and go down again," said Eddie Carnett, who pitched against Hutchinson as a member of the Los Angeles Angels before joining the Rainiers after the homegrown pitcher had left for the Majors. "He was a veteran pitcher when he came out of high school. I thought his windup was unusual, but it was something he did natural. Everybody in the league was talking about him. I was pulling for him, being a young guy myself."

People in Seattle urgently wanted to hear all of Hutchinson's pitching secrets. Near the end of that 1938 rookie season, he sat down and shared them in a lengthy newspaper interview—which was rare for any athlete back then—with Leo Lassen, who doubled as the Rainiers' play-by-play radio broadcaster and the *Seattle Post-Intelligencer* baseball writer. Describing his pitching routine, the pitcher spoke confidently without sounding boastful. "Seldom do I throw the ball as hard as I can, only when I am in trouble," Hutchinson said, explaining that he used a one-finger grip across the seam. "You think it's silly, but sometimes that plate looks so close that I could touch it. That's when I know I'll have my control. Sometimes it looks a block away."

He revealed that he didn't like pitching in San Francisco, because the wind and the cold left him sore and stiff. He warmed up for just twelve to fifteen minutes before a game, or enough to get a sweat going. He admitted to slapping his thigh nonstop when he felt edgy on the mound.

"I prefer to use my fastball in the tight spots because I have a lot of confidence in it when I have control," he told Lassen. "I see where a lot of the boys don't think so much of my curve ball. Don't worry about that, because I can throw it when I want to. When I get that slide on the ball, I don't have any trouble with it."

Hutch said he tried to save his arm whenever he got a big lead. He confided that he was working on a changeup. He also had a team preference at the next level after he was done playing for the hometown Rainiers. He wanted to wear pinstripes. "As for the future, of course, I want to go to the big leagues some time," he said. "I'd like to pitch for those New York Yankees, if I make the grade."

Eleven of the sixteen big-league teams sent scouts to follow Hutchinson on a final road trip through California. Had the free-spending George Steinbrenner been the New York owner back in that era, Hutch likely would have ended up in the Big Apple. He was considered baseball's most coveted minor-league prospect and had a long line of baseball suitors. Yet the then-cost-conscious Yankees were reluctant to enter a bidding war, which rarely has been the case since. They blanched at the initial asking price for Hutchinson: it was four players—specifically, a catcher, two left-handed pitchers, and an outfielder—and $65,000.

How much to acquire his rights and leave him in Seattle for the 1939 season, the Yankees countered? In that case, the Rainiers wanted a flat $50,000, insisting that Hutchinson was worth at least $35,000 per season to them in gate receipts alone. They needed to be properly compensated and were firm on the money demands.

Devine, the Yankees scout asked to bird-dog the young pitching sensation, spoke regularly with Rainiers manager Jack Lelivelt about acquiring the pitcher. He was determined to whittle down the price tag. In regular missives to the New York front office, Devine questioned Hutchinson's fastball and then his temper. He told his employers that although the Hutchinson family insisted that the Cleveland Indians and Chicago Cubs had made solid offers for the pitcher, he thought those claims were negotiating bluffs.

On August 30, Devine sent a letter to Yankees business manager E. G. Barrow, suggesting the Rainiers had greatly inflated the pitcher's worth for leverage. "I figured that Lelivelt has no such offers for Hutchinson and he is trying to use the friendly feeling of Mr. Sick toward the Yankee organization and in the meantime trying to throw a knife into us with such a price," Devine wrote. "If some other club pays this, it is all right with me."

On the same day, Devine sent another note to the Yankees' front office that was equally skeptical in tone. "The only way you could do any business on Hutchinson and be safe is to have Seattle give us an option on Hutchinson for delivery in 1940, and I would not be inclined to go over $25,000 in cash for an option," the scout suggested, concluding that the Rainiers would never go for such an offer.

Three days later, Devine sent another report to New York. The talent-seeker tried to maintain his hard line in assessing Hutchinson's raw talent, but begrudgingly acknowledged the pitcher was a winner. "Saw Hutchinson shut out Hollywood for eight innings the other night with nothing but a prayer," he wrote in a letter. "This lad has one of those years he cannot lose if he wanted to. I never saw a boy win so many games that has shown so little."

For someone supposedly so disinterested in the pitcher, Devine was still on Hutchinson's trail two and a half months later as the Pacific Coast League meeting convened in San Francisco. He met separately with Lelivelt and Sick. He complained to his superiors in New York that one man told him one thing and the other something totally different. He should have known better. They were playing hardball with him.

Before heading home for Thanksgiving, the Yankees scout filed yet another report to the New York front office, intimating there might be a new opening in advancing a deal for the coveted Seattle pitcher. "I understand that Mr. Hutchinson told the Seattle ballclub that if they did not sell his boy he would demand them to pay him a Major League salary next year," Devine wrote to Barrow.

All parties involved moved to minor-league baseball's winter meeting in New Orleans and serious bidding for the player began. New York deals involving one player and $40,000, four players and $20,000, and up to five players were tendered for young Hutchinson. Yankees prospects Johnny Babich, Johnny Bittner, Harry "Stinky" Davis, Chris Hartje, Frank Kelleher, and Jack Saltzgaver were offered in different groupings. Kelleher later played for the 1940 Rainiers, as did Babich in 1943 and '44, joining the franchise from different routes. A stipulation was added calling for the return of Hutch to Seattle should he need further minor-league seasoning.

On December 7, Devine sent a Western Union telegram to the New York front office telling them that he had not closed the deal for Hutchinson. "They refused this offer," a clearly frustrated Devine wrote to Barrow. A shift in the leading suitor occurred next. Three days later, wire-service reports came out of New Orleans that the Pittsburgh Pirates were close to acquiring Hutchinson for $50,000 and a large but undetermined number of players.

"There are several minor details to be worked out, but I'm confident the way will be cleared so that we can make the deal," Pirates president William Benswanger told assembled reporters. "I have an appointment with Emil Sick, president of the Seattle team, and I expect to have everything settled before I leave New York." The Yankees already were convinced a deal had been made. "Pittsburgh beat us to him," New York manager Joe McCarthy said, conceding defeat in the Hutchinson sweepstakes.

The Pirates made a big show of trying to trade for Hutchinson, according to The Sporting News. They offered most of their starting lineup for the kid pitcher, but the deal was squelched when the best player, first baseman Gus Suhr, made it known he would never report to Seattle. Suhr already had played in the PCL, with the San Francisco Seals, and wasn't interested in going back to the minors.

Everyone moved to the Major League meetings in New York, and it was clearly a seller's market in the Hutchinson sweepstakes. On December 13, a deal was made, and it was too rich for the Yankees and Pirates. It also was beyond the means of the Cubs and Boston Red Sox, who had made late bids for the coveted pitcher from the Pacific Northwest.

Hutchinson was at his parents' Rainier Beach home at 6102 Keppler Avenue, in between classes at the University of Washington, when the telegram arrived. His big-league future had been determined. He sat in a window and eagerly scanned the breaking news in his hands. All promises had been kept:

Made deal that sends you to Detroit 1939. Fine opportunity for you to realize your ambition and good deal for our club. Wanted you to know first. Will give you details when we arrive. Regards to your mother and dad.

Torchy, Jack and Emil

The Tigers handed over the bounty that was required to move the pitcher out of Seattle and was balked at by other big-league franchises: a $100,000 deal. Broken down, this amounted to $50,000 cash and $50,000 for the contracts of four players, including two big leaguers in starting center fielder Jo Jo White and journeyman infielder Tony Piet, and two minor leaguers in first baseman George Archie from Toledo and relief pitcher Ed Selway from Beaumont. Later, minor-league catcher Buddy Hancken was substituted for Piet, who decided to stay in Detroit and sell cars instead of moving to the Northwest. Piet eventually visited Seattle and the Rainiers' ballpark on a summer vacation and expressed outward remorse that he hadn't followed the others into this feel-good baseball situation.

The trade actually was more complicated than that. A year later, Hancken was released from his Rainiers contract, one of ninety-two players made instant free agents by baseball commissioner Judge Kenesaw Mountain Landis, who ruled that the Detroit Tigers and other big-league teams had manipulated contracts. As final payment for Hutchinson, Detroit sent right-handed pitcher John Tate to the Rainiers on April 2, 1940, making him the fifth player handed over, this last piece of the trade coming sixteen months after it was first announced.

"We would have rather kept Hutch for another year, but none of the Major League owners were interested in such a transaction," Sick told reporters, explaining the pitcher's departure. Losing your main box-office draw was difficult, but the bright lights were beckoning Hutchinson and the Rainiers couldn't get in his way. Besides, now there was enough talent in Seattle to field a championship team next season and for seasons beyond.

"We didn't want to let Hutch go for 1939 delivery, but Major League clubs wanted immediate delivery, and both manager Jack Lelivelt and I felt that Hutch deserved his chance," Sick said. "At the same time, the players we received will virtually build the Rainiers into the type of a team that will be a pennant contender every inch of the way."

Hancken was living in the offseason in Beaumont, Texas, painting the walls of a nearby oil refinery, when he learned of his inclusion in the Hutchinson trade from a local sportswriter. He later received a letter from the Rainiers, confirming everything he already knew. He got married, packed up his bags, and headed west to promising baseball prospects.

"It was a great trade," said Hancken, who served as the backup catcher to Gilly Campbell. "Hutch turned into a helluva big-leaguer and all of us got there to Seattle and won. We started a real baseball place up there."

Hutchinson was supposed to make Detroit a contender if not help the Tigers supplant the long-dominant New York. It figures that he had to make his big-league debut against the Yankees. It didn't go well. As was the case with his PCL maiden voyage, he wasn't ready for it. Hutchinson suffered through another horrendous baseball debut. On May 2, 1939, after sitting idle for the first month of the season as the Tigers babied their youthful, high-priced acquisition, he gave up six runs in relief. Over two innings, he faced eleven batters, retired just two of them, and was responsible for six runs in a 22–2 defeat to the Yankees on an emotionally charged day in Detroit. New York's Lou Gehrig, his health failing rapidly, had pulled himself from the lineup, ending his consecutive appearance streak at 2,130 games. Hutch allowed a run on a passed ball, walked five batters, and gave up four hits, including a three-run home run into the left-field seats by Charley Keller. His control hadn't been pinpoint throughout spring training.

He was sent to Toledo that night, with people at home wondering out loud why Hutchinson couldn't have stayed and played in Seattle longer if he was going to pitch again in the minors. "I think Hutch will do himself some good with the Mud Hens," Detroit manager Del Baker told reporters after making the move. "He needs regular work to regain his control, and he'll get it in Toledo."

Outwardly, Hutchinson tried to put on a brave face as he packed his bags for the minors, but tears were evident. "I'll be back," he vowed to the sportswriters buzzing around him in the locker room. "I'll be back as soon as I get some control. I had the same trouble at the start of last season with Seattle."

The rookie pitcher returned to the Tigers later in 1939 and made twelve more appearances, struggling though not nearly as much, as he registered three victories in nine decisions. He would enjoy consistent big-league success, though nothing like his Rainiers debut season, winning ninety-five games and losing seventy-one during a war-interrupted career. His best years were 1947, 1949, and 1950, when he finished 18-10, 15-7, and 17-8, respectively. He pitched in a 1940 World Series game against Cincinnati, and he started the season strong in 1951 and made his only All-Star Game appearance before settling for a 10-10 record. His competitiveness and intensity never wavered, a quality that didn't go unnoticed by his big-league employer. The Tigers urged him to become their manager in 1952 before he quit playing and had even turned thirty-three, and he pitched fifteen more times while making out the lineup card.

Looking to the catcher for a sign, Hutchinson curiously found himself throwing to Hancken, one of the players traded to the Rainiers for him, in the minor leagues at Buffalo in 1940. "All you had to do was put the mitt down," Hancken said of Hutch. "He knew what he was going to pitch from the time he got on the mound. He wasn't overpowering, but he was intelligent. He was a great pitcher. We never talked about the deal at all."

Somewhat lost in all of his mound and managerial work was the fact that Hutchinson became one of baseball's more consistent hitting pitchers, displaying the talent others earlier had promoted on his behalf. Often used as a pinch hitter by the Tigers between pitching outings, he finished with a .263 career batting average in the big leagues, collecting four homers and eighty-three runs batted in. Some thought he might have erred in not becoming an everyday player rather than a pitcher, following Babe Ruth's lead, but Hutch disagreed. "I pitch for a living, but hit for pleasure," he insisted.

Hutchinson's brief Rainiers tenure was designated a huge success, and, even without a pennant to his credit, a certifiable coup for Sick. The brewer's immediate reward for his intuitiveness was league-leading attendance: 309,723 pushed through the turnstiles, or 4,075 per game, which was more than double the Seattle Indians' final gate count. The Rainiers proved more popular than some of the nation's haughtier, big-league attractions in the East. Sick's minor-league teams had a deeper and more resonant relationship with communities, providing a heartbeat for people generally starved for entertainment options. The Seattle attendance, while accumulated over a schedule ten games longer at home, surpassed the totals of three of the sixteen big-league teams: the St. Louis Cardinals (291,418, or 3,770 per game), Philadelphia Phillies (166,111), and St. Louis Browns (130,417).

Spending nine innings or more at Sicks' Stadium was considered an important social engagement not to be missed, one often presided over by Sick himself, who was present most nights. Rainier would became the city's favored alcoholic beverage and its baseball namesake Seattle's main sporting attraction, even eclipsing the University of Washington's most popular and sacred offering, by a wide margin. "The Rainiers were even bigger than Husky football," said Pat Patrick, a Seattle batboy and clubhouse attendant. "They were our team."

Sick had to be thrilled with his first summer as Rainiers owner. Not only had he become a heroic figure in Seattle, which didn't hurt his beer sales any, he had made money on baseball. In the normally wet Northwest, his team had been rained out just once that season, a highly favorable development for business. Contrary to what Ruppert had forecast, Sick turned a profit well in excess of $100,000 that first season. The Yankees owner lived just long enough to see his Seattle friend cash in. In rapidly deteriorating health, Ruppert died a month after the 1938 baseball season ended. Sick had visited with his seventy-year-old friend in New York only a few weeks before his passing.

The rest of the Big Apple had taken notice of Sick's faraway accomplishments, of him instantly winning over a tough baseball crowd in Seattle. He had balanced the books and earned a healthy profit. Ruppert's baseball associates asked the Rainiers owner to become partners in their effort to acquire the Yankees, but he declined, citing his own health problems and his competing baseball interests. "We would have done very well with our purchase, but New York was so far away," Sick said. "I had my hands full in Seattle." A bigger challenge ahead would be fielding another competitive, fan-pleasing team without Fred Hutchinson on the mound.

4. Turning Tigers Loose

Ask Joyner White where he was from, and in his deep, southern drawl he would slur an answer in such an indecipherable manner hardly anyone had a clue where this place was on the map: Joe-Jah. When finally translated, people discovered this somewhat unconventional man in a flannel baseball uniform hailed from Georgia, from rural Red Oak. He was playing in the minor leagues in Indiana in 1930, when his garbled response led to a permanent nickname, with a slight variation, "Jo Jo," coined by the amused Evansville manager Bob Coleman.

Acquired in the Fred Hutchinson trade, White didn't have much of an arm and couldn't hit for power, but he could run and stir up things, and Seattle fans quickly adopted him as their favorite baseball personality. He was the one who made everyone laugh. He was the one who came into second base with his spikes high. He was the one who made the deal with the Detroit Tigers pay off and eased the loss of Hutch. Of the quartet of players brought in from that widely publicized 1937 transaction, first baseman George Archie spent just two seasons with the Rainiers, and pitcher Ed Selway and catcher Buddy Hancken only one each, but White roamed the Sicks' Stadium outfield for four consecutive years, and good things seemed to happen each summer.

White's energy and aggressiveness were big reasons the Rainiers would collect three consecutive PCL pennants and hang onto their emotionally involved fan base in Hutchinson's absence. He was the new franchise headliner. White kept things in perpetual motion, thrilling fans and upsetting opponents. He scored all the way from second base on infield outs. He stole home. He could easily leg out an inside-the-park homer.

"I had never seen anybody who could run like him," Seattle infielder Len Tran said. "He was quick. He would stride. He ran like a damn horse."

The man readily identified as Jo Jo utilized the fadeaway slide made famous by Ty Cobb, a Hall of Famer, another Detroit Tigers player, fellow Georgian, and his baseball hero. White perfected another slide that was more disruptive, cleverly knocking the ball out of the second baseman's mitt by kicking his opponent in the wrist. If he slid in hard and got a negative reaction, he wasn't afraid to throw a punch if challenged. The left fielder taught all of this baseball etiquette to his impressionable book-end teammate, right fielder Edo Vanni.

Adding to his allure, White was a homespun personality. In biographical information prepared by the Rainiers for reporters covering the team, the outfielder was asked about his reading preferences, and White's answer was the following: "Not a great deal—want to save eyes." Thumbed out on a questionable third-strike call, he was determined to let the offending umpire know of his displeasure, even if it meant speaking a language he didn't quite understand.

"Y'all is incompetent," White barked at the offending ump.

"Do you know what that means?" Vanni asked, sitting dumbfounded on the bench.

"No, but it sure sounded good," White replied.

People gravitated to this man, with young fans vowing to grow up and play left field just like White. Recognizing his drawing power, management made sure White's stay in Seattle was more lucrative than the big leagues had been, paying him $10,000 per season, as opposed to the $8,000 he had earned in his final year in Detroit. From a financial standpoint, the journeyman player no longer needed the Majors. "Why would I want to go back up there?" White told Vanni. "I'm getting taken care of pretty good here."

The Detroit trade acquisitions mixed in smoothly with the Rainiers holdovers. In fact, there was great harmony on this team. After victories in 1939, Seattle players hustled to the showers nightly to belt out their favorite musical tunes. One night in Hollywood, the team's postgame choir was in full chorus when a certifiable big-league talent joined in. Considering the movieland surroundings, it wasn't unusual for some high-profile entertainer or film star to wander through the clubhouse. Seattle manager Jack Lelivelt had met many celebrities during his previous stint with the Los Angeles Angels and encouraged them to stop by. Four or five players were in the shower when one of America's favorite crooners at the time, Bing Crosby, turned up in the dressing area. Hearing the off-key warbling in the back, an overly curious Crosby went to check it out.

"We only knew four songs, all religious songs, songs like 'In the Garden' and 'Let the Lower Lights Keep Burning,'" said Hancken, always one of the loudest voices. "Crosby came back and we surrounded him. Everyone was naked as a jaybird. It was one of the greatest things I ever did in my life. He knew all those songs. I was singing with Bing Crosby."

On another night in Hollywood, Hancken stood near the visitors' bat rack when comedian Bob Hope leaned over and asked him which bat he was going to use his next time up. This simple inquisition was meant more as a compliment, because Hancken had driven in the winning run with a sacrifice fly the night before. A photographer saw the entertainer and player chatting together, posed them for a photo, and later sent the image to the grateful catcher, who made it a lifelong keepsake. For the most part, such distractions were minimal for Hancken and his teammates. In Seattle, they became the celebrities.

The 1939 Rainiers chased the league-leading Los Angeles Angels for weeks, finally moving past them and into first place for good on July 31. A month and a half later, they clinched Seattle's first pennant in fifteen years, beating the Angels, 4–3, at home. This was front-page news, tempered only by competing stories suggesting that American involvement in world war wasn't far off, reporting that the Chamber of Commerce was offering priority interest to new business dealings with a "war basis," and detailing President Roosevelt's stern warning that Nazi Germany was not to pursue British or French holdings near the United States. Momentarily, Seattle players and fans were able to push the real world stuff aside and celebrate a championship in different ways. While ticket holders headed for the nearest watering hole to drink the city's favorite beer, the

Rainiers retreated to the showers after the final out and offered an enthusiastic rendition of "Roll Out the Barrel."

One ballpark witness, Florence Charlesworth, was so inspired by the city's long overdue pennant that she went home and penned the following poetic description of a landmark evening at Sicks' Stadium:

The field lights were bright and the evening was cool
The Rainiers were there but the "Tribe of O'Doul"
had broken their hearts and left them weak
as they rallied once more the pennant to seek
The ball was thrown out with the signal to start
I tried to relax but my poor anxious heart
was beating so wildly it filled me with fright
Until a clear ringing voice called out into the night
The next batter up will be Jo Jo White
I clasped my hands tightly and strained with my eye
I wanted to see that ball rise and rise
far out of the way of the Angels' reach
Then suddenly behind me I heard a loud screech
And Lawrence way out in the midst of it all
was right there at center to mow down that ball
Hal Turpin, the pitcher, at ease on the hill
had most of the Angels bowed down to his will
The score? Does it matter? We were four to three
The game was a "Pip," a sensation to see
I left with the feeling in all future years
I would always remember the courageous Rainiers

These 1939 Rainiers, finishing 101-73 and four and a half games ahead of San Francisco, were a team built on speed,

Bill Lawrence was a defensive standout for the Rainiers in center field.

Tigers speed, leading the PCL with 148 stolen bases. White supplied a team-best 47 steals while batting .287, and Archie, another Detroit newcomer, pilfered 27 bases and hit .330, his average surpassed only by shortstop and team top hitter Alan Strange's .335. All the pieces seem to fit this time, thanks to the boost from the Tigers. Replacing Hutchinson, holdover starting pitchers Hal Turpin (23-10) and Dick Barrett (22-15) had come out of the shadow of their former teammate and filled in admirably as stoppers.

A smothering outfield defense provided by the fleet White, Bill Lawrence, and Vanni, from leftfield to right, might have been this team's strongest attribute. White had played center in the big leagues, but that wouldn't happen in Seattle. The Rainiers used him in left because he wasn't going to dislodge the angular, 6-foot-4 Lawrence, who moved like a gazelle and tracked down virtually everything hit deep. He made impossible catch after impossible catch. The man nicknamed "High Pockets" was fearless around the outfield walls, particularly in the PCL's bigger ballparks. He could run forever and dared anyone to try to launch one over him. New York Yankees legend Joe DiMaggio, who played in the league for the San Francisco Seals before moving up, noted that the Seattle minor leaguer was the best defensive center fielder he ever played against. The Rainiers' pitchers felt so comfortable with Lawrence standing behind them, they weren't afraid to groove pitches. Understanding his special skill, the defensive whiz allowed his outfield mates to relax and know that help was always nearby.

"Edo, you cover the right-field foul line, and Jo Jo, you cover the left-field line, and I'll catch anything else in the ballpark," the confident Lawrence once instructed the others flanking him.

"The best center fielder I ever saw was Bill Lawrence, and I saw all the great ones," said Hancken, who later worked for the Houston Astros as a coach and publicist. "He had that long, loping run. He was tall. He always got there. No one ever hit one over his head and kept it in the park."

If only Lawrence could have hit with some authority, he might have enjoyed a long and fruitful big-league career. He was given

only a brief trial with the Detroit Tigers and batted just .217 in
forty-six at-bats for them in 1932. His plate development might
have been hampered by the curious fact that he hadn't played
sports at all at Lick High School in San Francisco, or at San
Mateo Junior College and Santa Clara College, both of which
were also located in the Bay Area.

There was just one drawback to the Rainiers' 1939 championship season. Even with all that hitting, pitching, and defense,
it wasn't enough to capture the President's Cup, the league's
four-team postseason event that provided a chance for players to
pick up a little extra money. Seattle lost four of six games to the
Angels in the first round and was eliminated. But Sick couldn't
complain about the playoff swoon. The music coming from the
showers hardly bothered him, either. The Hutchinson trade had
worked out well, bringing in enough talent to secure the pennant and hold fan interest steady, with attendance increasing to
355,792, a 46,069 boost without Hutchinson on the marquee.
The Rainiers, averaging 5,473 fans per game and playing eleven
more home outings, outdrew four big-league teams: the Washington Senators (339,257), Boston Bees (285,994), Philadelphia
Phillies (277,073), and St. Louis Browns (109,159). Sick awarded
his players gold rings for winning their championship after
banking another yearly baseball profit exceeding $100,000.

"My fondest memory was the night I caught the last out in
1939 and we won the pennant and a guy yelled, 'I'll give you fifty
bucks for that ball!'" Vanni recalled. "I was tempted to give it to
him, but the manager said, 'Better hang onto it; you might not
catch another one.'" He should have sold the championship
ball after all. Two more were coming.

Sick's 1940 Rainiers were even better, finishing 112-66 and

Manager Jack Lelivelt and his Rainiers celebrate winning
the 1940 Pacific Coast League championship.

nine and a half games ahead of Los Angeles, and enjoying a
season so dominant that this team perhaps ranks as Seattle's
greatest collection of minor-league players. On September 5,
the Rainiers pushed across two runs in the bottom of the ninth
to beat Sacramento, 3–2, and clinch the city's first back-to-back
pro baseball championships. Fittingly, George Archie ignited
the last-inning rally with a leadoff single to leftfield.

While the personable White had won over the fans the year
before, Archie also had enjoyed his moments as a Rainiers newcomer, padding his average with his own shimmering Fourth
of July fireworks show. In a holiday doubleheader sweep of
Hollywood on the road, he hit for the cycle in the opener and

George Archie was a Rainiers big hitter
acquired in a trade with Detroit.

barely missed repeating this baseball rarity in the seven-inning
nightcap. He collected the requisite home run, triple, double, and
single to complete the feat in an 11–4 victory in the first game,
which lasted nine innings. He was an agonizing single short,
the easiest hit of the four, in a 13–4 win in the second outing.
For the afternoon, Archie finished 7-for-10 at the plate, drove in
seven runs, and scored six. By coincidence, July 4, 1939, was a
day that also proved unforgettable for another first baseman.

In New York, the terminally ill Yankees great Lou Gehrig stood
before 61,808 fans and gave his famous "Luckiest man on the face
of the earth" speech, gracefully backing out of the game because
of the crippling disease that would be named for him.

Archie was no speechmaker. The Tennessee native wasn't a
big talker at all, finding himself far too busy playing baseball

to waste any excess motion moving his lips. Seattle was a good place for him. He had received just two at-bats with Detroit in 1938 before washing out, and the Rainiers were his chance at returning to the big leagues in a hurry. He just wasn't one to share his thoughts with anyone. "He might say six words in a day," Hancken said. "He was a flat-out good ballplayer, a good fielder, a good baserunner. He just never got a chance to establish himself in the Major Leagues."

There was no shortage of opportunity in Seattle. In 1940 Archie was the only Pacific Coast League player who appeared in every inning of all 178 games. He didn't miss an at-bat, even after he was accidentally beaned in the head by Rainiers pitcher Mike Budnick during spring training. The first baseman's tireless contributions didn't go unnoticed, earning him league player of the year honors, a tough sell considering the numbers the Los Angeles Angels' Lou Novikoff put up. Novikoff was the PCL triple-crown winner, supplying a monstrous .363 average, 41 home runs, and 170 runs batted in. Archie's average was 39 points lower, and he hit 33 fewer homers and collected 75 fewer RBI, but he led the league with 46 doubles and had a championship in his back pocket, making him more valuable in the MVP voters' estimation.

These Rainiers also made a clean sweep of all available team rewards, winning eight of ten postseason games against Oakland and Los Angeles to easily capture the President's Cup. Season attendance at Sicks' Stadium dipped a bit to 295,820, 4,482 per game, but it still led the league and, over eleven more home games, exceeded the total of three big-league clubs: the Boston Braves (241,616), St. Louis Browns (239,591), and Philadelphia Phillies (207,177). The beer baron was still making money on baseball, and he was more than willing to invest it back into the franchise. Contract negotiations were hardly contentious. Sick made sure everyone was happy, starting with Vanni. While playing in the considerable shadow cast by Hutchinson and White, the little outfielder had done what was expected of him in his first three Rainiers seasons, averaging .301, .325, and .333 at the plate. He finished third in the 1940 PCL batting race. He made himself a test case with the owner, haggling over his next contract offer. After receiving a $25 per month raise, which he deemed grossly inadequate, Vanni held out and didn't report to spring training for a couple of weeks, simmering at home in protest. The owner calmly settled things over the phone.

"Edo, what's the matter?" Sick asked over the telephone.

"I think the guy who typed up my contract put in the wrong figure," the player responded dryly. "He put the period in the wrong place."

"Come down to my office and I'll fix it," the owner said.

Vanni got what he wanted and reported to camp. Protracted holdouts were not part of the Rainiers' makeup because Sick was making money and spreading it around, and word of his generosity quickly circulated through pro baseball. "Seattle was one of the best teams to play for in the minor leagues because it always paid the best money," Rainiers pitcher Van Fletcher said.

While the franchise generated great sums of money for Sick, baseball was still a hobby for him. Selling beer was how he made his living, and the brewer took the opportunity to market his wares whenever he could. Years later, Charlie Metro found this out when he joined the team as its new outfielder.

"Son, do you drink beer?" Sick asked him in their first meeting.

"Sometimes," Metro waffled, not sure how to answer.

"From now on, you drink Sick's beer," the owner said firmly.

Sick's baseball teams traveled by train, and the owner saw to it that his players always had the best accommodations. The Rainiers were given a private railroad car, usually the first one located behind the baggage car and sealed off from other travelers. The setting was so secluded and private they could sit around in their underwear all day if they wanted. They played a lot of card games between rail stops. Most players would get fully dressed only to go to the dining car for meals.

"Old Sick was pretty good with the guys," Rainiers pitcher Rugger Ardizoia said. "We traveled first class all the time. What he did for us was real nice."

The team was winning pennants, Sick was banking a profit, and the players were happy and productive, which made for a harmonious work environment, over and above the shower room antics. Eying a third consecutive PCL pennant in 1941, the Seattle franchise had no reason to change anything, yet immediate change would become necessary, if not sadly urgent.

When hired as manager of the Rainiers, John "Jack" Lelivelt received a standard one-year contract from Emil Sick. The two men had had never met in person and really didn't know each other. When the Rainiers' new field manager sat down with the owner for the first time, at the league meeting in Sacramento, an instant connection was made. Lelivelt was so personable and knowledgeable and created such a favorable first impression that Sick tore up his contract on the spot and gave him a three-year deal instead.

"You're the kind of man I need at Seattle, so let's sign up for

Jack Lelivelt, Rainiers manager in 1938–40, was an able motivator.

three years and I hope it will be even more permanent," the owner said, paying Lelivelt $12,000 per season in salary and giving him another $5,000 in Rainiers stock. Three years, however, were all Sick would get from his hand-picked leader.

Lelivelt was a master motivator, someone who inspired people with a firm but fair hand. He never played favorites, never rushed to cut a player. He was so reliable on the bench and unflappable with the umpires, he never missed an inning with one of his Seattle teams, never got tossed from a game. He was referred to simply as "The Man" by his players. "He should have been a psychology professor in college," Vanni said. "He could size you up in a hurry."

Lelivelt gained immediate approval from the Rainiers for his handling of shortstop Bill Schuster and Jo Jo White, two dominant, potentially destructive personalities. One kept popping off to umpires, getting tossed out of games late; the other was initially playing poorly, unhappy that he was no longer a big-league player. The manager told them both he wanted an about-face or he wouldn't keep them, and they responded accordingly.

Lelivelt had braced himself for problems with White once the Hutchinson trade was finalized. In a letter sent to the Detroit front office on December 27, 1938, first asking for addresses and salaries of his new acquisitions, the Rainiers manager penned the following observation among others to the Tigers' general manager Jack Zeller: "I'm very much interested in knowing the result of your talk with White as to how he feels about coming out here."

White earlier had considered quitting baseball when the Tigers made him the centerpiece of the Seattle deal, hardly enthused about leaving the big leagues and moving down a baseball notch.

"That's tough and I don't know whether I'll go out there or not," he told Detroit sportswriters when first informed of the late 1938 deal. "There's only one place to play baseball. That's in the majors and that's where I want to play. I figured I'd been up here so long, I deserved a chance to stay in the majors with some other club."

Lelivelt made White feel important and wanted, easing the transition. Everything was negotiable with him, though he ruled with a firm hand when deemed necessary. The Rainiers' pitcher-outfielder Eddie Carnett considered Lelivelt an aristocrat in a baseball uniform, someone who reminded him of the regal Connie Mack, the Philadelphia Athletics manager. Standing on the mound, Carnett tested his manager just once in a game, when both were with the Los Angeles Angels, and found out conversation wasn't always necessary for Lelivelt to get his point across.

"I hurt my arm and I wouldn't give him the ball," the Rainiers player said. "He got another one from the umpire. He never said a word. He just got another ball and waved for someone to come on in relief." Later, the manager addressed the situation with the left-hander when emotions weren't running so high and no one else was around, informing Carnett rather emphatically, "Next time you better give me the ball, because you work for me."

A Chicago native, Lelivelt had a love of the game that left him with only a grammar school education. He skipped class to hang out on the highly competitive sandlots of the Windy City, causing his mother considerable worry that he might end up a failure. Instead, he used what he knew and made her proud. A proficient hitter, he bounced around the minors before playing in the big leagues with the Cleveland Indians, Washington Senators, and the New York Yankees. Injuries to both arches in his feet caused him extended hip pain, curtailing his playing career and sending him into managing.

Lelivelt made his baseball reputation by creating powerhouse teams over eight seasons with the PCL's Los Angeles Angels, most notably a 1934 club that put together a gaudy 137-50 season and was considered one of the greatest minor-league teams put together. When the Angels wouldn't reward him with the front-office responsibilities he felt were deserved in addition to his field managing duties, he left the organization before the 1937 season. Lelivelt was familiar with the Rainiers franchise when he took over. During his season away from managing, he had scouted for the Chicago Cubs, and one of the players he regularly sized up was a Seattle high school kid named Fred Hutchinson.

On January 19, 1941, Lelivelt returned to the Northwest for a fourth season and a third pennant run, tanned and rested after wintering at his new three-acre residence in Southern California. One day back on the job, he mailed out players' contracts and set February 18 as the spring training reporting date. Dinner that night was at the north Seattle home of club vice president Torchy Torrance. After eating, the two men left for a much-publicized Harlem Globetrotters basketball game at Civic Auditorium, which was next door to the ballpark the Rainiers had long abandoned. Torrance and Lelivelt were joined at the arena by Edo Vanni, and the three men settled into front-row seats for the sporting comedy. The manager had become so successful and popular in his newfound city that VIP seats were not out of the question. He remarked to his companions how good he felt and how anxious he was for the upcoming baseball season to begin. Watching the basketball game go back and forth, Lelivelt enjoyed himself, laughing heartily at the Globetrotters' court antics.

Near the end of the evening, however, Lelivelt turned pale. He now complained he wasn't feeling well, and his condition worsened as the game wound down. A concerned Torrance led the manager out of the downtown gym minutes before the final buzzer sounded, well ahead of the crowd. He drove Lelivelt to the Washington Athletic Club, the baseball man's temporary residence in downtown Seattle. Vanni went home thinking his manager was sick, really sick, but nothing more. On January 20, 1941, on a chilly Saturday night, the Rainiers' manager had suffered a massive heart attack and was taken to the now defunct Maynard Hospital. Just fifty-five years old, he died shortly before midnight.

Sick had envisioned winning more championships, and making and spending more money, but now his hand-picked manager was gone. All of baseball was shaken by the sudden demise of Lelivelt. Everyone in the game, at all levels, was familiar with the Rainiers' dugout leader. Lelivelt was a person who had dedicated himself to pro baseball for thirty-eight years, twenty-three as a manager and six as a big-league player. He had compiled a 1,861-1,439 managerial record, making previous stops in Omaha; Tulsa; St. Joseph, Missouri; and Milwaukee before turning to the PCL teams in Los Angeles and Seattle. He enjoyed more success than any other Rainiers manager, guiding them to three consecutive hundred-win seasons and those back-to-back pennants. Overnight, The Man was gone.

"It turned me sick to my stomach," said Vanni, who cried

Lelivelt's casket is carried out of his funeral by players and team officials.

when he received the news in a telephone call to his home. "Of all the managers I've ever seen, I'd put him No. 1, over Billy Martin and Yogi Berra. He got along with everyone. That was a very sad day when he died."

Lelivelt was a middle-aged man who seemed healthy enough, yet the prevailing medical theory, offered without benefit of an autopsy, was that a blood clot had formed from an old baseball leg injury that night and raced to his heart and killed him. A few days later, stoic-faced Seattle players served as makeshift pallbearers as they loaded Lelivelt's casket on a train bound for Van Nuys, California. Rainiers general manager Bill Mulligan was on board, making sure all arrangements were properly administered in bringing the field manager's body home. Torrance flew ahead to help Lelivelt's widow, Ethel, set up a funeral service.

Lelivelt's reputation as a baseball leader had been solid and widespread. Sick, new to baseball, considered no one else for his first manager among a dozen candidates, acting only on a strong recommendation from Col. Jacob Ruppert. His old Yankees friend was gone now, making the Rainiers' search more difficult this time. Yet the Seattle managerial job was considered a plum one throughout the baseball world. There was plenty of talent on the roster, an attractive ballpark, and a rich owner waiting for someone competent enough to surface from the search process. A long line formed for Lelivelt's job. The Rainiers intimated that they wanted to bring in a big name to run things, and, among thirteen candidates, was one of the biggest: George Herman "Babe" Ruth.

5. The Babe

Within thirty-six hours of Jack Lelivelt's death, Babe Ruth's name emerged as a possible successor for the Seattle managerial position, but this was overly wishful thinking. The Rainiers contacted him and were initially rebuffed. Ruth was sick for the second time during that winter of 1941, a concern for everyone on the East Coast. A heavy cold, sore throat, and 101-degree temperature had left him bedridden and the subject of New York newspaper stories, his celebrity status hardly diminished by the fact that he had been retired as a player for five seasons.

The Bambino's previous efforts to manage had been roundly discouraged at the big-league level. Traditional baseball men were fearful of hiring the former Yankees slugger because of his earlier disdain for authority and his rampant desire to live up to his reputation as one of the game's more free-spirited and unbridled personalities. "Babe couldn't manage himself, so how was he going to manage a team?" asked Edo Vanni, who would have played in the outfield for Ruth had the man been hired by the Rainiers.

However, others pointed out that the Babe had answered to another beer-producing man in Col. Jacob Ruppert, the Yankees owner, an arrangement that had worked out well in the end for all sides concerned. "I guess all the breweries, wineries and distilleries liked him," pitcher Eddie Carnett quipped.

Once the Rainiers made their early intentions known about the managerial vacancy, Ruth sent word through his wife, Claire, that he wasn't interested in the job. This news became public in brief wire-service bulletins circulated throughout the country. In his only nonplaying baseball position thus far, Ruth had served as a coach for the Brooklyn Dodgers in 1938, though he appeared to be little more than a glorified gate attraction and wasn't invited back for a second season. He didn't want to go to the minor leagues. Besides, he likely was weary of pursuing jobs in baseball after having being told no so often in his previous attempts to land work.

Yet after feeling better a few days later, Ruth had a change of heart. The Rainiers job now appealed to him. After all, hadn't these people called him? He applied for the Seattle vacancy, lobbying for the position with a long letter to Emil Sick that stated his interest and listed his qualifications. Maybe this was his big chance, an opportunity to be someone other than a home-run hitting circus.

Of the thirteen Rainiers managerial candidates, Ruth's wasn't the only notable name among them. Rogers Hornsby made a bid for the job, as did Paul Waner and Grover Cleveland Alexander. Former Chicago Cubs manager Gabby Hartnett also put his name in the mix. The five of them would each land in baseball's Hall

Babe Ruth autographed and sent this photo to *Seattle Post-Intelligencer* sports columnist Royal Brougham in 1933.

of Fame at some point. Ruth had others lobby on his behalf, namely, a Palatka, Florida, man named Ray L. Doan, who was a self-described "representative" (or early day sports agent) of the former Yankees player, and told the wire services that he was "sure Seattle could get Ruth if it wanted him."

In the Northwest, Babe's potential hiring stirred great debate in the press. Royal Brougham, the *Seattle Post-Intelligencer* sports editor who had befriended the Yankees slugger through the years, stumped for him in his column, declaring, "Babe Ruth positively would make the team the greatest drawing box office team outside of a few Major League cities."

To his credit and the surprise of some, because Brougham could be an out and out cheerleader for various causes, the journalist also cautioned against hiring someone just because he had been a top player, suggesting that other greats had failed when given the ultimate authority to run a team from the bench. "Even with the mighty Babe at the helm, the Rainiers would lose their lure were they to shuffle off into the depths of the second division," Brougham reminded in his column. "It always works out that way. Two of the most glamorous figures in baseball, Ty Cobb and Walter Johnson, were busts as managers. It takes more than a player's reputation to handle a ballclub, to instill in it a winning spirit and keep it hustling and playing in harmony. President Sick and his advisors are too shrewd to be enamored by a name."

Brougham must have had insider knowledge, because he wrote everything except the new manager's name. He concluded his thoughts on the Rainiers' search for a leader by slyly reporting, "Of course, the good old Bambino in a Seattle uniform would be a lot of fun and I hope they can coax him back to the game he dominated for so many years. But don't be disappointed if the Rainiers wind up signing some solid, capable, level-headed citizen and not a glamour boy."

On February 6, 1941, Sick received a long-distance phone call from Ruth inquiring about the job. Their exchange was printed in Associated Press accounts that turned up nationwide, most notably in the *Los Angeles Times*. It wasn't a long conversation, and there was a sad tenor to it. "This is Babe Ruth," the man on the other end said. "How are you, Emil, and what about that job of managing your Seattle baseball team? I'm in the market."

The next sound had to be that of a huge baseball ego deflating. Sick politely informed the game's most famous player that he had filled the position two days earlier with one of Ruth's former teammates, though the slugger no doubt had to scratch his head to remember the other guy. Bill Skiff, a Yankees catcher for just six games and eleven at-bats in 1926, had been hired. This had to be a major letdown for the Babe, especially since he had lost out to someone who had played an insignificant role in the New York clubhouse that he had presided over, who had failed to hit even one big-league homer, who had been made obscure like so many others in his considerable baseball shadow. "Well, OK, but I just thought I better ask," a discouraged Ruth said before hanging up.

The Yankees slugger would have been welcome in the Northwest. He had visited twice before, causing a great commotion each time. He had turned up in the region in the off-season, once at the height of his baseball career and another time at the end, headlining barnstorming games. On Saturday, October 18, 1924, Seattle came face to face with true sporting royalty for the first time when a train from the East pulled to a stop at King Street Station. The city hadn't seen a superstar of this order up close before. When the most important passenger on board appeared in the doorway before getting off the train, he wore a stylish overcoat. His jacket was buttoned snugly at the waist, and a white shirt and bow tie peeked out from an open collar.

Babe Ruth grasped a handrail with his right hand and doffed his cap with the other. A *Seattle Post-Intelligencer* photographer recorded this moment by snapping away.

Ruth had traveled cross-country for a glimpse of a city strange to him and to visit a place even more eager to eyeball the wildly popular New York Yankees baseball player in return. A few weeks removed from the end of an American League season that had permitted him 46 home runs, 121 RBI, and a .378 batting average, but no World Series, the slugger had agreed to participate in a series of charity exhibition games across the western half of the nation. He made stops in Minnesota, North Dakota, Montana, and Spokane before he reached the most far-flung point on his itinerary.

Always adventuresome, Ruth dined on rail-car meals of buffalo meat, a culinary first for him. He joked about adding a herd of this delicacy to his farm in New England as a means of getting positive batting results. "I ought to hit a hundred home runs next year on a buffalo diet," he wisecracked.

For three days in Seattle in 1924 Ruth was at full long-ball capacity while well fed in his ambassador's role. To facilitate this first-time tour of one of America's biggest celebrities, the *Post-Intelligencer*'s Brougham served as an escort for Ruth. Brougham had personally arranged for this leg of the trip, convincing the morning newspaper to finance the Bambino's stay in the city.

Ruth's first stop on Sunday, his one full day in town, was at Orthopedic Hospital on Queen Anne Hill. Ruth, wearing a tuxedo, showed up to cheerfully greet each patient at the children's care facility, patting heads and drawing huge smiles. While seated, he used one youngster's crutch to demonstrate a batting tip to him.

At 1 p.m., the Babe was ushered into Dugdale Park in Rainier Valley and greeted by a crowd of nine thousand. Those fourteen years old or younger were admitted free; others paid $1 for the right to ogle the famous slugger. Ruth, twenty-nine years old himself and halfway through a twenty-two-year big-league career, was as recognizable and as mesmerizing as anyone on the planet. He spoke to the assembled gathering, inviting the younger fans onto the field while hitting autographed baseballs into center, creating a mad scramble.

The main event was a nine-inning contest matching the Babe and a Seattle all-star team against Ruth's Yankees teammate Bob Meusel and a collection of statewide players. To appease the fans, the two big-league players batted twice each time through the lineup, also swinging for their respective pitchers as designated hitters. The VIP players received nine at-bats apiece.

For the next few hours, Ruth did what he did best, launching three mammoth homers out of the park, adding a double, and leading his side to an 11–10 victory. At 2:07 p.m., his first long ball soared out of the ballpark in right field and over a neighboring street and a gas station, sending a roar throughout Dugdale. "Babe Ruth smacked his first Seattle home run and the ball hit Mount Rainier on the first bounce!" Brougham wrote enthusiastically in the *Post-Intelligencer*. Late in the game, a small boy was so enthralled with the big man in the New York uniform that he slipped out of the stands and ran out to Ruth on the field. Treated gently by his hero, the intruder got a handshake and his head tousled before being pointed back to the seats.

While Ruth was putting on his fearsome hitting display in the city's south end, the ballpark's normal tenants and predecessors to the Rainiers, the Seattle Indians, were in Portland wrapping up a Pacific Coast League championship that same afternoon. In a classy move, the Yankees bopper dictated a telegram to the hometown team on the spot, addressing it to manager Red Killefer and imparting the following message, which was published on the front page of the *Post-Intelligencer* the following day:

The score boy has just put up the scores. Congratulations to the new champions of the Coast League.
Babe Ruth

A fancy dinner came next. That evening, *Post-Intelligencer* publisher E. C. Griffith hosted Ruth at the exclusive Rainier Club, inviting several city dignitaries to join them. The guest of honor spoke briefly. He explained why the Washington Senators had supplanted his Yankees as the World Series entry from the American League, but he made no excuses for this shortfall. "Don't alibi; that's one of my mottos," the ballplayer told the upscale dinner crowd. "The Washington club beat us out of the pennant, and I'll say they were the better ball team." Later, on the garden roof of the Washington Hotel, Ruth mugged for a much smaller gathering, playing a saxophone—not very well—alongside musically gifted twin brothers armed with the same instrument.

At noon on Monday, Ruth was still at his crowd-pleasing best with his visit nearing an end. He climbed atop the roof of the *Post-Intelligencer* for yet another goodwill gesture. With hundreds huddled around the newspaper building at Sixth Avenue and Pine Street, Ruth signed about a dozen baseballs and tossed them to his adoring fans, at first gingerly and then with more effort after realizing he couldn't hurt anyone with the sea of hands grabbing for each souvenir ball. Police kept close watch, chaperoning streetcars through the crowd but rerouting automobiles down other streets.

After speaking to students at Seattle College (now Seattle University) and enjoying a quick golf round at Jefferson Park, he climbed aboard a train, making another stop in Tacoma before gradually working his way down the coast to California. However, Seattle hadn't seen the last of Ruth in a baseball uniform.

In 1934 Ruth returned to the city for a second October fundraiser. At this time, he was a fading superstar who recently had parted ways with the Yankees. While he was in Seattle, it was widely assumed that he had retired, but Ruth would go on to play twenty-eight more games in the Majors for the Boston Braves the following season before reluctantly giving up his baseball career for good. For this trip, Ruth was part of a huge delegation of big-league players that made a brief stopover in Seattle before departing by ship from Vancouver, British Columbia, to Hawaii and then a thirty-game Asian tour. Ruth's traveling companions included Lou Gehrig, Jimmy Foxx, Earl Averill, Lefty Gomez, manager Connie Mack, and one Moe Berg, the latter a back-up catcher who, it was suggested later, had been sent on this trip as a government spy.

With a crowd of 7,500 gathering on an overcast day at dusty Civic Stadium, Ruth at first indicated he would play just three innings, but he went the full nine, unwilling to disappoint anyone. In his all-star team's 9–6 victory, he had trouble running the bases. He no longer could hit on cue or with gusto, striking out with the bases loaded late in the game. But he made sure everyone went away happy. "You can't hit 'em when you can't see 'em," Ruth said for all to hear, drawing laughs, when he fanned.

A teenaged Vanni worked as the Civic Stadium clubhouse attendant on the visitors' side for that 1934 exhibition game. He waited on the Bambino while getting his autograph and had a front-row seat for the big man's crude but endearing antics. "He was really funny," Vanni said. "He'd break wind in the clubhouse. He just let 'em rip. He drank beer and farted a lot. He was a big guy, a helluva nice guy, and treated everyone with respect. He was just one of the boys."

An indecisive Ruth was simply too late in making a bid for the Seattle manager's job in 1941, and it cost him. While the Bambino was convalesced at home following his winter illness, Skiff was hired a mere week after the search for Jack Lelivelt's successor had been put in motion. Sick still maintained strong New York connections, and in making this decision he consulted with Yankees manager Joe McCarthy, who had recommended Skiff, not Ruth. The former catcher's credentials looked impressive enough to the Rainiers, counting seven years of previous managerial experience and two seasons as the Yankees' farm system field supervisor. Skiff had even coached on Lelivelt's 1930 Los Angeles Angels staff, so there was a welcome connection to the deceased manager. The new guy was given an annual salary of $7,500 from Sick, a sum that might not have been enough to satisfy Ruth anyway.

"I don't think it would have worked out because Ruth was really a flamboyant person," said Bob Stagg, a Rainiers catcher in 1940–42. "We sort of had the team picked out and we needed someone more disciplined. Skiff was a good man."

While the idea of hiring Ruth was tempting, Sick likely envisioned only the worst-case scenario for his Rainiers had the man known as the great Bambino joined the franchise, as had others throughout baseball. Ruth had done too much damage to his reputation with his carefree, alcohol-fueled ways, though he always proved intoxicating to fans. Sick could have reversed course on Skiff, but he stuck with the low-key hire.

"Babe was too high strung," Vanni said. "They felt they couldn't tell him what to do. But that was the way all those guys lived with the Yankees. They ruled the roost. Even Joe McCarthy couldn't handle Ruth."

On August 21, 1947, six years after losing out on the Rainiers job, a rapidly deteriorating Ruth turned up in Seattle for a third and final charity benefit, this one a speaking engagement at Sicks' Stadium. Yet he was so frail and weakened by throat cancer, with his voice reduced to a raspy whisper, he couldn't leave the Olympic Hotel. Brougham, who had become a good friend through the years, hastily made other arrangements. The resourceful journalist interviewed the baseball legend in his room, and their easy exchange was carried over KOMO radio and piped to the kids gathered back at the ballpark.

Ruth signed off by telling everyone he would return to the city, health permitting. It was a promise he couldn't keep. This proved to be one of the final trips that he would take anywhere. All of his excesses caught up with him. The baseball giant died almost exactly a year later in New York, sending the nation, including Seattle, into deep mourning.

In hindsight, the Rainiers missed a great opportunity by not hiring the Yankees legend. From a publicity standpoint, it might have been the worst mistake Sick made in his long-running baseball business dealings. Skiff would win a third consecutive pennant with Lelivelt's holdover talent, but the franchise floundered and grew stagnant with the onset of World War II and failed to recover quickly after it was over, forcing Skiff's ouster. Considering Skiff's rather forgettable legacy, it might have been worth it for the Rainiers to risk putting Ruth in a Seattle uniform, sitting him on the bench, and letting him call the shots, offsetting a grim world that was fast approaching.

"I think it would have been a good thing," Carnett said. "Take a manager everybody likes, and the players would have busted their backs for him. He was a good drawing card. They should have given Babe the chance. Sometimes I think baseball is pretty cruel."

6. Balls and (Air) Strikes

Jack Lelivelt never saw his country pulled into the real-life run-down that was World War II, and he wasn't around for the outcome when Germany and Japan were tagged out. Yet for the final seven months of his life, the Rainiers' baseball manager was aware something big was going to happen because of what was taking place around him. Overnight in Seattle, Lelivelt had a bunch of new neighbors. While his Rainiers were in the middle of the 1940 Pacific Coast League pennant race, the city, if not the region, joined the escalating arms race, creating a palpable population spike. Once France fell to Nazi Germany that June, Congress moved ahead with war preparations, which involved awarding rich defense contracts to the Northwest's airplane maker, the Boeing Company, and its military boat builder in nearby Bremerton, the Puget Sound Naval Shipyard. An official war declaration was still eighteen months away, but the gates to Seattle had been flung wide open.

With guarantees of steady employment, people still scuffling from the Depression started to pour into the city. From 1940 to 1943, Seattle's population rose to 480,000, an increase of 112,000. Many of the newcomers were displaced baseball fans, people who needed to be entertained, families eager to find another team to call their own. These wartime immigrants adopted the Rainiers, with the earliest arrivals sharing in a 1941 season that was hardly lacking for summertime drama after the look of the Seattle ballclub was altered radically from the previous year, far more than anyone would have envisioned for the two-time defending champions.

The accomplished Lelivelt was gone, leaving the manager's job to Bill Skiff. The former Yankees catcher had less than a month to learn his roster, make sure everyone was signed to a contract, and prepare for spring training in California's San Fernando Valley. League MVP first baseman George Archie was gone, returned to the big leagues after his breakout season, picked up by the Washington Senators for the sale price of $7,500. Right-field fixture and hometown favorite Edo Vanni was as good as gone, missing all except nineteen games after breaking his left leg while sliding hard into second base in San Diego, suffering one of nineteen injuries that would disrupt this Seattle team and leave it significantly wounded.

Skiff's Rainiers were 34-34 and fifteen and a half games out of first place on June 17 and close to calling the season a bust, when everything magically righted itself. Players pulled out of slumps. Players were healthy again. Players started producing. The grandstand grumbling that had surrounded Skiff and his ineffectual lineup was muted when the ballclub took off, winning 66 percent of its games over the final two months to secure

Eventual Hall of Famer Earl Averill came home to play his
final pro baseball season with the Rainiers in 1941.

a third consecutive, albeit improbable, pennant. The Rainiers had a championship in hand on September 11 after a double-header sweep of Los Angeles, beating the Angels 14–3 and 5–1 on the road, and they would finish 104-70, four games ahead of Sacramento and San Diego in the standings.

Pitching had rescued this team, with veterans Dick Barrett and Hal Turpin coming through with 20-12 and 20-6 seasons, respectively. Les Scarsella, Archie's replacement at first base, had done his part, too, bouncing back from a slow start to lead the Rainiers with a .322 batting average and 110 RBI. Providing a sentimental sidelight, eventual Hall of Fame inductee Earl Averill, at the end of a highly decorated baseball career, returned home to play a final season in the minors with Seattle after drawing his release from the Boston Braves. The Snohomish native didn't have much left, but the team gave him 223 at-bats out of respect and he batted .247, 71 points below his career big-league average, before heading into retirement.

The Rainiers also had to dig deep to stay alive in the 1941 postseason, securing the President's Cup for a second year in a row. They were pushed the full seven games in each playoff series with Hollywood and Sacramento, each time faced with elimination, and winning the final two contests of each series to pull through. Even with the unsettling distraction of looming war, attendance remained steady at 273,855, 4,641 per game, thanks to the city's sudden population boost.

With three pennants and impressive gate receipts in hand—the team had led the league in attendance each of the four seasons under his ownership—Emil Sick was singled out as a true base-ball liberator, nationally and regionally. The Sporting News named him minor-league executive of the year, and league secretary

Harry Williams, one of Sick's biggest fans, publicly and privately gushed how the Seattle man "had saved the Pacific Coast League."

Sick, not Skiff, took most of the bows for the 1941 turnaround. The new manager patiently waded through a difficult season but failed to please everyone, a situation that nagged at him throughout a six-year managerial stint with the Rainiers, the longest tenure anyone would have in that role. "Bill Skiff was a different kind of guy," Vanni said, trying to be kind. "He was a Yankees guy coming in, didn't want to rock the boat and he did a good job. But with the team we had, we could have run it ourselves."

Even the man who hired Skiff never seemed totally satisfied with him. "Although he was no Jack Lelivelt, he performed yeoman service for us," Sick said, offering his second manager only a backhanded compliment. With what was coming next—a country totally besieged by war for four years, requiring extra creative thinking on the part of anyone trying to field a pro baseball team—Skiff would have little opportunity to make anyone forget Jack Lelivelt.

Five weeks after Pearl Harbor was turned into a battleship graveyard and five weeks before the opening of spring training camps, baseball officials were prepared to shut down the game only to have President Franklin Roosevelt veto this idea and implore as many teams as possible to keep playing at every level. Continuation of the national pastime was good for the country's morale, the nation's leader reasoned. While eager to comply with the war effort, Sick was nervous about the prospects for his Rainiers, fears that would be realized as his model franchise lost all of its momentum and turned unrecognizable at times, even to its staunchest fans.

"With the declaration of war between the United States, Germany and Japan, the future of baseball looked pretty dim," the Seattle owner concluded. "Attendance figures left much to be desired."

Still, empty seats and stringent operating restrictions weren't immediately apparent for the Rainiers as American servicemen were thrust into the fighting elsewhere. The Seattle team played its 1942 season opener against the Oakland Acorns in front of twelve thousand people—for the first time, the traditional day game was moved under the lights, for war purposes. Although blackouts or dimouts would later be enforced, Sick's team was encouraged to play this game at night to allow as many wartime workers as possible to attend and create a patriotic gathering. The first real indication of the drastic changes wartime would cause for Rainiers baseball was evident in the different uniforms now being worn by a handful of current and former Seattle players who were invited onto the field for opening night ceremonies. Edo Vanni and fellow outfielder Levi McCormack, and pitchers Hunk Anderson and Paul Gregory each were dressed in Navy blues and on leave, and accompanied by club vice president Torchy Torrance, appropriately attired as an officer in the Marines. Together, these men formed the letter V and drew a huge ovation on an emotional evening, one that started with a leaguewide remembrance of Pearl Harbor and ended with Seattle coming up with its own victory, 4–0.

A fourth consecutive pennant would elude the 1942 Rainiers, who finished in third place with a 96-82 record, which certainly was no fault of Barrett and Turpin, who were superb on the mound again and matched each other quality start for quality start. Barrett won twenty-seven of forty decisions, Turpin twenty-three of thirty-two. They finished one-two in the league in earned run average, with Barrett the leader at 1.72 and Turpin close behind at 2.07. The Sporting News rewarded Barrett by naming him minor-league pitcher of the year, but the publication easily could have picked either Seattle pitcher.

Primarily relying on a knuckleball, Turpin supplied the best single outing of the two, throwing the first no-hitter in Rainiers history by beating San Diego, 3–0, on the road early in the season—coming as close to a perfect game as one could without getting it. He lost the gem on a two-out, full-count walk in the bottom of the ninth inning to Padres batter Cedric Durst, formerly a member of the vaunted 1927 New York Yankees, on a questionable umpire's call. Where other pitchers readily would have dressed down the man behind the plate for seemingly taking away something so special, Turpin shrugged, offered no protest, and stoically retired the next batter to complete the no-hitter.

Turpin, who owned and tended a southern Oregon farm in the offseason, had little time to verbalize much between getting the crops in and the hitters out. The joke was that the man with all of the off-speed pitches would say hello to start a season, win his twenty games, and say good-bye when he left, and that was it. Bunches of words weren't forthcoming with this guy. He traveled in silence outside the ballpark, too. Turpin and the equally tight-lipped George Archie earlier were road roommates. One could only imagine the total lack of conversation between those two players in their hotel rooms.

Curiously, Turpin was asked to speak in front of a large crowd for the first time as part of a wartime charity gathering at Sicks' Stadium, and Rainiers fans were eager to see how he would handle what was sure to be an uncomfortable moment. His words were short and to the point. "I'm a farmer, but I guess my farm won't be worth two cents if we lose this war," he said. That was it. Still, the pitcher received enthusiastic applause and a headline the next morning in the *Post-Intelligencer*'s sports pages that described his landmark speech this way: "Yep, Turp Made It!"

Once the 1942 season ended, the Rainiers lost a big part of their identity, thanks in part to the impact of war. With the big leagues scrambling to fill rosters, popular left fielder Jo Jo White, coming off four productive seasons in Seattle, was purchased by the Philadelphia Athletics, while Barrett, after his commanding performance, was summoned by the Chicago Cubs. Franchise headliners now were hard to find. Former pitching sensation Fred Hutchinson had moved from the big leagues to the Navy, where he was joined by Vanni and isolated from his profession. Archie had washed out of the big leagues again and was in a service uniform. Aging center fielder Bill Lawrence soon would retire after the 1942 season, return upon urgent request the following year and play in eighty games, and then quit for good. That left Turpin as the only one from the glory years to rally around.

As the fighting escalated in the coming seasons, the Rainiers struggled to keep up. Starting times for weeknight games fluctuated from 3:30 to 8:15 p.m. during the war years, with the government banning night games altogether for eighteen months, and issuing a directive, beginning on August 20, 1942, that play had to be concluded by dark. Contests were postponed or canceled because of travel restrictions, with troops drawing priority seating on trains up and down the West Coast. An idle Sicks' Stadium often was used as a staging area for wartime training exercises, cordoned off so munitions could be exploded in the middle of the diamond. On game nights, fans were not permitted to drive down Rainier Avenue, the main thoroughfare to the ballpark; instead, they were asked to circle around the surrounding neighborhoods in search of an alternative route so as to leave the other road clear for military vehicles. Rosters were cut to twenty players on the road, and then twenty players at all times, which was not that much of a hardship considering the problems the team encountered finding enough athletes capable of performing at the Triple-A level.

Sick did his best to hold things together. He became creative with his finances, buying up outstanding team stock and consolidating his baseball holdings with his Seattle brewery to limit his tax obligations. He rented out vast stadium storage to brewery interests, taking money from one business to support the other. The progressive owner also provided wartime support to the families of his absent employees, continuing to pay Seattle baseball players who had been called away to fight half of their regular salaries. The Rainiers weren't always sure who was coming back and when, and the war continually left them guessing over a player's baseball availability. The following letter was sent from Torrance, the club vice president, to outfielder Bill Matheson on December 26, 1941, less than three weeks after the Japanese had bombed Pearl Harbor:

Dear Bill,
Is there any reason why we can't expect you to report to spring practice on a date to be designated later? I mean, is there any

chance you will be in the service by that time, or do you expect to be on hand? I would like the information before January 4th if possible.

Yours very truly,

Torchy

Filling out a lineup card was a constant challenge. The team used whoever was available, with players told they might have to play multiple positions during the season. For example, Eddie Carnett pitched and played in the outfield for the Rainiers. Players headed for or already in retirement were resurrected. Players with minimum or no pro experience were handed uniforms. The talent pool was not deep at all. Big-league teams annually drafted and purchased the best players from minor-league rosters, yet in 1944, for the first time since Sick had acquired the franchise, no Seattle players were taken.

Len Tran, a Rainiers second baseman after the war, joined the Marines and shipped out to the South Pacific on a destroyer, trained to fire heavy artillery guns. Once on Guam, he took a break from this life-and-death existence, with permission, to walk fifteen miles, one way, to watch displaced Major Leaguers serving in the Fifth Fleet put together an impromptu baseball game on the island. Luckily, he snagged a ride on the way back from this welcome interlude. "It was the thrill of my life to see big-league players, who, until then, I'd only read about," Tran said.

Some players avoided the war by receiving deferments, designated as the only ones who could support their families or provide jobs that specifically were needed to keep the country going, such as teaching; or, they had overcome some other sort of personal hardship, such as Charlie Metro. An eventual Seattle outfielder and big-league manager, Metro had survived a coal-mining accident as a teenager that had killed seven other men in Pennsylvania, and that was his out from World War II. "I never went into the service," Metro said. "I was classified 4-F. I was lucky. I guess they felt that coming close to dying once was enough."

Not everyone in a military uniform was always in harm's way. Vanni admittedly spent a lot of service time playing baseball. Consider this 1944 entry from a World War II newsletter titled *The 3 and 0 Umpire*, prepared for Seattle's baseball-minded soldiers stationed elsewhere: "Edo Vanni, diving into a foxhole when the big Jacksonville storm struck, thinking some Japs were hitting line drives . . . Edo drove the Japs back with a beautiful .379 batting average and was chosen the most outstanding player in their league."

In Vanni's absence, the Rainiers often resembled a senior center for aging baseball players. Byron Speece pitched for Seattle from 1943–45, and he was a doddering forty-eight when he concluded his wartime stint with the franchise, just three years younger than Sick, the man in charge. Acquired from Portland, the seasoned right-hander was a submarine-style pitcher, using his underhanded delivery to make a collective seventy-five appearances and compile a 26-25 record. Speece, an Indiana native who previously played for the Washington Senators, Cleveland Indians, and Philadelphia Phillies, had been out of the big leagues for sixteen years, a baseball lifetime, when he first joined the Rainiers, but he was hardly a one-man freak show. Using the baseball elderly was standard practice by the Seattle franchise. Joining Speece on the 1945 pitching staff was the well-traveled Sylvester Johnson, a forty-four-year-old man who was 6-3 on the mound, and the soft-throwing Turpin, who, at forty, posted an 18-8 record in what would be the last of his nineteen pro seasons, all spent in the minors, with retirement beckoning.

The Seattle ballclub made an exhaustive fifty-nine player transactions in 1945, and some of them smacked of desperation. Jack Meister was just sixteen when he was signed directly out of Queen Anne High School with two seasons of schoolboy eligibility remaining and sent to the Class B Vancouver Capilanos. Even Hutchinson and Vanni hadn't turned pro until they were eighteen and graduated. Responding to escalating protests over Meister's premature jump to the pros from Queen Anne baseball coach John Cherberg and Seattle Public Schools athletic director Leon Brigham, Rainiers general manager Bill Mulligan argued back, "If we didn't sign him, some other club would have." Finally joining the Rainiers in 1947, Meister pitched in just one game for his hometown team. It was clear he should have played longer in high school. In a miserable three-inning stint, he gave up eight runs on six hits, walked eight, and struck out one batter.

Earl Torgeson was seventeen when he joined the Rainiers late in the 1941 season and he was given just a handful of at-bats. A superb first baseman from rural Snohomish, he was known for his gruff demeanor, thick glasses, and smooth batting stroke from the left side. He was mature enough to hit for a .312 average in 1942, and once crushed a ball so hard it went through the top of the wooden outfield fence at Sicks' Stadium, leaving a sizeable hole, a feat that landed him a home run. Umpires ignored the visiting team's plea that the ball should have been ruled a ground-rule double, apparently impressed by the ferocity with which it left the ballpark.

Near the end of World War II, word arrived home that Torgeson had been wounded during fighting in France, but his injuries were not touted as life or baseball threatening. Turns out, the worst of it for the future big-leaguer was being mistaken for a dead body and getting flipped over while lying in an impaired state among several corpses in a truck. Torgeson recovered sufficiently to play fifteen seasons in the big leagues with five teams, appearing in the 1959 World Series with the Chicago White Sox. He returned home and entered politics, with his career ending in scandal. As Snohomish County commissioner for four years, he was accused and later cleared of charges of willful neglect of duty. The smudge on his name was permanent. He ran for office twice more and couldn't get re-elected.

With so much roster churn, just four players held down Rainiers spots for each of the four war seasons: pitchers Carl Fischer, Turpin, and Johnson; and Matheson, Vanni's replacement in right field. As an Oregon farmer living in the rural community of Yoncolla and the sole provider for his family, Turpin was given a free pass on the war while he pushed a plow. At times, he had to push baseball aside, too, leaving the team in 1943 at midseason to tend to his farm because no one else was available, and reporting late in 1945 for the same reason.

Wartime interest in the Rainiers bottomed out in 1943, with just 143,477 fans, or 2,391 per game, willing or able to watch a stripped-down team forced to play too many day games. Nerves were frayed by the escalating war and attention was now diverted elsewhere at President Roosevelt's request. People couldn't easily get away from the frenzied activity at the Boeing plant on

Marginal Way, which was camouflaged from the air in case of a mainland attack. Workers were asked to roll out B-17s, or Flying Fortresses, at an incredible rate for combat, producing five thousand just two years into the conflict, twelve thousand overall. In hours that typified the wartime demand, Walt Milroy, an aspiring baseball player and teacher from Seattle, worked six consecutive weeks without a day off on the Boeing final assembly line, with his marathon run of shifts ending only when he joined the Navy, just as the first B-17 was nearing completion.

Making baseball matters worse, these Rainiers weren't very interesting to those who saw them in 1943, at least early in the season. They tumbled into last place before righting themselves and finishing third with an 85-70 record. Once the season ended, Skiff's job security was roundly debated in the Seattle press, but he received another contact extension. His job, it seemed, was simply to keep things together as best he could under trying circumstances.

A year later, night games were restored. There was a welcome spike in attendance everywhere in baseball, and the Rainiers' 326,549 total, or 4,796 per game, more than doubled from the previous season. Trouble was, the 1944 team still wasn't very good, finishing 84-85 and out of the playoffs. The losing season and postseason absence both were uncomfortable firsts for the Sick ownership. Again Skiff was panned in the press and rumored to be on his way out, but the front office stood behind him.

"I'll build from the ground up if I'm manager next year," Skiff said before he was rehired again, the urgency noted in his comments. "I'll get a new team. There are too many things wrong with this one to fix it up. If Mr. Sick gives the word to go ahead I'll begin making wholesale changes right away."

One player he decided to go without was Dick Gyselman, trading him during the 1944 season to San Diego. The slender, smooth-fielding player called "The Needle" had been Seattle's third baseman for a decade, starting with the Indians, and was a fixture on the Rainiers' pennant-winning teams, even topping the PCL with fifty-three doubles in 1938. With each departure, Seattle's glory years seem to fade away more and more.

Baseball's great suffering was almost over. In 1945 the war ended on each side of the world and each side of the season, with Germany surrendering in May and the Japanese following suit in August. After peace was declared and people took to the streets in celebration, the Rainiers became relevant again, if only briefly, finishing as the PCL runners-up behind Portland, compiling a 105-78 record, the last of five 100-win seasons for Sick. The owner finally had a chance to see how much Seattle's wartime population boost would pad his attendance, and it was significant. Without any worries or pressing deadlines to complete plane or ship orders, a franchise-record 434,133 fans, or 6,201 per game, passed through the gates. On August 15, the day the conflict came to a halt in the South Pacific, a lot of people chose to do their celebrating at the ballpark, with 13,621 filling up Sicks' Stadium for a doubleheader split with the Los Angeles Angels, the Rainiers losing 4–2 in the opener and bouncing back with a 10–6 victory in the second game.

Everyone seemed to have a lighter, healthier outlook now that world order was restored. On option from the St. Louis Browns, pitcher Chet Johnson was a Ballard High School graduate and native son, someone who had worked in a Seattle shipyard by day and pulled on a Rainiers uniform whenever possible, and he was determined to enjoy himself when on the baseball diamond in 1945. In compiling a 14-12 record, he was a nonstop entertainer on the mound. When facing a good hitter, Johnson would turn and motion for his outfielders to move back. Once he threw a strike past the batter, the animated Johnson would turn and motion for everyone to come in closer, drawing snickers throughout the crowd.

As the 1945 season wound down, travel restrictions were eased and baseball contemplated returning to normal, yet logistics remained tricky at times. Playing in the final round of the newly rechristened Governor's Cup series, the Rainiers twice had to postpone the opener at Sicks' Stadium. The San Francisco Seals, the eventual postseason champs in six games, couldn't arrive in time for Wednesday night's opener, the result of travel complications. On Thursday night, both teams were in the ballpark and fans were in the seats, waiting for the first pitch, when everything was waved off again. It seems the Seals' baseball baggage had turned up in Portland and couldn't be retrieved until the following day.

Nineteen forty-six was supposed to be a year of baseball renewal, an opportunity for Sick to reclaim the personal glory and cash flow he had given up once bombs started falling on Hawaii. There was an abundance of baseball fans living in Seattle, with more on the way home from war, and people were eager to head to the ballpark again. It was time for Sick to get the franchise up and running at highly competitive levels again.

There would be no more excuses. Skiff, the man with his constant detractors, would be given the opportunity to show what he was capable of doing without the shadow of Lelivelt or the pall of war hanging over him. There was just one problem:

the Rainiers were worse than ever, skidding to seventh place and a horrendous 74-109 record, forty-one games behind the pennant-winning San Francisco Seals.

No longer the free spender he'd been in his earliest years, Sick was part of the problem. Determined to restore his financial bottom line, he liquidated some of his coveted young baseball talent for significant returns. Torgeson was the biggest bat sacrificed: he was shopped to the Boston Braves before the 1945 season, with delivery promised in 1946 after he had fulfilled his military obligation and appeared in 103 more games for Seattle. The outfield prospect fetched an impressive bounty of $60,000 and four players, outfielder Bill Ramsey, infielder Tony York, catcher Hugh Poland, and pitcher Lou Tost. Gone was a unique player in Torgeson, the first in a Rainiers uniform to wear glasses on the field, the better to see all those blasts to the power alleys, and lost was a local drawing card, something Sick previously had demanded when putting together teams.

The helter-skelter Rainiers used fifty-eight different players in 1946. Typical of these was Lou Novikoff, who was past his prime and living off his earlier reputation as a heavy hitter for the Los Angeles Angels. The hot-tempered man known as "The Mad Russian" still had anger problems but little else to offer when he stood at the plate. He had rapped out forty-two home runs for the Angels six years earlier; he hit two in eighty-four games for the Rainiers, dropping to his knees and kissing home plate after supplying one of them. Teammates noticed he needed something extra to get through the season. He often showed up at the ballpark smelling of alcohol.

Theatrical by nature, Novikoff was called out one night after sliding into second base and went after the umpire in a fierce tirade, ranting to no avail. Spotting the image of another arbiter painted on the Sicks' Stadium outfield wall in an advertisement, one with outstretched arms signaling a positive outcome, Novikoff took off running toward it, slid in at the base of the endorsement on the warning track, turned to the real ump and bellowed, "See, I was safe, you sonofabitch!" The emotional player, of course, took the rest of the day off, at the ump's request. "The size of that umpire sign was two garage doors wide," said Carnett, a Rainiers teammate. "Lou ran 250 feet to dead left-center to get there. The fans just went crazy."

Novikoff couldn't hit a baseball like he once did, but he managed to make solid contact elsewhere. With the team waiting in Portland to board a train for Seattle, he grew annoyed with the recently acquired Tost and the recently returned Edo Vanni, who were bickering on the depot platform. A few drinks had fueled Tost's argumentative ways. Hearing enough, Novikoff lost his temper, walked over, and punched the unsuspecting Tost, leaving him with a black eye and broken teeth, unable to pitch the following day as scheduled.

"Tost nearly rolled under a Pullman car," said Tran, a witness to the punch. "Novikoff was kind of unpredictable. He was a real wild man. He had a short fuse. That was typical Lou."

It was unclear what the argument with Tost was all about, but Vanni couldn't have been too happy with the way his pro baseball career had been short-circuited by World War II. He missed four seasons while serving in the Navy, this after earlier sitting out another with his broken leg. Before the huge gap in the little outfielder's play, *The Sporting News* had reported that the Pittsburgh Pirates were prepared to offer $100,000 for Vanni, with a quarter of the sale price going into the player's pocket

The Rainiers' second baseman Al Niemiec never backed down,
whether arguing with umpires or suing his team.

if the deal was consummated. Instead, the Navy obtained his
services for free for the next four years. And once his service
obligations were over, Vanni was no longer a good Triple-A
player. He made the Rainiers roster in 1946, but his skills failed
him the following season and he was shipped to Double-A Birmingham in the Southern League. He spent the next decade
shuffling through Class A ball in several Northwest cities as
a player-manager. As for the Pirates, he was left only with the
yellowed clipping of what could have been, a keepsake tucked
in a scrapbook, nothing more.

"That's what killed me," said Vanni, who made the best of a
deeply disappointing situation. "You can't get it back. But I was

alive, what the hell. So what? I came back. I got into management. I can't complain."

Not everyone took it so well. Al Niemiec was the Rainiers' regular second baseman during 1940–42, a decent .266 hitter when he was called off to serve as a Navy lieutenant. When he returned to Seattle in 1946 at the age of thirty-six, he fully expected to reclaim his old job and steady paycheck. The Rainiers apparently felt Niemiec's play was anemic, because he played in five games in April and was released. The chagrined war veteran sued the team in a highly publicized case, claiming that the G.I. Bill of Rights had guaranteed him one year of employment upon return, regardless of his playing capability, and that the ballclub had violated these rights. The infielder could be a tough guy when necessary. In the middle of the 1942 season, Niemiec and his former Rainiers teammate Gilly Campbell, a catcher now wearing the colors of the Los Angeles Angels, brawled for fifteen minutes near the pitcher's mound in the first game of a doubleheader at Sicks' Stadium. The umpires and the rest of the players just stood aside and watched until Niemiec and Campbell exhausted themselves throwing punches; then, the game resumed as if nothing had happened, with the combatants spared ejections.

However, there was a decisive outcome for the lawsuit. With all of baseball watching, Seattle federal judge Lloyd L. Black ruled in favor of Niemiec, chastising baseball in general for turning its back on some of its returning war heroes. In June, Black awarded the unwanted player $2,884 in lost salary, which equaled to $577 per game for the five he had played—an amount, as Royal Brougham snidely pointed out in his column, that made Niemiec, not Bob Feller or Hank Greenberg, the game's highest-paid player that year. The judge also ruled the Rainiers were under no obligation to put Niemiec on the field again. He would remain in the area after playing briefly in the PCL for San Diego, and Sick, maybe feeling guilty, gave him another job, working for the brewery and selling beer. Ultimately, the two would settle their differences.

With war pushed aside, baseball was back in business, but the Rainiers' fortunes continued to lag. While damaged European and Asian landscapes were under steady repair, the Seattle franchise remained in ruin. Sick was a businessman who had a long history of making money, even in baseball, even when he was told it couldn't happen, and he grew impatient when the city became vibrant and progressive again, but his team did not. Niemiec would not be the only one employed by the Rainiers to fail to survive the 1946 season, have his departure chronicled in bold headlines, and wind up in court.

Sick had seen enough losing. On June 11, 1946, he asked for Skiff's resignation and then fired him when the manager refused. He distanced himself from the man he had hired instead of Babe Ruth and stood behind during the lean war years. Sick's team was 26-46 with no hope of recovery, and he had to do something. "We retired Bill Skiff," was how the Rainiers' owner put it.

What galled him the most was that although Seattle was now spending money and building homes by the thousands, which resulted in new roads and schools, his franchise sat stagnant, failing to join in the postwar reconstruction. After years of relying on a solemn baseball man, Sick needed someone to infuse excitement into his team, someone whose attitude would coincide with the upbeat times, and he had a replacement picked out well in advance of creating the managerial opening, though this person had never held this position of power before. Jo Jo White was his number one candidate.

The former Rainiers outfielder had washed out of the big leagues again and returned to the Pacific Coast League, this time with the Sacramento Solons, and was still capable of grabbing everyone's attention. He had finished as the league's 1945 batting champion, claiming the title with a robust .355 average. Sick wanted him back in Seattle in the worst way, and was willing to do whatever it took to reunite the man and the city. Understanding this, the Solons asked for significant offensive firepower in return, and a deal was struck for outfielder Bill Ramsey, who was the Rainiers' only .300 hitter. The transaction was a little more complicated than that, requiring an additional Seattle move. Ramsey was on loan from the Boston Braves, and the Rainiers first had to purchase his contract before shipping him to California's capital city.

The widely popular White returned to Seattle amid great fanfare as a playing manager. Oddly enough, Skiff was out of a job but not on his way, forced to remain in the city that had turned its back on him and testify in the Niemiec lawsuit. Still, the change at the top had been made, and bringing the folksy southerner back to the Northwest seemed right. Yet a disturbing thing happened when White was put in charge of his old team—he wasn't a great leader at all.

"He was a better player than a manager," said Metro, a Rainiers player for White in 1946 and someone who later managed in the big leagues with the Kansas City Royals and Chicago Cubs, and made White one of his Royals coaches. While Sick had refrained from hiring Babe Ruth based primarily on name recognition, he had fallen victim to it with White. Jo Jo had plenty of chances to succeed, too. He enjoyed brief moments of managing glory but couldn't build any long-term momentum. He didn't play much in his second trip through Seattle, primarily using himself only as a pinch-hitter in dire situations. Maybe he should have stepped up to the plate more to preserve his second baseball career. There was no quick fix in 1946, with the club stumbling to a 48-63 record after White took over.

Sick had big plans for the franchise in 1947, White's first full season as manager. The Rainiers entered into their first formal player-working agreement with a big-league team, the Detroit Tigers, agreeing to a deal that called for five roster additions from the American League club for Seattle. However, the Tigers provided no Fred Hutchinson-like bounty this time, and the arrangement was short-lived, with none of the loaner talent amounting to much during a disappointing 91-95 season. The only interesting deals were the outside re-acquisitions of pitcher Dick Barrett and Dick Gyselman, White's teammates from the Rainiers' three pennant winning seasons, but these guys were well past their prime and proved to be emotional hires.

Sick didn't need any big-league help, anyway. Publicly at least, he wanted to be in the big leagues and, at the 1947 winter baseball meeting, the Rainiers owner and his PCL peers pushed this idea, boldly asking top-level baseball officials to consider recognizing them as a third Major League and presenting a five-point plan. The idea never got out of the batter's box. Baseball higher-ups rejected the proposal, turned off by the prospect of sharing elite baseball status with the West's unwashed, and of coast-to-coast travel, with commercial jets still nearly a decade away. Baseball expansion wouldn't be considered for thirteen more seasons. In the interim, franchises would be moved, and even encroach on PCL territory, but not added.

Counterproposals were swapped until opening day of the 1948 season, with the final one suggesting the PCL and Texas League enter into some sort of merger and evolve into the third big league being proposed. Again, it was swing and miss. However, there was casual mention for the first time that the big leagues might be interested in expanding into Los Angeles and San Francisco. But take in an entire Triple-A league? No way.

Sick privately had conceded that most West Coast ballparks, including his handsome Seattle facility, didn't meet big-league standards and that most of his fellow owners didn't have enough money to purchase talented enough players. He mainly went along with the third Major League concept in order to preserve or enhance the PCL from a business standpoint, asking for better bargaining rights in retaining players longer or receiving a better sales price for them. He repeatedly voiced his concerns that the big leagues, which annually drafted and purchased minor-league players, were not paying fair market value for PCL talent.

"We don't want to hold back a player's advancement, but they were moved up before the present draft arrangement for big money years ago, players such as Willie Kamm, Earl Averill, Jimmy O'Connell, Mickey Cochrane and many others," the Seattle owner pointed out.

The Majors idea stalled out, as did White's Rainiers in 1948. In June, there was great hope for the new manager when his second-place team hosted the first-place San Francisco Seals in a weeklong series, and 77,674 fans poured into the ballpark for the seven games, 10,000-plus per outing, a franchise record that wouldn't be surpassed. White's position appeared secure as Seattle won four of the contests, moving to 37-25 and within two games of first place. "For a young fellow just breaking in as a skipper, Jo Jo isn't doing such a bad job," Brougham wrote in the *Post-Intelligencer*. But the good vibe wouldn't last long. White's Rainiers started to slide and finished 93-95 and in fourth place, still drawing 452,448 in attendance while failing to break .500, leaving Sick sick of it all. The team was popular, just not very good.

Sentiment would carry White only so far. In June 1949, after he had been on the job for the equivalent of three seasons, he was fired while his 55-54 team was in San Francisco. The removal of this franchise pillar was emotional and difficult. The Seattle newspapers treated his ouster like an obituary. Reporters seemed to share in White's disappointment, offering condolences rather than writing about his shortcomings. A *Seattle Times* headline summed up his dismissal this way: "His Only Fault? Not Enough Players Like Himself." Management, in considering the potential revenues lost, was a little more willing to speed White on his way.

"Jo Jo was a colorful figure that we all liked," Sick said. "He had been a very grand baseball player, full of competitive spirit, but as a manager he was a little inexperienced and I decided to change him."

White was done in after the Rainiers dropped nineteen of twenty-five games. The slump started with a humbling 17–0 defeat in Los Angeles and ended with nine consecutive losses at home. Bill Lawrence, the artful centerfielder from the earlier pennant-winning Rainiers teams and a coach on White's staff, was installed as interim manager for the rest of the season. "The

Jo Jo White, the Rainiers' manager from 1946 to 1949,
holds a team meeting in the clubhouse.

strain of the recent homestand and the loss of nine straight was
plenty tough on the old nervous system," White told reporters
in his usual whimsical manner.

The manager's chief drawback was his laid-back approach,
which ran counter to his fiery style as a player. Despite his elevated status, he remained one of the guys, always joining in
their poker games on the train, always winning more than his
share, always regaling everyone in the clubhouse with one of
his long-winded stories. More distance from the troops would
have been advisable. He had the players' friendship but could
not inspire their best effort, and it cost him everything.

"He was square and fair to you," said Carnett, a supporter.
"If he had two guys and one wasn't the best player but was
trying harder, Jo Jo got rid of the better ballplayer because he

thought the other guy was better for the team." Countered Hillis Layne, White's third baseman and more circumspect about the leadership that was in place, "Jo Jo was always hesitant to say anything about anyone."

White landed squarely on his cleats again after leaving Seattle, joining the Hollywood Stars at the age of forty as an outfielder only. The Rainiers had barely said goodbye to him when he was back at Sicks' Stadium within a few weeks, his return stirring another round of newspaper headlines. His every at-bat and fielding play during that first game back were charted in detail in the *Post-Intelligencer*. Relaxed and smiling again, White singled twice in that outing, but his new team lost to Seattle, 1–0, in ten innings.

Still, Sick had felt it necessary to make the change, certain he had left White with more talent in 1949 than any other Rainiers team assembled since Jo Jo had been a full-time player seven years earlier. Veteran pitchers Guy Fletcher and Charley Schanz posted workmanlike 23-12 and 22-17 records, respectively, each logging more than three hundred innings. Providing a potent bat was first baseman Heinz Becker, who initially wanted nothing to do with Seattle. Acquired before the season from Kansas City of the American Association, the German-born Becker had a fear of earthquakes, and as he knew Seattle had experienced ground-shaking before, he was outwardly hesitant to report to this seismically active place. After repeated discussions with management, he was assured that nothing like that would happen, and he joined his new team. On April 13, 1949, Becker was preparing to play in his second game in Seattle when a huge noontime quake rocked the Northwest, from British Columbia to Southern Oregon, killing seven people and injuring sixty-four,

Catcher Sammy White played just twenty-nine games for the Rainiers
before the Boston Red Sox traded for him.

and causing millions of dollars of damage. Becker eventually
would adjust to his new surroundings and enjoy a solid season,
leading the Rainiers in batting at .313 and in RBI with 101. However, for the first month of the season, he took a backseat at bat
to another White who wasn't long for Seattle, either.

Sammy White, a Seattle native who had come to the team

directly from the University of Washington, hit .345 in twenty-nine games, which was all big-league scouts needed to see to start frothing and proposing deals. In May, the Boston Red Sox acquired him, sending three players and $75,000 to the Rainiers, a trade that happened so quickly even White was caught off guard. "You're not kidding me, are you?" he responded when informed of the transaction by a *Post-Intelligencer* sportswriter.

Sammy White shouldn't have been surprised by the interest in him, because no one else was. He had more options available to him than most aspiring pro athletes. An accomplished Washington basketball player who had helped his team advance to the NCAA tournament, he received NBA contract offers from the Minneapolis Lakers and Washington Capitols. He could accept $10,000 per season to play for the Red Sox or draw $8,000 annually from one of his pro basketball suitors. He chose the better salary and the more established pro sport, and would spend eleven seasons in the Majors with three teams.

While the different Whites were coming and going in 1949, the Rainiers were saddled with a third consecutive near-break-even season, finishing 95-92 and fourteen games out of first place, and missing out on the playoffs again. However, the fans hadn't given up on them, with a minor-league and PCL best 545,434 coming through the doors, and an average gate of 7,370 setting a franchise record. This was even more remarkable considering that a new invention, television, had broadcast Wednesday and Thursday night games and Sunday doubleheaders on home stands over the station KRSC.

War had turned Seattle into a much bigger place and helped launch its aviation interests. Midway through the 1949 baseball season, Seattle-Tacoma International Airport was completed, and soon the Rainiers would be abandoning trains and turning solely to air travel. However, despite these benefits, the war had also altered the look and feel of Sick's baseball team, with service time and career interruptions robbing it of much of its personality.

Letting go of Jo Jo White was difficult enough, but Seattle would soon be asked to turn a cold shoulder to another headliner who had built his own devoted following, someone who had been connected to the local franchise longer than anyone else. A month after the manager's forced departure, an ineffective Dick Barrett pitched in his final Rainiers game and asked for his release, which was granted.

7. Kewpie Dick

When he first showed his face in Seattle in 1935, Dick Barrett's hairline was receding and his waistline was expanding. These were hardly indicators that his stay with the local baseball franchise would be lengthy. Acquired by the Seattle Indians with third baseman Dick Gyselman in a trade that sent third baseman Joe Coscarart to the big-league Boston Braves, practically as a throw-in to complete the deal, the balding and chubby pitcher from Pennsylvania wasn't very good on the mound initially, losing his first six decisions. He wasn't even really named Dick Barrett, having borrowed his father's first name when embarking on a semipro career, forsaking his given moniker of Tracey for something more conventional.

Barrett would never part ways on a permanent basis with his newfound baseball home. He turned that miserable 0-6 beginning into a sparkling 22-13 record for the 1935 Indians. He fittingly was rechristened, and his new identifying tag "Kewpie" became an unforgettable nickname widely circulated throughout the Pacific Coast League, making him forever a cartoonish and mythical figure.

"There was no better competitor," his former Rainiers teammate Edo Vanni said. "He had a heart you couldn't believe."

Barrett's body was difficult to fathom as well. He was listed at 5 feet, 9 inches, and 180 pounds, but his weight was well over 200. Indians teammates started calling him "Kewpie" during that 1935 spring training. His lack of a muscular frame might have had something to do with it. One story had him labeled in this manner because his ruddy face and roly-poly body reminded everyone of the popular dolls made at the time. Another explanation was that this good-natured guy became known as "Cupid" while generously babysitting a teammate's young children; the kids' garbled rendition of the label, it is said, evolved into his well-known trademark. "Sportswriters dearly love to hang a nickname on a player and stick to it," Barrett said, explaining that the calling card hadn't been adopted voluntarily.

He would play twenty-six seasons of pro baseball, eleven in Seattle. He pitched and won the first game for the Rainiers franchise, and he pitched in the first game held at Sicks' Stadium. He tossed a seven-inning perfect game, the only one of its kind for the Rainiers. He won 206 of 342 games combined for the Indians and Rainiers. The numbers, however, don't come close to describing the long-running fascination fans in the Northwest held for the rumpled right-hander. Barrett was the only Seattle athlete of his era whose 1949 release warranted a full-fledged, front-page newspaper story. He was voted the most popular Rainiers player after the franchise had been in existence for fifteen years, which meant he had a bigger following than

Fred Hutchinson and Jo Jo White, who were galvanizing personalities in the city. People idolized Barrett not only because he was frumpy but because he seemed to want to pitch forever. He never looked to the bullpen for help, and he could throw every third day. He was always offering to work both ends of a Sunday doubleheader.

"I was supposed to pitch with him in a doubleheader, and he said, 'Ed, you don't mind if I pitch both games?'" his Rainiers teammate Eddie Carnett recalled. "I told him I didn't mind a bit. Talk about a great competitor."

"It's fun to call any game Barrett pitches because he likes to play baseball," broadcaster Leo Lassen pointed out.

Fans also warmed to Barrett because of his daredevil penchant for getting in and out of trouble. More times than anyone preferred, he had to escape a bases-loaded situation, something that happened so often his loyal followers started to believe that he did it on purpose, inspired, perhaps, by the difficult task facing him and a desire to become a baseball Houdini. He faced so many full counts that the media began to compose poems about him, most notably, Lassen: "Roses are red, violets are blue. Barrett is three and two, what will he do?" he harmonized from the radio booth.

Barrett relied on two different curveballs to get the job done. The first was a slow bender. The other was a sharp-breaking ball that required the use of two substances, a brown sticky material and resin, which he rubbed together, creating nothing but trouble for the unsuspecting hitter.

"He had this Sunday curve and a strikeout curve," Carnett said. "The second curve was this thing that exploded out of his hand and broke right down. He'd just rub that stuff on it a little."

"I remember that thing dropping down pretty fast," said Ford "Moon" Mullen, a teammate of Barrett's both on the Rainiers and the Philadelphia Phillies.

Kewpie was a fastball pitcher early in his pro career, simply willing to challenge the hitter and not worrying about much else. In 1940 he hurt his back twice in spring training, which forced him to try a more cerebral approach. He became more effective, more of a curveball specialist.

"I don't try to strike everybody out now," he told the *Post-Intelligencer* that season. "I don't take such a wide pivot in my delivery, have sight of the plate at all times and am saving myself a lot of grief by slowing up now and then, because, I suppose, I am forced to do so."

Barrett won at least twenty games in seven of his first eight seasons in Seattle. He formed a fearsome pitching duo with Hal Turpin, who matched his twenty victories on four of those occasions. In 1940 Barrett and Turpin were 24-5 and 23-11, so simultaneously dominating that the *Post-Intelligencer*, for the first time, began to provide daily charts comparing their stellar statistics, something that would be repeated in future seasons.

"There are two men wasting their talents outside the Major Leagues: Barrett and Turpin," their teammate Bill Lawrence said. "Even at their age, they would help win a pennant for any one of several clubs in the National and the American."

Kewpie Dick was at his best in 1942, compiling a 27-13 record and a 1.72 earned run average, the latter figure penciling out as pro baseball's lowest. Barrett started that season fast, winning his first three outings, all on the road, before losing at Hollywood. He came home and tossed consecutive shutouts, a three-hitter against the Oakland Acorns and a four-hitter against Hollywood's Stars, and he went twenty-four innings before allowing a run.

Demonstrating his endurance in his tenth start, Barrett pitched all fourteen innings of a 3–1 victory at Los Angeles, one inning shy of his Rainiers best. He was hardly weary in his next outing, either. He beat the San Francisco Seals, 2–0, at Sicks' Stadium, missing a no-hitter only when Kermit Lewis legged out an infield single up the middle that was gloved by Rainiers second baseman Al Niemiec. Less than a month later, Barrett barely missed out on another no-hitter at home in a 3–1 victory over the San Diego Padres over seven innings. Improving his record to 14-4 that game, he allowed a one-out single up the middle to Jack Whipple in the sixth inning but nothing more.

On August 7, Barrett became the first pitcher at any pro baseball level in 1942 to record his twentieth victory, beating Portland 6–0 on the road. In a seven-inning outing, he spaced out seven hits and struck out eight batters. Barrett maintained serious pitching momentum through his final regular-season start, earning his twenty-seventh victory with a five-hit, 5–0 shutout at Oakland, his sixth scoreless performance. That night, he broke the record for victories by a Seattle pitcher in a season, surpassing Jim "Jumbo" Elliott, who had twenty-six victories in thirty-six decisions for the Indians in 1926.

In the 1942 postseason, Barrett was beaten in his President's Cup opener by pennant-winning Sacramento, but he came back with victories over the Solons and Los Angeles. Going for a thirtieth overall victory on the mound and the Cup clincher on the final day of the championship series, he was denied in an 8–3 loss to the Angels, suffering through perhaps his worst opening inning of the season. In the first game of a doubleheader, he gave up five runs before registering three outs. Luckily for Barrett, the Rainiers, who finished as the PCL's third-place team during the regular season, bounced back to secure the Cup in the nightcap. His final outing that season did nothing to taint his collective work. On December 21, 1942, *The Sporting News* singled out Barrett as the minor-league pitcher of the year. "Gee, what a swell Christmas present!" Barrett gushed when informed of his national award.

Barrett, always pushed by Turpin, had a number of seasons worthy of attention. From 1938 to 1942, he was a combined 111-62, Turpin 106-50. Although their numbers were similar, their styles were radically different. The deliberate Barrett took forever to get through a game, fidgeting and laboring over every pitch. Turpin preferred to zip through his starts as quickly as possible. The team used this information to strategic advantage at the concession stands. Since more beer was sold on Saturdays than any other day of the week, Barrett always pitched the Saturday night home games, helping to keep the concession windows open longer than usual. The more he waffled, the more suds were sold. Turpin often finished off a game in an hour and a half. He was usually given Sunday assignments on the weekend, because alcohol wasn't offered at the ballpark that day.

As good as he was in Seattle, Barrett never made a breakthrough in the big leagues. He had four chances. In 1933 the Philadelphia Athletics brought him up for fifteen games and he split eight decisions. A year later, he drew fifteen more outings with the Boston Braves and went 1-3. After his big splash with the Rainiers, the Chicago Cubs and Philadelphia Phillies summoned him to the top level in 1943 and 1944, but he was barely ordinary, winning just twenty-two of fifty-three decisions over those two seasons.

"Kewpie" Dick Barrett, shown here getting a drink of water,
usually preferred something stronger.

Barrett's stated big-league goal practically came straight from
a menu, which might have been part of the problem: "To get in
the majors for a least a sandwich. I am tired of going up there
for a cup of coffee." Barrett ended up going hungry, though he
was confident in his abilities.

In 1943 the *Post-Intelligencer*'s Royal Brougham sent the pitcher
a Western Union telegram that asked him to compare his big-

league experiences to those in the minors. From Philadelphia, Barrett wrote the sportswriter back, declaring, "[The] only difference in pitching is that you face more good hitters each day than you do in [the] minors, which is balanced by better fielding. [Stan] Musial of St. Louis is [the] best hitter I have faced. The fans back here are pretty enthusiastic but not near as fair and broadminded as our Seattle fans."

Weird stuff seemed to stunt his baseball career at times. Barrett claimed that Athletics manager Connie Mack fully intended to use him as a starting pitcher until finding out that he was moonlighting as a pro football player to pick up a few extra bucks. In another strange incident, a companion on a bird-hunting trip accidentally shot Barrett in the knee, forcing him to spend three months in a hospital. "I guess he mistook me for a ring-tailed rooster," Barrett wisecracked.

The veteran pitcher was back in the minors for good after his final fling with Philadelphia. He had too many personal demons to succeed as a big leaguer. There was a reason his cheeks were beet red and his body so puffy, sometimes unbearably so in spring training. He was a nonstop drinker, an unapologetic alcoholic, a lush. While players several generations later would be castigated for pumping up their bodies with performance-enhancing stimulants, Barrett tore his down, unable to stop the damage. Working as an insurance salesman during the off-season, Barrett would travel with two suitcases. One was filled with clothes, the other with hard liquor. During the baseball season, he used to carry around a flask of Seagram's whiskey. When the players went out after a game, if the drink prices were too steep for him at some bar or tavern, Barrett would pull out his personal stash and pour his own.

"He'd drink that stuff like water," former teammate Rugger Ardizoia said. "He'd have big pimples all over his body because of it. If that man didn't drink, what a ballplayer he would have been. Man, he could throw."

"I know he liked to drink," Carnett said. "He wouldn't turn one down."

One night after a 1940 game in San Francisco, Barrett drank so much that he passed out in a bar. His teammate Bob Stagg was asked to bring him back to the hotel. The catcher made Barrett take a cold bath in the early hours, anything to speed his recovery and get him ready to put on a baseball uniform again. The next day Kewpie wasn't scheduled to pitch and sat on the bench nursing a serious hangover. The Rainiers were losing big, and the manager wasn't pleased with either the pending outcome or the condition of his top pitcher.

"I'm going to get even with him," Jack Lelivelt told the others, before wheeling on Barrett and barking, "Barrett, you're in!" The disbelieving pitcher trudged to the mound and labored on every pitch in a lost cause, just trying to get through the surprise outing as best he could. It was the ultimate challenge. "He pitched three innings, still drunker than hell," Stagg said.

Barrett played for Seattle teams from 1935 to 1942 and again from 1947 to 1949. He was supposedly washed up the second time around, and he was certainly older, fatter, and balder. Yet on May 16, 1948, the forty-one-year-old pitcher threw a perfect game in the nightcap of a doubleheader at Sicks' Stadium, beating the Sacramento Solons over seven innings, 3–0. Only one ball, a liner from Babe Dahlgren in the second inning, threatened to fall safely during this pitching gem, but the Rainiers' second baseman Tony York made a leaping grab for it and saved everything. Barrett struck out five batters, was rarely behind in the count, and went to 3-2 on only one batter, Alex Kampouris, striking him out.

His teammates did everything possible to preserve his pitching masterpiece. Jo Jo White's eight-year-old son, Mike, was seated on the Rainiers' bench when he looked at the scoreboard during the sixth inning and suddenly realized what was taking place.

"Jeepers!" the manager's kid bellowed, but he could not get out much more than "Sacramento hasn't got even one . . ." before four hands, belonging to four different Rainiers, smothered the end of his sentence, preventing any jinx from setting in and ruining the effort.

Perfection was complete when Barrett enticed Ted Jennings, the third player in the Solons' batting order, to ground out to York. Seattle players ran to the mound and mobbed the pitcher, hugging him and slapping him on the back, while the crowd of 6,945 gave him a standing ovation. "They say it was too bad that it was only a seven-inning game, but after 23 years of waiting for one to come along, I'll settle for that," Barrett told reporters. It was only the PCL's second perfect game, the other having been thrown by Oakland's Cotton Pippen, who had retired every batter he faced against Sacramento five years earlier.

People were so smitten by the aging Seattle pitcher and his heroics that they arranged for a "Dick Barrett Night" three months later. On August 20, 1948, a night on which he was pitching against San Diego, Barrett was saluted in a pregame tribute, and plied with gifts. He received a new Chevrolet sedan from the fans, boosters, and the team, and climbed inside and posed for a newspaper photo. The team also gave him an engraved gold wristwatch. His West Seattle neighbors bought

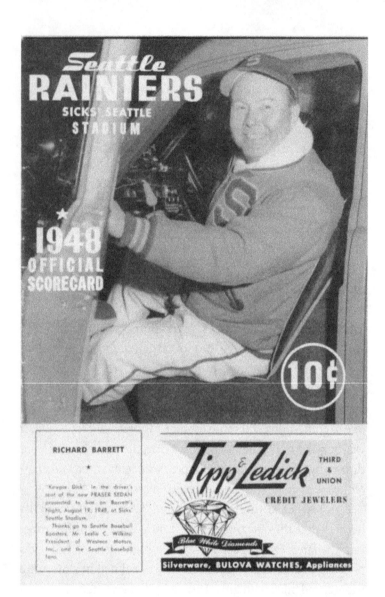

Pitcher Dick Barrett is featured on a Rainiers program cover.

him a hunting rifle. He received a bonus check from the Rainiers and a personal check from general manager Earl Sheely. The boosters couldn't resist and handed him a blond toupee, which presented another photo opportunity. The Padres gave him a glass arm. A men's club handed over a silver coffeemaker. Even the umpires got involved, impishly handing the pitcher a three-foot-wide home plate.

Telegrams by the dozens arrived at the ballpark, and Barrett heard from former teammates, opposing players, opposing managers, and the league office. Several messages were affectionately addressed to "the Round Man." All were highly effusive in praise, especially a Western Union salutation sent from PCL president Clarence Rowland:

You have set an outstanding example of performances on our diamonds not only giving winning efforts with a high degree of consistency, but by your great show of heart at all times. Never an alibi for that close game lost. Never anything but praise for your rivals and never a gloat over a victory. By these traits and by your remarkable record you have stamped yourself as one of the truly greats in Pacific Coast League history.

On his big night, Barrett went out and pitched six-plus innings in front of 8,006 fans, receiving no decision in a game that went thirteen innings and wasn't over until midnight. The Rainiers won it for him, 6–5.

Sentiment took a serious pounding the following summer. Barrett came to training camp in awful shape and was used sparingly once the season unfolded. Finally on June 6, 1949, he asked for and received his release. Emmett Watson, briefly a Rainiers teammate and pitching batterymate six seasons earlier, chronicled

Dick Barrett joined the Rainiers' radio broadcast team,
sharing the booth with Rod Belcher.

Barrett's requested departure in a front-page story in the *Seattle Times*. "I think I can still pitch," Barrett told Watson. "Naturally, I hate to leave Seattle, which I consider my home, but baseball is my business and I have to go where I can work at it."

A day later, San Diego signed the pitcher. A month later, Barrett beat the Rainiers twice in a weeklong series played at Sicks' Stadium, part of his combined 12-6 season for the two franchises and last bit of Triple-A glory. After pitching next for Western International League (WIL) teams in Victoria and Vancouver, British Columbia, which was Class A ball and a decided step down from Seattle, he was out of the game for good as an active player in 1953 and briefly served as general manager for Yakima's WIL team.

In 1957 Barrett and the Rainiers were reunited when the

ballclub invited him back as the color announcer on the radio team, sitting him alongside play-by-play man Rod Belcher. The former pitcher was as jovial as ever and passed himself off on the air as a gourmet cook at home, describing his epicurean appetite. In the booth, Barrett proved knowledgeable about baseball and its history, and he made people laugh. He slipped up a few times, too.

"He was interesting to work with, but you had to be careful of him in the broadcast booth," Belcher said. "He'd say funny things. Once a black player was knocked down and nearly hit by a pitch, and Barrett came on and said, 'Oh, that almost made a white man out of him.'"

It was a temporary gig. Barrett moved away from baseball again and started to drift. He tried a number of jobs over the next few years, among them working for a mill, the parks and recreation department, a public relations firm, the ferry system as a ticket-taker, and as a restaurant greeter. The next time anyone heard about him was in December 1963, and the news wasn't good. The one-time community hero was hardly recognizable, turning up in a Seattle courtroom and answering to a shoplifting arrest. Standing in front of a municipal judge, he was unable to hide his shame.

Suffering from diabetes and a liver ailment, the now fifty-seven-year-old Barrett explained how he and his wife were barely making it on a $48 monthly welfare check. Sheepishly, he told of entering a West Seattle grocery store and picking up three pieces of chicken and some chicken livers, and stuffing them in his pocket. He grabbed a six-pack of beer, too, but paid for that on his way out the door. Barrett didn't get forty feet before a store employee stopped him. Police arrived, arrested him, and booked the pitcher in the downtown jail, and he spent a sleepless night behind bars. He received a $50 fine and a thirty-day sentence, which were both suspended because he had no prior criminal record.

"I never gave up in a baseball game and I'm not giving up now," he said, expressing remorse that kids would see his struggles. Adults felt sorry for him, and *Post-Intelligencer* accounts of Barrett's plight led to an outpouring of support, with checks earmarked for him arriving at the paper. It was needed relief for a man who was used to pitching complete games, sometimes two in one day.

8. TV, Rajah, and Jungle Jim

Baseball's reaction to the 1949 invasion of television into the ballpark was no different than the nation's response to its first UFO sighting, which was reported two years earlier between the Northwest peaks of Mount Rainier and Mount Adams: traditional baseball men everywhere, including Seattle owner Emil Sick, were initially spooked. Two cameras set up at Sicks' Stadium transmitting grainy images to homes across the city in concert with a solitary broadcaster shivering in a makeshift wooden booth hardly seemed like something to fear. Yet throughout the Pacific Coast League, this technological advance had caused attendance to decline notably, specifically in Los Angeles, where more than five hundred thousand households had sprung for TV sets, and fans were so enthralled they weren't leaving their living rooms.

Pacific Coast League president Clarence "Pants" Rowland was so upset with the sudden revenue loss he considered the new broadcast medium a one-year experiment that had failed baseball and even told his teams on the eve of the 1950 season that "it's time to pull the plug on television." Rowland had been nicknamed "Pants" because his belt had broken and baseball trousers had fallen once when he was racing around the bases as a player. Now it seemed as if someone was pulling them down on purpose, and he didn't like it. Rather indignantly, he noted how a TV station could both sponsor a game broadcast and support the team and then undercut the effort between innings by telling the public to buy a set and watch the action at home. Still, no one reached for the off button.

Bill O'Mara, a one-person broadcast team for KRSC-TV— which, after a year of operation, became KING-TV—had auditioned for the job after reading about it in the newspaper, as did a host of other curiosity-seekers, including Oregon State College's basketball coach Amory "Slats" Gill. Experience, of course, was not necessary—or possible. O'Mara, who had roots in North Dakota, was a slight, thin man. Originally known as Bill Rhodes, he changed his surname to O'Mara after he was hired, because the Bon Marche department store was sponsoring the baseball telecasts and one of its chief competitors was another outlet called Rhodes. He took his grandmother's maiden name, attached an O to give it a boost, and he had a new identity. At first, it probably didn't matter what anyone called him.

"From the beginning, I was totally unknown to everybody and TV was totally unknown to everybody," O'Mara said. "What we inherited was a listening audience. When they switched over to TV, they weren't really watching the picture at first. They were still listening."

KRSC's first baseball telecast came on the second night of

1949's season-opening home stand against Sacramento. It wasn't the biggest news in town, coming hours after a major earthquake had shaken up the city, but the show had to go on. The Rainiers kept O'Mara and his cameramen busy in the booth that night, blowing a 7–0 lead and losing 15–8. There were just a few television sets in Seattle, plus everyone was assessing significant quake damage, so there was no telling if many people at all watched the landmark telecast.

Many simply found TV hard to accept, most notably, the Rainiers' longtime radio broadcaster Leo Lassen. He felt threatened by it. Baseball, in his mind, was a radio game, meant to stir the imagination of those outside the fences. TV was set up next door to Lassen's booth, and he tried his best to ignore it and anyone connected to it. Gradually, everyone would warm to TV, even Lassen, because it wasn't going away.

"Leo would pass me on the runway and I would say hello to him and he wouldn't say anything," O'Mara recalled. "This went on for a year. He never gave any indication that I was there. But the second year, he would nod to me, and by the time we got to the third year, he would say hello."

With a studio set up in the back of the ballpark booth, there were commercials that didn't work, notably, a wheel spinning out of control for a Bardahl Oil advertisement. It didn't take long for male cameramen to regularly train their lenses on comely women seated in the crowd, a practice that was never followed by any commentary. Production was comical at times, with floor director Al Houston once forced to step in front of the camera in order to get O'Mara's attention, with the home audience sharing in their animated discussion about what would come next. The sale of televisions also had to be promoted at every opportunity

Paul Richards was the Rainiers' manager in 1950
before heading to the big leagues.

to keep the broadcasts alive. "Each month, we had to have a
count and see how many sets we had sold," O'Mara said.

Unlike the California teams, the Rainiers experienced only a
slight attendance dip once TV broadcasts were up and running.
Sick, always the calculating businessman, noticed there were
more empty seats, but he also was banking on TV broadcast

revenue, slowly understanding the give and take of this venture. A bigger concern for him was putting a competitive team up on these new illuminated screens.

After firing manager Jo Jo White and releasing pitcher Dick Barrett, the Rainiers changed a lot of stuff in a hurry entering the 1950 season, and they now had a new manager in Paul Richards, a man moving through the ranks fast and who would later manage the Chicago White Sox and Baltimore Orioles. Before he could get to the big leagues, Richards was forced to suffer through an awful summer in Seattle. His team stumbled badly from the beginning, losing twenty-three of twenty-five games in April, nine in a row at one point, and never fully recovered.

In one particularly dismal outing, Edo Vanni, playing a limited role in his final season as a Rainiers player, was told by the manager to come off the bench and play in left field after five opposing home runs had been launched out of Sicks' Stadium in a hurry. Vanni couldn't resist being a wise guy, and with a straight face, he asked the manager, "Which side of the fence?" Now thirty, Vanni was released after a handful of games, not for the quip, but for losing his batting stroke, and he headed for the Class A level to assume a player-manager role.

Things were so bad for Richards's team that on one night, Royal Brougham, the *Post-Intelligencer*'s civic-minded sports editor, challenged his readers to help grease a turnaround by providing a show of support at the ballpark. In other words, they were invited to attend a pity party. The resulting crowd of 5,573 was more enthusiastic than overwhelming in size, but the Rainiers snapped a nine-game losing streak that night with a 5–3 victory over the Sacramento Solons. The club went on to win twenty-three of its next thirty-six outings, and Seattle finished

Hillis Layne crosses home plate after hitting a game-winning
home run for the Rainiers.

eight games below .500, a reasonable showing considering the
miserable start. If the TV cameras needed someone in a Rainiers
uniform to zoom in on for a close up, the pitcher Jim Wilson
was usually chosen. He won sixteen consecutive games while
compiling a 24-10 record, much of it done with a sore right arm.
His reward was a return to the big leagues, with his sale to the
Boston Braves once the season ended.

Richards's Seattle team had been loose and relaxed when it
showed up for spring training in Palm Springs, if not a little feisty.
During an exhibition game in the California desert against the
New York Giants, as they were then named, Rainiers coach Eddie
Taylor was hanging over a dugout railing when he pulled out a
watch and started swinging it back and forth on a chain. This
was done for the benefit of Leo Durocher in the other dugout.

"Remember this? Remember this?" Taylor chirped impishly until the Giants manager became so angry he ran through the infield, cut across the mound, and headed straight for the instigator. Rainiers players intercepted the big-league manager, forming a shield between Durocher and their watch-wielding coach. A nerve had been struck, which was the intent. Early in his playing career with the New York Yankees, Durocher had been accused of stealing a watch belonging to the great Babe Ruth, something he always vehemently denied.

Richards got along with this group of Rainiers about as well as Taylor did with Durocher. He wasn't popular at all with most of the players, keeping everyone on edge with caustic comments and his growing impatience as the losses mounted. It got so bad the Seattle players were ready to mutiny. "We lost about 10 straight [it was nine] and one of the players, and I won't tell you who he was, said, 'I wish we could lose 20 straight because of him,'" Rainiers third baseman Hillis Layne revealed. Layne wasn't a big fan of the manager, either. Richards never warmed to him, releasing the veteran infielder during the season, allowing Portland to quickly sign him on the rebound. The Tennessee native previously had been Seattle's best hitter, winning the 1947 PCL batting crown with a .366 average and finishing second in the 1948 race at .342. A clutch hitter, Layne once promised his teammates he would come up with a home run to end an extra-inning game in Los Angeles, then proceeded to blast one over the right-centerfield fence. He liked nothing better than to step into the batter's box at Sicks' Stadium and catch a glimpse of Mount Rainier before turning his attention to the opposing pitcher. "I enjoyed Seattle better than I did the American League," he said. "I know I wanted to play there forever."

Rainiers funnyman Bill Schuster would do just about anything for a laugh.

Layne was a cerebral type who played next to shortstop Bill Schuster, his polar opposite. Schuster was made for TV. He approached the game in a far different manner than anyone else in the Pacific Coast League—as a nonstop showman willing to do anything to draw attention to himself. At Sicks' Stadium, he climbed up the protective screen and shook it, and then waved to howling fans and crowed like a farm hen, which brought him one of many pet names: "Schuster the Rooster." After tapping an easy-out grounder to the first baseman, he veered off course, ran to the pitcher's mound, and slid in. After hitting what he thought was a pop-up to left field, Schuster threw his bat down in disgust and took off running for third base instead of first; the ball went over the outfielder's head and Schuster was thrown out before he could retrace his steps in the traditional manner around the bases.

After slapping the ball to Seattle first baseman Len Gabrielson for an apparent easy out while playing for Los Angeles, Schuster went only halfway down the baseline before he reversed himself and ran to home plate, sliding in. Rather than touching the bag, Gabrielson played along with the charade and threw the ball home so his catcher could make the tag. The play wasn't over; Schuster still had to argue the call.

After hitting a home run in Los Angeles, Schuster crossed home plate and kissed a blonde-haired woman in the stands before disappearing into the dugout. After a teammate struck out to end an inning, Schuster ran from the on-deck circle toward the opposing pitcher, who braced himself on the mound, expecting the worst; the Seattle player instead energetically shook his hand and complimented him on the final pitch.

Finally, during one flaky Schuster at-bat, time-out was called and the opposing catcher hustled away in one direction and the home-plate umpire went another, confusing everyone else in the ballpark. There was certain madness to this moment as the Rainiers player stood there alone, smiling broadly. He always ate way too much garlic on purpose. Unapologetically, he had polluted the air.

Schuster was one of the reasons a sixth-place Seattle team led

As the Rainiers' manager, Rogers Hornsby often didn't
leave the dugout when making a pitching change.

the PCL and all minor-league teams in attendance for the second
consecutive season in 1950, pulling in 492,647 fans, or 6,398
an outing. The next closest minor-league team was Montreal,
which topped the International League with 391,001. Victories
came at a premium for the Rainiers, but laughs were endless at
Sicks' Stadium. The serious-minded Richards barely could put
up with this stuff from Schuster, but he resigned at the end of
the season to take the top job with the White Sox, leaving the
matter unresolved. Schuster wouldn't survive the next guy in
charge. This man was of baseball royalty, and there would be
no joker in his court.

One could almost hear the trumpets blaring when Rogers
Hornsby arrived at spring training in 1951 as the Rainiers' new
manager, or picture him stepping out of a horse-drawn buggy,

surrounded by fawning and fanning attendants ready to jump at his command. He was one of baseball's earliest Hall of Fame inductees, elite hitters, and overbearing egos. On the first day of camp, the white-haired man gathered everyone around him in Palm Springs and spelled out what was coming in a long-winded opening speech that left everyone shuffling uneasy. He also made sure everyone knew exactly who he was and what he had done.

"I don't know who you guys think the greatest hitter in baseball is, but this is what I accomplished," the new manager said, listing all of his records in a deliberate, methodical manner while twirling a bat under the hot sun.

"He was a great ballplayer," said Hal "Skinny" Brown, a Rainiers pitcher who would enjoy a fourteen-year big-league career, which started at the end of that season with the Chicago White Sox. "I don't think he was too great of a manager."

To his credit, the man known as "The Rajah" directed the Rainiers to the PCL championship that season, the first pennant in a decade for the franchise. However, in the process, he nearly smothered everyone with his brutish style. Everything was all about Hornsby. No player was exempt from having his confidence shattered. No one was excused from being publicly humiliated by this man.

"Rogers had a fine capacity to judge player talent and somehow got the utmost out of players," Sick said. "On the other hand, Rogers was not the most tactful man. He was very outspoken and often critical when talking to the press, and to an extent our public relations suffered."

Upon accepting the Rainiers job, Hornsby announced rather pointedly, "I am not diplomatic," and he would offer repeated proof of this during his tenure. To replace a pitcher, the Seattle manager never left the dugout, a courtesy every other baseball man in his position extended his players. From the top step, Hornsby summarily waved for one guy to exit the game and another to replace him. There was no reason to interact with the person on the mound. This gruff guy had no time for a struggling player.

Hornsby was a seven-time batting champion, a two-time triple-crown winner, and someone with a Cooperstown induction on his resume. Even at the advanced baseball age of fifty-five, he could still step into the batting cage and send line drives scooting to all fields, drawing an admiring crowd. "He had exceptional eyesight, like Babe Ruth, in making contact," Rainiers utility player Len Tran said. "He didn't hit many foul balls."

Observers actually whispered that Hornsby might be Seattle's best hitter, though no one wanted him to hear that. There was no sense in enlarging the man's sense of entitlement, because he already was demonstrating plenty. Lefty O'Doul, the San Francisco Seals' manager at the time and later a kinder, gentler Rainiers manager, was no fan of the rigid Hornsby leadership style, a point made clear when he said, "He treats his men like mules."

Hornsby, whose unusual first name happened to be his mother's maiden name, had a huge weakness for horses. He was a compulsive gambler who often stopped to place wagers at Longacres Racetrack in suburban Renton before reaching the ballpark. However, he wouldn't take many chances on players. Putting together a roster, Hornsby arbitrarily got rid of some of the Rainiers' biggest names from the season before. Among them were proven pitchers Guy Fletcher and Vern Kindsfather and that hyperactive shortstop Bill Schuster. The crusty manager didn't like their looks or, in Schuster's case, his comedic routine, and wanted them gone.

Fletcher was two seasons removed from a 23-12 record that included a twelve-game winning streak, compiled with a losing Rainiers team backing him, when he was ceremoniously dumped. Hornsby couldn't have liked the pitcher's attitude, because the right-hander could be as grumpy as The Rajah. Fletcher had a tendency to blame stuff on everyone except himself, once growling to a groundskeeper, "What's wrong with this mound?" Hearing this refrain too many times, the man with the rake shot back, "Look in the mirror! That's what's wrong with the mound!"

Kindsfather won twelve of twenty-one decisions in Seattle in 1950, but was shipped to the Double-A Memphis Chicks of the Southern Association without much of a look or explanation shortly after the season began, given only a harsh note from Hornsby that read, "You've been sent out." In 1952 Kindsfather rejoined the Rainiers and was their pitching ace, producing a 21-11 season on the mound.

"He was a rough old gruff guy, and I don't think he ever knew my name," Kindsfather said. "It was, 'Hey, you, come out of the bullpen.' It was never, 'Hey, Vern, you're going to do this or you're going to do that.' That was the one thing I really disliked about Rogers. He should have talked to his players. He was excellent in his playing days. He expected excellence, but if he didn't get that, he wasn't too friendly."

Excited at first to have a member of baseball nobility as his manager, outfielder K Chorlton brought his wife over to meet the man during a break in spring training. The Rajah sat in a hotel lobby, his nose buried in a newspaper. Chorlton approached and made polite introductions. Hornsby barely looked over the top of the page, maybe grunting once.

When the team arrived in Seattle after opening the season with a long road trip, Hornsby noticed there were heaters installed under the bench in the home dugout at Sicks' Stadium. Richards, his predecessor, had been responsible for this game-night accessory, attempting to make everyone more comfortable during an unseasonably chilly season in 1950. Hornsby had them ripped out, explaining that heaters made his players soft.

Veteran pitcher Marv Grissom survived Hornsby's brutish style by winning twenty games for him, a situation for which the player took full advantage. "He was a hard-nosed manager, I guess the same as he played," Grissom said. "I just gave it back to him." Pitchers were not allowed to throw a slider, which Hornsby sarcastically described as a "nickely curve." He told Grissom to stop using that particular breaking ball, even after the veteran pitcher had struck out twelve Portland batters one night, six going down on called third strikes, all on sliders. In another Hornsby edict, pitchers were expected to sit in the dugout after getting removed from the game. They might learn something, Hornsby reasoned. Grissom repeatedly defied this order and reclined in the clubhouse. He would have preferred to cool down with a beer, but Hornsby didn't allow beer in the dressing areas, even for a team owned by a brewer. Hornsby drank nothing stronger than coke, and expected everyone else to follow his lead. Either way, Grissom didn't return to the dugout as ordered, causing Hornsby to summon the pitcher into his office and remind him of the steadfast rule. "I don't care," Grissom told him. "I'm better off sitting in the clubhouse than trying to start an argument with some umpire that

K Chorlton had his career derailed after cussing out
Rogers Hornsby in the dugout.

probably made what I thought were a bunch of bad calls against
me and was the reason I had to leave early." Hornsby responded
with an expletive and waved off the pitcher, permitting the defiant moment only because his top pitcher was well on his way to
a 20-11 record, and he didn't want to mess that up.

Paul Calvert was another pitcher who stood up to Hornsby and got away with it. Calvert always was the last to board the team bus. His anal manager usually was first in a seat. An extra impatient Hornsby finally noted the discrepancy in their promptness, snapping at the pitcher as he walked past. Replied Calvert, in his usual droll fashion, "Rogers, somebody has to be last." Hornsby looked away, unwilling to push the issue any further. Calvert's positive play had allowed him a full reprieve in this instance. The Canadian-born pitcher, hardly an imposing figure in thick black glasses and with his wispy build, had thrown a no-hitter in late May, beating Sacramento, 4–0, in the first game of a doubleheader at home.

Chorlton was afforded no second chances by Hornsby. The young outfielder could run faster than anyone on the 1951 team but was unable to escape the wrath of The Rajah. If only Chorlton could have caught everything sent his way. One night, he dropped a fly ball in left field with one out and nobody on base. He heard footsteps behind him as he trotted back to his position and turned to see his teammate Walt Judnich approaching, waving him in. "That old sonofabitch sent me out to replace you," Judnich told Chorlton as they passed in the outfield.

Embarrassed twice on the same play, Chorlton let his frustration erupt once he was in the dugout, swearing up and down at Hornsby. Big mistake. Hornsby cut the insolent player from the roster that night, and that was just the beginning of his pettiness. The manager called around, making sure Chorlton was properly blackballed by others and banished to the lower minors. Career advancement was difficult after that, and a painful lesson was learned. "You don't cuss out a Hall of Famer," said Chorlton, who was not the only one exiled by Hornsby. A few

Rogers Hornsby had compassion for Dave Kosher,
who was physically disabled but became a scout.

weeks later, Judnich, the replacement left fielder and a former
big-leaguer, left the team for a third and final time, unable to
deal with his hard-boiled manager.

Hornsby went after everyone in the ballpark in a bullying
manner. After catching some of Lassen's authoritative radio

commentary in the dugout and not liking it, the manager dressed down the broadcaster in public: "I manage the ballclub and you talk about it," the manager barked at Lassen, who stood there meekly and said nothing in return. "Don't get it mixed up again. If you do, I'm going to come up to that booth and show you."

Hornsby spared no one with his impertinence, least of all his boss, Emil Sick. After guiding the Rainiers to the pennant, he turned his back on all contract negotiations, ignoring all Seattle overtures for an extension while fielding big-league offers. He had considered jumping the Triple-A team at midseason, when the St. Louis Browns called and asked about his availability. Sick had made him honor his contract, and now Hornsby was getting even. The Rainiers owner finally gave the manager an ultimatum on a new deal, heard nothing, and publicly declared he was done with the great Rajah.

Hornsby was a complicated man. While goading and shaming players and ignoring management, he showed a rare soft side to a disabled Seattle man, Dave Kosher. Learning that Kosher was interested in baseball, the Rajah put a uniform on him in spring training and let him coach the bases. He encouraged him to get more involved in the game, and Kosher would become a respected baseball scout for the Chicago Cubs, Los Angeles Angels, and Cleveland Indians.

"He was a mean sonofabitch, but he gave Dave a life," said Walt Milroy, who scouted players for a couple of National League teams when he wasn't doing color commentary on Rainiers TV broadcasts and coaching high school basketball. "He wasn't a likeable person at all. I had to forgive him for the other things because of what he did with Dave."

The St. Louis Browns proved persistent and hired Hornsby

away from Seattle for the 1952 season. Back in the big leagues, the manager didn't make it past midseason. A team revolt was behind his ouster. In Associated Press reports, former Rainiers outfielder Earl Rapp told how players were so upset they were ready to come to blows with the insensitive one on the bench. On the day of the firing, Rapp's teammates made a big show of presenting the Browns owner with a hastily purchased silver cup that included the following inscription: "To Bill Veeck, for the greatest play since the Emancipation Proclamation."

On the rebound, Hornsby was hired to finish out the season by the Cincinnati Reds, but fired the following year. Again, sour player relations were cited for his downfall. With no place else to go, Hornsby asked to return as the Rainiers' manager in 1955, but never had a chance at reclaiming his old job. He had the gall to ask Sick for an eight-year guaranteed contract.

The Rajah gradually drifted away from managing, taking a succession of baseball coaching jobs and even joining the staff of the 1962 New York Mets that labored through their historically inept 40-120 season. A year later, Hornsby entered a Chicago hospital for cataract surgery, suffered a stroke, and died at the age of sixty-six. At the news of his passing, former Rainiers and ballplayers everywhere were hardly overcome with overwhelming sadness.

Hornsby was remembered only for blunting possible big-league careers with his harsh ways. "He had no class at all," the banished Chorlton said.

Players were there to serve The Rajah, nothing more. Hornsby wanted his own hand-picked players and didn't care how he got them. He wasn't too concerned about players' negative track records, either, because he figured that wasn't anyone's business

Rainiers outfielder Jim Rivera was the Pacific Coast League's
most valuable player in 1951.

but his own. He had failed to mention in 1951 that his newly
acquired center fielder, Manuel "Jungle Jim" Rivera, had previously served time in an Atlanta prison after his army court martial
in Louisiana for the attempted rape of a colonel's daughter.

Rivera played like Pete Rose, diving, hustling, and getting
dirty at every opportunity, only he had more power at the plate.
He never shaved for a game. This largely unknown player from
the Bronx was a baseball late-bloomer at the age of twenty-nine,
having originally been a pro boxer. He startled everyone in Seattle
by turning in the most complete offensive showing in Rainiers
history. He topped the league with a batting average of .352,
40 doubles, and 33 stolen bases, and chipped in 16 triples, 20
homers, and 112 RBI. He was an easy choice for Pacific Coast
League player of the year.

Rivera put on a show whenever he could that year. In a pre-game carnival at Sicks' Stadium before the team played Sacramento, he won $100 by barely beating the Solons' fleet Bob Boyd, who would become a Rainiers player the following season, in a seventy-five-yard foot race. Yet Rivera never came close to repeating any of his 1951 numbers in the Majors, while playing for the Browns and Chicago White Sox. He was a realist about what happened in Seattle. He had enjoyed a career year, and it took place in the minors.

"You know how it is, where sometimes you're up there and you can see the ball and everything on it, and the next time you can hardly see it," Rivera said. "You have to have good tempo at the plate. It wasn't the big leagues. In Triple-A, you get the fastball; in the Majors, you get the curveball. I just got along with everybody in Seattle."

Rivera got along with some people far better than others. He was a self-appointed ladies' man and had such an urgent need for female companionship he could hardly wait for games to end. After games, he'd pull on a suit, of which he had many, and he drove a shiny Cadillac (and repeatedly asked the clubhouse boys to wash it and watch it). He spent all of his off hours on the prowl. "Jim was what I would call flamboyant," said Rocky Krsnich, a Rainiers third baseman. "He was a very talented guy. I remember him being able to tap dance."

Hornsby instituted a midnight curfew for his players on the road, but there was a good chance he looked the other way when it came to Rivera, a rough-around-the-edges character who had grown up in a Brooklyn orphanage and seemed intent on making up for any lost time. As long as the outfielder's batting average ranked among the league leaders', he could tap dance all he wanted and as late as he wished.

"Jim used to say to me, 'Come with me, we're going out,'" pitcher Art Del Duca said. "He was really wild. He had women everywhere. He had nice clothes, nice suits. He was out all night. I went out with him once and, when it was 1 a.m., I said no more. He would be out all Saturday night and I'd see him come in for the doubleheader the next day and he would just be dragging."

Seattle provided its own set of temptations without all of the legal complications. There were no headlines linking Rivera to anything sordid, no images of him in handcuffs. Elsewhere, he had trouble staying on his best behavior. In 1952, when Rivera was with the White Sox, he was arrested for allegedly raping a soldier's wife in Chicago. A grand jury failed to indict him. To those who asked, Rivera downplayed his off-field problems, insisting there were extenuating circumstances, that he was a repeated victim. "When he got accused of raping that colonel's daughter he said he wasn't around but took the rap," said Rainiers catcher Earl Averill, son of the Hall of Famer, of Rivera's earlier incarnation.

Though Hornsby wasn't all that forthcoming about Rivera's previous legal troubles, media members covering the Rainiers eventually became aware of his checkered past. Nothing was disclosed in print or on the air, however: in that less intrusive journalistic era, baseball reporters and broadcasters tended to look the other way when it came to athletes' personal lives, no matter how gruesome they were.

"Everybody understood where he came from and what he did, but there was no mention of that," said O'Mara, the team's TV broadcaster. "He was playing baseball and that's all we were talking about. As long as the ballclub was happy with him, that's what mattered. The players and the reporters who covered the team were a little closer back then. There was a difference in approach."

To most Seattle players, Rivera represented a great mystery. They had no idea what he did with his time outside the foul lines. Rivera's only known transgression came in the clubhouse, when he and catcher Joe Montalvo, supposedly his closest friend on the team, started a fierce argument over, it was believed, a Seattle woman both were interested in. In a shocking move, the angry Montalvo pulled out a knife and swung it at Rivera a few times before the incident was quickly defused by other teammates.

"Sometimes you play all year with a guy and you don't really know him," Grissom said. "You see him at the ballpark and that's the end of it. That's the way it was with Rivera."

Behind the lead of Hornsby and Rivera, the Rainiers secured the pennant, finishing 99-68, six and a half games ahead of the Hollywood Stars. On September 5, 1951, they wrapped up the championship with a 4–2 victory at home over Oakland, a moment capped off by a classy scene in which the losing manager, Mel Ott, came out and gave Hornsby a warm handshake, one Hall of Famer to another. The Seattle players added to their spoils by blitzing through the Governor's Cup, beating Los Angeles two out of three games and Hollywood in a five-game series. No one was complaining about The Rajah at that moment.

"We had such a good time," Rivera said. "Winning the championship was important, because the fans were the greatest."

All of the main characters left the Rainiers after the title run, each of them rewarded with trips to the big leagues after having spent just a solitary season in Seattle. Rivera, Brown, and

Grissom joined the White Sox, with the center fielder bringing a $67,500 sale price, and Hornsby was finally headed for St. Louis.

Utility infielder George Vico actually made the most memorable exit, though the full details of it were known only by a few amused teammates at the time. Vico, who had big home-decorating plans for the off-season, relabeled several boxes of Rainiers bats and slyly had them shipped to his California home. He made a bar and bar stools out of the redirected bats, using old gloves for seats, and players who later sampled Vico's finished handiwork said the baseball decor was cleverly done.

Having grown weary of the increasing demands of the pompous Hornsby, Sick moved on without him. He had seen his baseball franchise come full circle, picking up a long overdue pennant. The Rainiers were as popular as ever, leading the PCL and all minor-league teams in attendance for the third consecutive season—drawing 465,727 fans, 6,559 per playing date. The next closest team in the minors again was Montreal, pulling in 391,107 fans. Seattle's prodigious crowd counts in 1952 marked the last time the franchise would outdraw a big-league club, once more shaming the Browns, who attracted just 293,790 and were now foolishly counting on Hornsby to give them a future boost.

It had taken a full decade, wading through war and warming to TV, but Sick had rebuilt his franchise into something special again. It finally had a pennant to match the unparalleled interest. The challenge was in keeping it there, and there were plenty of obstacles looming. The big leagues were threatening more loudly to move franchises to Los Angeles and San Francisco, and Sick, practically a one-man opposition to the idea, promised to sue everyone if that happened. He envisioned the PCL dismantling if the territory was invaded and his Seattle baseball empire crumbling.

A peace offering was made at the 1951 winter meeting in New York when the PCL was granted an "open classification," a designation allowing the Rainiers and other league members to hang onto their players longer than other minor-league teams and ultimately push for big-league entry with their teams. Players couldn't become draft eligible for the big leagues unless they had five years of experience and a $15,000 fee was offered, $5,000 more than required of International League and American Association personnel. An open classification, or outlaw league, as some referred to it, could apply for Majors status if it had a combined 15 million population, ballpark capacities of 25,000, and annual attendance of 3.5 million—numbers that easily ruled everyone else out. Still, the PCL in 1950 played a mammoth 200-game schedule, trying to build a larger fan base.

"The crowds were marvelous," Chorlton said. "The only place that didn't draw was old Seals Stadium in San Francisco. The fog would roll in, and if you were in center field, you couldn't see the pitcher from the waist up." Weather was not the only deterrent in the Bay Area. That particular Seals team finished in last place for the first time in twenty-five seasons.

Sick was in a combative mood every time he went to a baseball meeting, but he was trying more to protect his interests than pursue the big leagues, in his estimation an unrealistic pipe dream. Moving to the Majors came down to a matter of money, and a majority of PCL owners were carrying debt and leasing their ballparks. "Aside from a few owners, most of the clubs were not in any position to build proper and adequate ballparks, or to finance Major League ball," Sick said. "I was very dubious of this so-called advance of ours."

Television screens offered only black and white images at the outset, and for the first three seasons that Rainiers broadcasts were offered, fans saw one color. In other words, the baseball franchise didn't have any African American players, and wouldn't have one until its thirteenth season, and then only briefly. In spring training of 1951, four seasons after Jackie Robinson broke baseball's color line with the Brooklyn Dodgers, the Seattle club signed its first black player, pitcher Ford Smith, but he left midway through spring training. The stated reason for Smith's departure was an inability to agree on salary terms, but hardly anyone believed it.

Hornsby was in charge and didn't try to hide his racist tendencies, which were out in the open. Fred Lieb, baseball writer for *The Sporting News* for nearly four decades, would report that the Texas native was once a member of the Ku Klux Klan. Whether or not that was true, it is certain that The Rajah wasn't interested in integrating baseball, and he made it clear this wasn't going to happen on his watch with the Seattle franchise. "I'll win without them," the manager informed Del Duca, likely using less flattering terms. "I don't need those guys."

As the Dodgers flourished at the big-league level with integrated teams, featuring such black stalwarts as Roy Campanella, Don Newcombe, and Robinson, Seattle fans were asking why their baseball team hadn't made a similar breakthrough. Royal Brougham, the *Post-Intelligencer* columnist, posed this question to the Rainiers and was told that the previous manager, Jo Jo White, a Georgia native with a decidedly racist background, had made it clear he wasn't going to mix with blacks. The club said it was simply waiting for a top local black prospect to emerge, which sounded like a convenient dodge.

Once Hornsby was gone and replaced by a more open-minded manager in Bill Sweeney in 1952, the Rainiers pulled off their racial blinders and were rewarded immediately for diversifying. Two black players, Mississippi native Bob Boyd, an outfielder, and Alabama transplant Artie Wilson, an infielder, engaged in a season-long battle for the PCL batting championship, a competition that wasn't decided until the final day of the season. Boyd, who was nicknamed the "The Rope" because of his ability to hit line drives, edged his teammate by batting .320 to Wilson's .316. Boyd, who also led the league in stolen bases with thirty-three and triples with eighteen, went 5-for-8 in a season-ending doubleheader against Hollywood to wrap up the Rainiers' second consecutive batting championship, matching Rivera; Wilson was 3-for-9 on the final day.

The Rainiers might have been behind the times nationally, but they were right on schedule with the rest of a northern city thought to be more racially sensitive than most. The University of Washington didn't embrace its first black varsity basketball player, Dick Crews, until 1955, and the football team didn't bring in an integrated recruiting class until that fall, when running back Credell Green, brother of future big leaguer Pumpsie Green, was among four black players who arrived from Contra Costa Junior College in California.

It would be foolish to think that the arrival of Boyd and Wilson didn't generate hard feelings or objections among players or fans, but any who did feel resentment were careful to keep their displeasure to themselves. Big batting averages had a way

Bob Boyd, *left*, and Artie Wilson, *right*, were the Rainiers' first black players and finished 1-2 in the 1952 league batting race.

of making people color blind. The only outward mistreatment Boyd and Wilson received came in spring training when a California restaurant refused to serve them. All of the Rainiers got up and left in protest.

"The fans were wonderful and I never had no problems, not even in some of the towns where other guys did," said Wilson,

who became a Portland car salesman after retiring from the game. "Seattle was a nice place. The fans were awful good. Nobody mentioned race."

Wilson received his one, brief shot at the big leagues with the New York Giants the season before and become a baseball footnote. After appearing in nineteen games, he was sent to the minors to make room on the roster for a rookie named Willie

Mays. Boyd also was a big-league rookie in 1951, playing for the Chicago White Sox, and his big season with the Rainiers earned him another shot at that level and led to a nine-year career with four teams. These two bonded right away as Seattle teammates.

"We went to training camp and we said that one of us had to win the batting crown," Wilson said. "We worked at it the whole season. One week I was on top and the next week he was on top. I had no grudge that he won."

While Boyd and Wilson made the batting race interesting, the 1952 season marked the return of Kindsfather from his Hornsby exile and the kid from Vancouver, Washington, was superb on the mound, winning twenty-one of thirty-two decisions for the Rainiers. He won twice in one day, starting the first game of a doubleheader and relieving in the second. He even was credited with a victory after crossing a state line. Pulled from a game in Portland and on the losing end, an angry Kindsfather walked out of the ballpark, got in his car, and drove to the other side of the Columbia River to his off-season home, all of this without the manager's permission. After arriving at his house, he learned the Rainiers had made a comeback that inning and he had been awarded an unlikely victory. No one was aware he had left early, certainly not the team brass. It was a secret the pitcher carried with him for years. "I wasn't in the clubhouse after the ballgame and it wasn't a nice thing to do, but I was mad," Kindsfather said.

A second consecutive pennant eluded the Rainiers, who were competitive enough, finishing 96-84 and in third place. More disturbing were attendance figures, which plummeted in alarming fashion, dropping nearly by half to 287,333, or 4,078 for each playing date. In 1953 attendance dipped precariously again, to 224,562, and this for a second-place team that posted a 98-82 record. Everything bottomed out on a chilly Tuesday night in September, when a franchise-low of 432 brave souls showed up at Sicks' Stadium for a 5–2 Rainiers victory over the Sacramento Solons.

The 1953 season also marked the loss of two Seattle front-office staples, past and present, and a popular trainer. Before the season got started, Bill Mulligan, original Rainiers general manager and working in that capacity for the Portland Beavers, suffered a fatal heart attack during abdominal surgery in Portland. After the season, current Rainiers GM Earl Sheely died of a heart attack at the age of fifty-nine, ending a seven-year run in the front office. One of his more celebrated deals was the midseason sale of his son, Bud, a catcher hitting .340 for the 1951 pennant-winning Rainiers, to the Chicago White Sox. After nineteen seasons with the Indians and Rainiers, trainer Lew Richards, described as the team "house mother" or confidante, left to enter private practice. Constant change now was part of the game in Seattle.

Television and baseball had gone head to head for a couple of years now, and the new medium was winning the battle for an audience. In 1952 Rainiers telecasts were cut back to Wednesdays only for the first time, supposedly to circumvent the ticket-buying slide, and in 1953 it was announced that no games would be shown, before a late deal was struck. Feeling the pinch, Sick raised the broadcast rights fees to offset his losses. KING-TV, however, was no longer a slave to the game's needs and was willing to consider other broadcast options, ones that would be more popular with viewers. The station was now inundated with calls from infuriated people whenever their favorite TV shows were pre-empted in favor of a Rainiers game. Fortunately, a better baseball product, inspired by a leading man from Seattle, soon would improve the ratings.

9. Hutch Returns

The Boeing Dash-80 airliner, prototype to the 707, taxied onto the Boeing Field runway on July 15, 1954, and, with four engines whining, gracefully lifted into the sky over Seattle on its first test flight, signaling the beginning of the American "jet age." Across town in Rainier Valley, the Rainiers couldn't get off the ground, leave the gate, or even make it to the terminal.

While the commercial airplane builder was poised to transform world travel and pull the small-town label off of Seattle, the city's once beloved pro baseball team felt ignored and unloved. Former big leaguer Jerry Priddy had been hired as a player-manager, shortly after hometown son Dewey Soriano, a one-time Rainiers pitcher, had been installed as general manager. Together, they produced a team that would finish 77-85 and twenty-one and a half games out, and excite no one. It mattered little that this was the first season the Rainiers offered popcorn cards of the players, a cherished collectible. Attendance was the most dismal in franchise history, 151,071, or fewer than 2,000 per game.

Veteran pitcher Tommy Byrne, a left-hander between stints with Yankees, was the only Seattle player who had any prolonged success, using a new slider perfected during the winter to post a 20-10 record, making him the last of the fifteen players who would win twenty games for the Rainiers. A highly proficient hitter, he also slugged seven home runs. He didn't finish the season in the Northwest, though, with New York repurchasing his contract on the first day of September. He was grateful for the second chance in the PCL, even if it meant playing in front of a lot of empty seats.

"I thought it was closer to the big leagues than the International League or American Association, which used younger players," said Byrne, who was thirty-four when he played for Seattle. "I always thought the Pacific Coast League enhanced baseball that way, because it had a bunch of old Major League players out there."

Still, that was part of the problem. With TV now regularly bringing the big leagues to Seattle living rooms, the local baseball fan wasn't as interested in watching the game's rejects attempt to restore their careers. Sick lost $100,000 each season in 1953 and 1954, a figure he had banked multiple times during his earliest years as franchise owner. Yet his team was not on its fiscal deathbed. As the 1954 season came to a close, a consortium of Seattle businessmen headed by banking executives Wilbur Seruby and Joe Swalwell and real-estate magnate Henry Broderick approached Sick and made him an offer for the Rainiers. Typical of these heady times in Seattle, these city leaders were convinced this Triple-A team was a valuable asset and that they could run it better.

Addressing the matter publicly, Sick said he would need

$200,000 in cash up front, 10 cents on each admission to cover ballpark rental, a league guarantee that the rental would be paid even if the others couldn't cover it, and assurances that Soriano would retain his job. He seemed to be playing hardball, but the long-time owner had no real intention of selling his team, and was maybe even put off that others thought he was incapable of still making baseball work in the city.

Within a month of the season's end, Sick announced that Priddy wouldn't be back and that Soriano, a year younger than Byrne, the pitching ace in 1954, would return and be entrusted with finding another way to sell baseball in Seattle. The general manager had a pretty good solution in mind for 1955.

Soriano had worked his way up from peanut vendor to pitching prospect to baseball executive at Sicks' Stadium, earning a ship's pilot and captain licenses along the way. He was considered ambitious and resourceful; plus, he had influential friends. At the time of his hiring, one of the congratulatory phone calls he received was from a former high school teammate. "Be sure and call on me if you need any player help," Detroit Tigers manager Fred Hutchinson generously offered. "We old-time Franklin High pitchers need to stick together."

Soriano, who had once graded out with the Yankees as a better pro pitching prospect than Hutch, had served three tours of duty as a player for the Rainiers, taking the mound in 1939–42, 1946, and again in 1950–51. His second stint had resulted in his sale to the Pittsburgh Pirates for $30,000 and two players, his best chance at reaching the big leagues, but a lingering knee injury prevented him from getting there, and he wisely turned his interests to baseball front office work.

As the Rainiers considered applicants to replace Priddy, the irascible Rogers Hornsby asked for his old job back. Four years had passed, and The Rajah had bounced from team to team in the big leagues, alienating people at every stop. Seattle had been the only place willing to put up with him for long. Hiring Hornsby was a tempting idea, considering he had delivered a pennant, but this wasn't enough to put him back on the payroll. There was someone else out there who also had put fans in the stands, and he had left the franchise on impeccable terms.

Soriano put in a call for help to Hutchinson. Not for players—for Hutch himself. The general manager talked his old friend into taking the job, surprising everyone in the Northwest. Hutchinson was a no-nonsense man who insisted that things be done in a strict and orderly fashion. This approach had forced him to look at other managerial opportunities when they arose, though no one expected him to accept this one. Hutch had been the Tigers' manager for three seasons and wanted a two-year contract extension. One year was offered. He asked for considerably more input in the team's personnel decisions. None was provided. Without a second thought, he bolted from the Motor City and went home. "Loving Seattle as he did, I am sure he would not have considered managing any other minor-league club," Sick said.

Seventeen seasons after he was a Seattle pitching sensation and baseball's minor-league player of the year, an older and more polished, but no less driven, Hutch created a second wave of local baseball euphoria by taking control of the team when it needed him most. The Rainiers were in the throes of six managers in six seasons, and not all of these guys had conducted themselves as professionally as the club would have preferred, least of all

Fred Hutchinson steps off an airliner after returning
to his hometown to manage the Rainiers in 1955.

Priddy. Early in the 1954 season, the Seattle player-manager had
not only brawled with San Diego catcher Willie "Red" Mathis,
he had injured Mathis during a nasty ninth-inning exchange at
Sicks' Stadium. A pitch hit Mathis on purpose and he tossed
his bat onto the infield in anger. Mathis and Priddy exchanged
words, punches were thrown, and the two men wrestled hard
into the first-base screen. Suffering a broken arm, Mathis was
lost for the season. Put on a short leash, Priddy was fined $100
and admonished for his behavior.

A month after the 1954 season ended, Soriano flew to the
Midwest and made a determined pitch for the services of his old
pal. The two men sat up until 3 a.m. hashing out the possibilities.
They were lifelong buddies. They shared a lot of history. They
had won championships together from grade school to high

school, so why not in the Pacific Coast League? Hutch could have stayed in the big leagues—the Baltimore Orioles wanted him—but he chose his hometown over ego, accepting a salary half of the $40,000 annually paid him by Detroit.

"Three or four big-league jobs are OK, but the rest of the cities are tough," Hutchinson said, explaining his return to the *Post-Intelligencer's* Royal Brougham. "You suffer all season with a poor team, and many of the owners won't or can't afford to buy players needed to make the club a pennant contender. When the team flops, the manager is the goat. Then there is the terrific heat back there. I don't know whether I would take another job up there. It would have to be a pretty good deal."

Jokingly asked how much of Sick's brewery he now owned, the new manager answered, "The south wing, I guess." Seattle was overly excited about Hutch's hiring, willing to give him anything he wanted, with adulation a good place to start. Besides the expected run on tickets, the club announced that KTVW-TV would broadcast every Rainiers home game after telecasts nearly had been eliminated in recent seasons. Keeping the momentum going, the new manager practically gutted the 1954 team, bringing in mostly older, former big leaguers he could depend on. There were no superstars, no Jim Riveras or Fred Hutchinsons on the roster, just veterans who would do exactly as told and perform, and fans would accept these retreads because the manager did.

"He was one of the best guys I ever played for," said outfielder Art Schult, a big leaguer before and after joining the Rainiers. "We went to spring training and he took one look around the dressing room and saw a veteran team, players who had been around awhile." Hutchinson kept things simple, telling his players, "You guys all know how to play the game, just give me nine good innings."

One thing hadn't changed: the ferocious Hutchinson temper remained intact and ready to flash at any time. Players fed off this intensity or were entertained by it. One night in Hollywood, the Rainiers manager took out his anger on a large collection of coke bottles stacked under the stands and sent the whole thing flying. He also kept a midsized punching bag hanging with an umpire's cartoonish face fastened to it in his clubhouse office at Sicks' Stadium and took thunderous whacks at it, especially when one of the men in blue enraged or ejected him. The club encouraged the use of this boxing prop, hoping to save on clubhouse damages.

John Oldham, a twenty-one-year-old rookie pitcher, had the locker closest to the manager's office and witnessed several over-the-top Hutchinson tirades. He saw the manager tear off his shirt, popping buttons and shredding fabric. He saw him tear off his pants, popping zippers or more buttons. He quickly learned when to shower and when not to after a game, taking a cue from his teammates. "It was scary," Oldham said. "When he was in that kind of mood, guys wouldn't go in the shower room until he got out. That was the respect, and fear, the guys had for him."

He also learned to give Hutchinson even more space. After a loss in Portland, Oldham followed the manager into the visitors' clubhouse, only to watch him take another step to the left and send shaving materials flying off a shelf with an angry sweep of his hand. Some of it struck the defenseless young pitcher in the head. "I was stupid," the pitcher recalled. "Guys were laughing at me later, saying, 'Are you going to follow Fred in there again?' I remember being scared to death."

Oldham actually had few problems with Hutchinson. On the mound, he threw hard and wild, which only seemed to endear him to the manager. Opposing players couldn't dig in against the tall right-hander, and this was the way Hutch used to pitch. Only with Oldham, who stood 6 feet, 4 inches, the wildness was often unintentional. The youngster made his Rainiers debut in Oakland, brought in specifically to face three consecutive left-handed hitters, George Metkovich, Jim Marshall, and Joe Brovia. Nervous on the mound, he unintentionally knocked down Metkovich before striking him out. He did the same with Marshall. Brovia decided to try a different approach with the kid pitcher, arriving at the plate and asking the Seattle catcher to pass along the following message to the mound: "Tell the kid to throw the ball over the plate and I will not swing." Oldham knocked him down, though not on purpose, and then struck him out.

Oldham was admonished by his manager for what he said, not what he threw. In a game with a man on first base, he gave up a single, and while backing up a play at third base, he let fly a string of expletives. Hutchinson hustled out to the mound after the play was over and asked him pointedly, "Did you know what you just did?" Oldham responded with a stammer, "I gave up a single." That wasn't the answer Hutchinson wanted. "No, you just embarrassed Emil Sick," he said. "Next time, you back up third, watch your language!" The manager had been on the receiving end of similar lectures himself. Nearly two decades earlier, when Hutch slipped up and yelled obscenities that could be heard high into the seats, which was quite often, his mother would get on him later.

Hutchinson was a serious baseball man who sat alone in the

Bill Sears, holding a drum, performed many duties as the Rainiers' publicist.
(Bob Peterson photo)

third-base dugout at Sicks' Stadium hours before any scheduled activity, soaking up the tranquil atmosphere. He was at peace in the ballpark when he wasn't losing. He might invite batboy Pat Patrick, but only Patrick, to share in these moments and hear his wisdom. Others witnessed only Hutch's volcanic side, even if innocently caught up in the action. The Rainiers' publicity director Bill Sears learned about this the hard way.

"Fred had a single vision and that was baseball, and that was winning baseball, and anything else was BS," Sears said. "When he pulled on that uniform and went out on the field, there were no ifs, ands or buts. It was, 'You better not screw up or I'll be looking down your throat.'"

Sears received one of these oral exams. He was taking photos from the far corner of the Rainiers dugout one night when a Portland outfielder's throw overshot the intended infield target.

The ball almost hit Sears, but caromed off the cement bottom of the nearby fence. Seattle catcher Joe Ginsberg was thrown out trying to score from second base. This brought a Hutch eruption, with the manager racing to the umpire, claiming the wayward ball had hit Sears and should have been ruled dead. The arbiter disagreed. Sensing the man's great discontent, Sears wasn't sure what to do when Hutch returned to the bench. The fuming manager decided for him, sending the publicity director scrambling for an alternative seat. Sears was innocent, but it didn't matter. "Goddamn it, Sears, you cost us a run!" Hutchinson roared. "Get out of the dugout!"

Hutchinson didn't have a twenty-game winner or a .300 hitter. He relied on a decent-fielding, light-hitting shortstop in Leo Righetti, whose son, Dave, later would become a prominent big-league pitcher. He counted on first baseman Bill Glynn for his glove and clutch hits, not hampered by the fact that Glynn's thirteen home runs were the most on the club. Spotting a chance to add another veteran bat, he acquired another shortstop, Vern Stephens, when the player became available at the big-league level, and then turned him into a third baseman. Stephens made the deal look good, hitting a grand slam in his first Rainiers at-bat.

Hutch's center fielder was Bobby Balcena, the first player from the Philippines to play pro ball in the states at any level and land in the big leagues, if only briefly (seven games and two at-bats with the Cincinnati Reds in 1956). At 5 feet, 6 inches, and 160 pounds, Balcena was the smallest player on the team, but he was fitter than everyone else, asking the team to install a chin-up bar in the training room, a request that was approved. "I was trying to do twenty-five one day and was dying," Patrick said. "Without any effort, he did one hundred."

Balcena, who hit .291 during the 1955 season, endeared himself to everyone, typically giving away a glove to a batboy, a bat
to a loyal fan. His locker was located next to the training room
and he greeted everyone who walked past. He was good with
kids, who grew attached to him. Seattle's Filipino community
leaders adopted him and held a luncheon at the King Cafe in
his honor.

"He was one of the nicest little guys that I played with," pitcher
Duane Pillette said. "He gave you every single thing he had and
he always wanted to do more, and he apologized if he didn't
do more."

Not so well liked was hard-throwing pitcher Ryne Duren.
He frightened opposing hitters with his wildness, squinting
through thick, dark-tinted glasses toward the plate. He scared
the kids who worked for the team even worse. Hours before a
game, Patrick discovered a huge rat scampering through the
stands and told ballboy Jimmy Johnson about his find. Duren
overheard this, climbed into the seats, and trapped the rodent
in his glove. He brought it down to the right-field bullpen and
ordered Patrick to dangle the animal by its tail over the plate
so he could hit it with a fastball for grisly sport. Patrick had no
stomach for this and ran off, leaving Johnson cornered for this
distasteful duty and uneasy the entire time. "Two things had
entered my mind: one, this rat is bigger than me; and, two, he
couldn't hit the broad side of a barn," Patrick recalled. On this
day, however, Duren threw one down the middle and the helpless rodent didn't have a chance.

Everything was a big showy act for this pitcher from Wis-
consin. Duren pretended to be blind whenever on the mound,
fumbling and reaching for the rosin bag as if he were someone

truly sightless locating a curb with a cane. His first warm-up pitch typically sailed over the catcher's head and the second one always was in the dirt. Batters were being set up. Duren also was a mean drunk, someone who purposely hit players and let everyone know it. He was not highly thought of among his Seattle teammates. After leaving the Rainiers for the big leagues, Duren was beaned by an opposing pitcher, and players at Sicks' Stadium heard about this gruesome news from a radio always turned to Leo Lassen's broadcast in the home dugout. They broke into applause.

Hutchinson was able to put all of these diverse personalities together and win with them. He played eight different guys at second base. He had just one catcher available most of the season because the first-stringer and fan favorite Ray Orteig was out with an injury. In a 6–3 victory over Hollywood, Hutch and opposing manager Bobby Bragan engaged in a baseball chess match, making a combined thirty-three player moves over their nine innings together.

The Rainiers manager also demonstrated great healing power with his players. The Baltimore Orioles sent him sore-armed Lou Kretlow at midseason and the hobbled pitcher recovered to post a 14-3 record for Seattle. As the player most responsible for pointing Hutchinson's club toward the pennant, Kretlow threw four consecutive shutouts wrapped in eleven victories in a row. Apparently all Kretlow needed for a speedy recovery was a forced sabbatical between pitching jobs. Driving coast to coast to reach Seattle, the left-handed pitcher and his family got stuck for a week in Cut Bank, Montana, when the transmission blew out on their car. He got his vehicle and arm fixed all in one stop.

"I didn't realize that all I needed was a week off for my arm to rest," said Kretlow, who was Baltimore's opening-day pitcher that season before he was exiled to the Rainiers. "I didn't know how quick it would come back so I could throw. Hutchinson helped all the guys. He treated the players good, I'm sure of that."

Hutch also got the most out of a well-traveled pitcher named Elmer Singleton, who won nineteen of thirty-one decisions for him. Singleton's victories included a seven-inning no-hitter over San Diego, with a lone walk spoiling his bid for perfection in the 2–0 victory over the Padres. Collecting nine shutouts in all, Elmer's pitching repertoire included something sneaky and undetectable.

"Elmer threw a spitball," said Howie Judson, fellow Rainiers pitcher. "That was his main out pitch. He bounced around the big leagues and didn't throw hard enough to stay up there. When he got ahead of you, he'd load the spitball up and get you out. He got pretty slick at it."

Singleton perfected that illegal pitch by himself. Unintentionally, Hutchinson supplied one of his other, less experienced, pitchers with something new to throw, and all he did was bark out an idle command, trying to make a point more than anything. "Freddie wanted to help all the young pitchers he could, and he said, 'When you go out there, throw that first one way over the catcher's head; that'll scare the hell out of the hitters,'" veteran pitcher Larry Jansen recalled. "He didn't mean it, but Oldham went out there in a game and threw his first pitch off the screen."

Hutchinson even found time to step on the mound and go through the motions himself. He pitched three innings of an exhibition game against the Wenatchee Chiefs of the Northwest League and showed why he was retired, giving up six runs.

Bob Fesler, attempting to make the transition from
softball to hardball, was a Rainiers curiosity.

Hutch was a traditional baseball man, but he was willing to try
anything to gain an edge. For the final three weeks of the 1955
season, he added his hot-tempered predecessor, Priddy, to the
active roster. The guy had been fired as Seattle manager the year
earlier, was badly out of playing shape, and management didn't
want him back, but the Rainiers desperately needed a second

baseman, he was available, and the manager's wish was granted. Priddy made Hutch look like genius, providing twelve hits in thirty-six at-bats in the heart of a pennant race.

Then there was the grand Bob Fesler experiment. In 1954 Sears, Soriano, and Priddy went to dinner to discuss the club's seriously lagging attendance figures. They tossed around ideas on how to get more people out to the ballpark. These were lean times calling for creative measures, and Sears suggested they work on the local softball crowd, because these were essentially baseball-minded people, and offer them something to talk about.

The PR man suggested he ask the sport's most dominant local player, Fesler, to face Pacific Coast League hitters in a pregame challenge: five Rainiers and five Hollywood players would take swings at his softball pitches and see how they fared.

Priddy's immediate reaction was negative. Sears, familiar with the local softball scene, bet him a steak dinner that Fesler would not permit a hit, that no one among the selected pro batters would get even a "loud" foul off him. Intrigued by this unusual promotional plan, Soriano overruled Priddy and encouraged Sears to proceed.

A large, festive crowd showed up, many of them softball players still in uniform, coming directly from their own games to see this well-publicized match-up. Knowing their game wasn't as easy as it looked, they were expecting to be entertained by this bat and ball crossover, and they didn't go home disappointed. With his underhand whip, Fesler struck out every batter he faced, including Priddy, though the player-manager actually foul-tipped a ball.

"What do you think of Fesler now?" Sears asked.

"Oh, yeah," Priddy answered with irritation.

"You owe me a steak dinner," Sears reminded.

"I fouled one off," Priddy protested.

"I said 'loud foul,'" Sears replied.

"I heard it," Priddy said, reneging on the wager.

Fesler was not done pitching at Sicks' Stadium. In 1955 the team invited him back for another pregame face-off and attendance boost. Hutchinson was now in charge and watched with great interest as the softball player sawed off another hardball lineup with his whiplike, underhand deliveries, striking out all nine Rainiers and Sacramento Solons players he faced. When the manager asked Fesler if he thought he could do the same with a baseball, Hutch received an affirmative, almost cocky, answer. Fesler changed balls, the manager grabbed a bat, and the experiment continued. Attempting only to bunt and failing to make contact, Hutchinson was another strikeout victim. He raised a white flag, concluding, "I've seen enough." The Rainiers asked Fesler to pitch batting practice and then signed the twenty-seven-year-old pitcher to a contract. Two nights later against the San Francisco Seals, he made his first start. Hutchinson was convinced this move might revolutionize baseball and was heard to say, "Wait until Ted Williams studies this guy."

The downside to Fesler was that the Seattle catchers had trouble putting a glove on his unorthodox offerings, and Glynn at first base was deathly afraid of Fesler's odd-angle pickoff move. The upside was that the softball pitcher was also hard to hit with a hardball in his hands, and the possibility was mentioned that he could throw every day if necessary, because there was so little strain on his arm. In Fesler's favor, the guy was no wallflower when it came to taking on a totally unfamiliar world. He exhibited no fear. "I understand you're pretty good," Hutchinson said, spotting the softball player putting on a Rainiers uniform in the clubhouse. Fesler's response: "Damn right, I am." Hutchinson didn't smile much around his players, but a little grin creased his face as he walked away. Fesler compared favorably in style to Carl Mays and Ad Liska, previous submarine-style pitchers who had made it to the big leagues and enjoyed success. To get ready for his big night, Fesler worked out at the ballpark with retired Rainiers pitching great Dick Barrett and brought four pitches to the mound: a sinkerball, a screwball that broke into right-handed batters, a sweeping curve, and another breaking ball he labeled his "Atomic Pitch."

On August 10, 1955, Fesler made his professional baseball debut in the middle of the PCL pennant race. He started the first game of a doubleheader for the league-leading Rainiers against the last-place San Francisco Seals. The ballpark atmosphere was electric. A Ladies Night crowd of 13,996, heavy on male softball enthusiasts, was totally engrossed in the action. Fesler struck out the first player he faced on three pitches and a roar echoed through Sicks' Stadium. Then the fairy tale began to unravel. Fesler suddenly lost all focus and walked five of the next eight batters. He was called for a balk and provided a pair of wild pitches. He took a liner off his shin. He was charged for five runs and unable to finish the first inning. Fesler might have escaped this calamity with minimal damage, but Rainiers center fielder Carmen Mauro misplayed a two-out fly ball, running in as the liner sailed over his head for a three-run double, in the Rainiers' eventual 5–3 loss.

Some players resented Fesler's presence. They thought he made a mockery of their game. It was suggested later that Mauro might have let the ball fall in safely for a hit to discourage further use of this unproven player, but other people strongly disputed that contention. Just three and a half games up in the standings entering the doubleheader, the first-place Rainiers were in no position to purposely give anything away, and a move like that simply wasn't in character for the outfielder. "Carmen Mauro was too much of a gentleman to do that to anyone," Patrick maintained. "I thought he just lost the ball."

Pitching two innings of relief in the nightcap, Fesler gave up four more runs in a 13–5 defeat, making his doubleheader debut a disaster. Now pitching from sixty feet, six inches, rather than softball's more economical forty-six feet, he threw a lot of balls in the dirt. Yet in spite of his struggles, Fesler drew some compliments from the opposing side. "He was wild, just like we figured he'd be, but he was a rough one when he got the ball over," Seals manager Tommy Heath said. "He can really make that ball do some tricks." Fesler's only high point during his doubleheader debut came when he took his only at-bat of the second game and lined one off the left center-field wall for a double, crunching one off former big leaguer Gene Bearden, earlier a member of the Rainiers.

Three days later, Fesler pitched again. In a 7–1 loss to the Hollywood Stars at Sicks' Stadium, he threw an inning of relief and gave up a hit, a walk, and a run, but his control was much improved. Fesler wouldn't take the mound again until the final day of the regular season, starting the second game of a double-header against the Los Angeles Angels. In four innings, he struck out four batters, but he also served up four runs and uncorked three wild pitches in a 9–0 loss. His season stat line wasn't encouraging: a 0-2 record and 16.47 earned run average. "He was all right for a while, a novelty at first, and then the hitters caught on," Rainiers pitcher Steve Nagy said.

With everything upbeat again, Sicks' Stadium was a fun place to be. Fans wanted to see a player knock one through the baseball-sized hole in the left-field fence and win an against-all-odds $100,000 payoff. A woman won a mink coat on Ladies Night. One well-meaning fan seated close to the action, Charles E. Sullivan, had the players' attention at all times. A Seattle florist and diehard fan, Sullivan handed over a ten dollar bill on the spot to any player who hit a home run or pitched a shutout, with players unashamedly veering over to the man's box seat after crossing home plate and offering an outstretched hand for their reward.

Hutchinson had once celebrated his nineteenth birthday by pitching his nineteenth victory in front of a sellout crowd. In 1955 his thirty-sixth birthday drew another ballpark party, a night that proved memorable though provided no on-field heroics. An older Hutch received a station wagon, a set of golf clubs, a TV set, a wristwatch, and clothing. His team gave him a 13–5 victory over Hollywood. Taking part in the pregame festivities honoring Hutch, Bragan, the Hollywood manager and an intense competitor, was handed a microphone on the field and brazenly introduced his team as "the 1955 Pacific Coast League champions." That did not go over well. Next up, Hutchinson thanked everyone in the stands for coming and providing gifts, and then rebutted Bragan's previous claim. Pointing to his Rainiers and visibly angry, Hutch said in a serious tone, "There are twenty-one fellows on this side of the field who will dispute that."

A month later, Hutchinson proved good on his word, having

Batboy Pat Patrick and manager Fred Hutchinson pose for a victory
shot the day before the Rainiers clinched the 1955 pennant.

never once thought his Rainiers wouldn't win the pennant. In a photo celebrating the moment and published in the Sunday editions of the *Seattle Post-Intelligencer*, the triumphant manager was shown hoisting up Patrick, who was smiling and raising a victory salute. Truth was, Sears had put the manager and batboy in this classic pose on Friday, the day before the Rainiers actually had the championship in hand, and the publicity director snapped the image himself. Saturday night newspaper deadlines were too rigid to wait for a live shot, but the *Post-Intelligencer* editors knew the championship was coming, and wanted the moment recorded, and the confident Hutch complied.

On September 10 the Rainiers provided a pennant to match the waiting photo, beating the Los Angeles Angels, 3–1. White seat cushions rained down on the field. After their heroes had gone inside, fans chanted for their return. At a certain point, it was obvious the players weren't coming out of the clubhouse again. They were guzzling an excessive amount of champagne and Rainier beer in a celebration that would last well into the evening. After the ballpark revelry, the alcohol covering the spacious dressing room floor was an inch deep. At 2 a.m. clubhouse boys were still cleaning up this mess when they heard someone banging outside, trying to get in. Considering the late hour, they looked at each other quizzically before Johnson, the ballboy and designated rat-holder, unlocked the door and peeked outside, discovering the Rainiers' merriment hadn't stopped. "Elmer Singleton said he forgot something," Patrick recalled. "He had a drink in his hand, threw it in Jimmy's face and went away laughing. It was, 'Welcome to the party.' He wanted to make sure we were part of it."

The Rainiers finished 95-77 and topped the league in

attendance again, more than doubling the fan count from the season before with 342,101, or 5,030 per outing, an impressive total considering every home game had been televised. There was no more President's or Governor's Cup—the playoff series, held late in the fall and unable to compete with football season, had been discontinued for lack of fan interest—but more reward was coming. Singled out for his hiring of Hutchinson and the resulting success of the team, Soriano was named minor-league executive of the year by *The Sporting News*.

Hutchinson seemed happy and content with his triumphant return home. He threw a victory party for the Rainiers at the Colony Club downtown, and Fesler, the frazzled softball player, was the center of attention again. An excellent dancer, he put on a memorable show for everyone, demonstrating all sorts of crazy moves, not unlike his unorthodox pitches. His manager just shook his head at the guy's antics. A few days after securing the pennant, Hutch sat back and talked about restocking his team, about making another title run in 1956. While sorting through several congratulatory telegrams, the manager remarked that the Rainiers urgently needed another starting pitcher and a catcher. He had two more years to go on his Seattle contract. Not surprisingly, given the Rainiers' luck, he didn't last another month.

In need of a similar quick fix, the St. Louis Cardinals and their brewery owner August Busch, naturally a close friend of Sick's and known to him as Gussie, hired the manager away and summoned him back to the big leagues. Seattle was growing up fast, and now it would have to carry on without the guy who had given the city two glorious baseball summers. Hutchinson boarded a prop plane to the Midwest, a primary mode of travel that would soon be phased out by sleeker and faster jets built in his hometown. Four years later, he would move back to Seattle for a second stint as the Rainiers' manager, just as the first Boeing 707s were put into service and delivered around the world. With so much progress made in such a short time at the jet-making plant, which was located a few miles west of Sicks' Stadium, Hutchinson had to be dismayed if not annoyed at how others could make such a mess of his hometown franchise in his absence.

10. The Secret Stairs

Eager neighborhood kids gathered outside Sicks' Stadium before every home contest, staring skyward, ready to scramble at any moment. Retrieve a baseball coming over the fence, and it was good for a ticket inside. Pat Patrick was in the middle of this nightly mayhem, which was as much a part of the home-game routine as players taking batting practice or groundskeepers chalking the foul lines. The son of a longshoreman, the kid lived at 1803 19th Avenue South on Beacon Hill, a half-dozen blocks from the ballpark, easy walking distance. Patrick and his older brother, Mike, first turned up outside the gates when they were just ten and eleven. Soon they were full-fledged members of a determined pack of enterprising, pubescent boys who understood the ground rules as they applied to the outfield fences.

The Rainiers wanted their baseballs back. This wasn't the big leagues, at least not yet, and those balls were expensive. They represented white gold. The ballclub went so far as to designate a taller, older kid named Bruno Boin to chase down all fence-clearing home runs and foul balls or make certain his peers handed them over. Boin was athletic enough for this important chore, later becoming a standout basketball center for Franklin High School and the University of Washington. Still, he had his limitations. "He was the enforcer, but he was slow," Patrick said.

Getting inside to watch his heroes play at Sicks' Stadium was hard work and required a certain amount of luck, but, at age thirteen, Patrick found a more surefire way. He filled out an entry form for a 1955 Rainiers batboy contest, a promotional venture concocted by the team and publicized by the *Seattle Post-Intelligencer*. Contestants were asked to write a letter, extolling their best attributes, and these were passed along to a panel of judges, which included former big-league and Rainiers ballplayers Earl Johnson, Al Niemiec, Jeff Heath, Dick Gyselman, and Dick Barrett. Patrick quickly learned he was among the twenty-two finalists. One name had been drawn from each parks and recreation field house across the city. Patrick was asked to pose for newspaper photos, just in case he was the lucky one. He was told to watch the *Post-Intelligencer* for a story that would reveal the winner. "Every day, I'd look inside the newspaper box," the future bank chief executive officer said. "I didn't have money to buy the paper."

On a Saturday morning, he received huge news. Patrick excitedly spotted a blurb with his name splashed across the front page of the newspaper. The sports page had three huge photos of him, all contrived, in which he was holding up a Rainiers jersey, hugging his mother, and sitting at a table doing homework; these were accompanied by a story about his good fortune. "New

Rainier Mascot, P-I Contest Winner, Pat's The Name" was the
top headline. The following Monday, Patrick was in class at
Sharples Junior High School when the daily announcements
were made over the public-address system. He was one of the
lead items. He was an instant celebrity among classmates.

This was the start of a steady, five-year working relationship
between the Rainiers and one of their most loyal followers.
Patrick received a $250 scholarship check for winning the Post-
Intelligencer contest. He was introduced to the players and had
access to all eighty-six home games that first season. He even
had keys to the ballpark. Patrick also had his marching orders,
both from the ballpark staff and from the players, such as, if
Rainiers outfielder Bobby Balcena wanted a hotdog, a free hotdog, the batboy would immediately fetch it for him.

Often the best part of the job was when the Rainiers were on
the road. Patrick and other youngsters would clean up the stadium and then hold pickup games on the same diamond where
their favorite players inspired them. Saturday nights during
home stands were special, too. After a concentrated cleaning
effort spent preparing the ballpark for Sunday's doubleheader,
Patrick and his peers were rewarded with all the concession-
stand food they could eat. The menu offerings were hotdogs,
popcorn, crackerjacks, and soda pop. Often, a Rainiers player
or two would join in the free feast.

"We just sat around and ate and ate until we were sick," said
Patrick, who didn't graduate from college but would run three
Seattle-area banks. "It was quite an experience to see how different folks worked together. When cleaning the stands and
eating together, it all went away, the hierarchy."

Patrick did his assigned work without fail, and he got to

know everyone involved in the operation. He also checked out every corner of the ballpark when he could. During the 1956 season, his second year on the job, the batboy spotted wooden steps he hadn't noticed before. Practically hidden, they led up to a darkened corridor next to the visitors' clubhouse. There were no lights, only mystery. Rather than asking anyone about this discovery, Patrick decided to investigate on his own after a game. He slyly darted up the mysterious steps, discovered a locked door at the end, and pulled out the set of stadium keys he had been given and purposely not handed back. He opened the door and slipped into a most unusual place.

Deep in the ribs of the ballpark, beneath the first-base grandstands, he had come upon a one-room apartment, no bigger than a cheap motel room. There was a fold-out couch, a kitchen area, a bathroom, some chairs, a small refrigerator, and a couple of paintings on the walls. It was kept clean. Before he could leave the secret hideaway, however, Patrick heard footsteps approaching and panicked. As the door opened, he ducked down behind the only thing that would hide him, the couch. A familiar Rainiers player, a married man, entered the room, accompanied by an unfamiliar woman. Patrick stayed out of sight and remained quiet as the two undressed and took advantage of what the couple thought was a private moment. "I was both pleased and scared to death," said Patrick, who vowed to himself never to reveal the identity of the player.

Undetected, Patrick waited until the couple was gone before he exited the ballpark hideaway. Later, he told friends what he had seen, speaking in general terms of course, not naming any names. Word got back to general manager Dewey Soriano, who threw a fit over this clandestine sexual activity taking place on

Rainiers trainer Carl Gunnarson was fired after the team learned he was letting players use a ballpark apartment for assignations.

the premises, started asking questions of others, made some discoveries, and ordered abrupt changes. Rainiers head trainer Carl Gunnarson, a former Portland Beavers pitcher who had been with Seattle for two-plus seasons, was fired on the following Monday. It seems the man in charge of the team's medicinal needs was running a casual escort service on the side for players' private needs. The secret apartment had become a second source of income for him. The intended purpose for this room was much less intimate: to temporarily house scouts, coaches, or players in for a tryout. Gunnarson had opened it for extracurricular socializing, something not prescribed by the team.

"Quite a few people used it, visiting guys, players that we were going to talk to, and it wasn't all that fancy," said Bill Sears, the

Rainiers' publicity director, of the unadvertised ballpark living quarters. "But you know, those trainers that worked for the club didn't make much money."

Patrick was shocked to see one of his bosses let go in such a harsh manner and so suddenly. Later he tried to open that apartment door again. The lock had been changed. It was clear that Fred Hutchinson was back in the big leagues, far away from this ballpark scandal, and it was probably best that he wasn't around for this discovery, that it had come on someone else's watch. The no-nonsense manager would have ripped out every last wooden step leading to that baseball love nest.

Outlandish behavior for the Rainiers in 1956 was not confined to a hideaway apartment. To replace the rigid and unquestioned rule of the departed Hutchinson, the team pursued James Luther "Luke" Sewell as the next manager, outbidding two other minor-league organizations for his services, waiting another painstaking week for him to accept a final offer, and loudly trumpeting the deal. Sewell, however, was not worth all the trouble. He was a disaster. Players revolted against the new leader in spring training. Players revolted again a month and a half into the season. Players got him fired with a month remaining on the schedule—with the club in second place, sixteen games above .500!

Sewell's bench credentials seemed substantial enough. After a twenty-year journeyman career as a big-league catcher, he had spent eight seasons in the Majors as manager of the St. Louis Browns and Cincinnati Reds, even guiding the Browns to the 1944 American League pennant and losing the World Series to the crosstown St. Louis Cardinals in six games. "I know that in one way I'm sort of on a spot, but I'm not coming out to Seattle to lose," the new leader said when his hiring was announced.

Yet telltale signs suggested otherwise. When the Rainiers signed him to a one-year, $18,000 contract, Sewell, who had been replaced at each of his previous big-league stops, was managing Toronto of the International League and considering a lateral move, still far from the spotlight, to Richmond. New York Yankees shortstop Phil Rizzuto, former Yankees pitcher Ed Lopat, and former Philadelphia Athletics manager Eddie Joost were the other managerial candidates the team considered.

Seattle players didn't like the new guy from the beginning. Sewell was a know-it-all who had strange ideas. Upon over-hearing a Rainiers player discussing his urgent need to obtain seasickness medicine for an upcoming Ocean Shores fishing trip on an off day, the manager told him that the best remedy for this malady was to stand on one leg. His baseball decisions often were rash and impulsive. Typical of his rambling thinking was the following letter sent on January 6, 1956, to pitcher Bill Brenner, who was eventually one of his coaches and the man who would succeed him as interim manager during the season:

Dear Bill:

Inasmuch as spring training is "just around the corner," and being fortunate enough to have been appointed your manager for 1956, I would like to make several suggestions at this time which I feel sure will be most helpful to all of us in getting off to a good start as we want to win another pennant in Seattle this year and will no doubt run into very strong opposition along the way.

We plan on a training period of approximately five weeks, and our exhibition games will start about ten days after the reporting date, so to avoid sore arms and pulled muscles in these early games, don't you think two weeks or more of throwing and running before reporting for training will help you avoid these setbacks? Of course some of you will have been playing winter ball and won't need this work, but those of you who haven't been doing anything since the season ended, should do this running and throwing. Those of you who live in the warmer climates can work outdoors, but those of you who live in the colder climates and find it too cold to work outdoors, should work in a gymnasium. Also you should report to training camp at approximately playing weight, as trying to get weight off during spring training takes up valuable time that should be spent on other phases of the game. Therefore, those of you who have gained weight since the season closed should go on a diet immediately and get this extra weight off within the next thirty days.

If I can be of any assistance to you in any phase of this pre-training camp conditioning, please feel free to write to me, otherwise I will be looking forward to seeing you in San Bernardino.

Sincerely yours,
Luke Sewell

In spring training, players complained about Sewell and his curious ways, but the front office interceded and backed the new man in charge. The players were told to be patient, to get to know him. Things took a more serious turn on May 13, during the second game of a doubleheader against the Portland Beavers at Sicks' Stadium, when Sewell tried to replace veteran pitcher Howie Judson and they had words on the mound. Rather than hand the ball

over, Judson fired it into the dirt. It was only the third inning, the
right-hander had given up just one run, and he wasn't ready to
concede anything and willingly walk off the mound.

"He was always taking me out too early," complained Judson,
a big leaguer for seven seasons with the Chicago White Sox and
Cincinnati Reds before winding up in Seattle. "He was going
to take me out of the game early again, and I threw the ball on
the ground."

After the incident, the two men were called to Soriano's office
and they argued some more. The disagreement on the mound
resulted in a $50 fine for the pitcher and an hour-and-fifteen-
minute team meeting two days later before a game against the
Hollywood Stars. Players were forced to miss batting practice but
allowed to air out many in-house complaints. The Rainiers, in
the first year of a player-working agreement with the Cincinnati
Reds, one that was supposed to fortify the assembled talent,
had been picked to repeat as Pacific Coast League champions.
Instead, they chased the Los Angeles Angels throughout the
summer, which became a source of growing frustration. This
was not a close-knit group on the field, a state of affairs that
became painfully evident during a 10–5 loss to the Sacramento
Solons at Sicks' Stadium.

Art Schult, a Brooklyn native and former Yankee trying to
work his way back to the Majors, was one of Seattle's better
players. The strapping 6-foot-4 outfielder kept the Rainiers
well supplied in home runs that season, crunching out three
in a game against San Diego. On August 7 against Sacramento,
Schult, batting third in the order, was knocked down and hit by
Solons pitcher Gene Bearden in his first two trips to the plate
after Seattle had built an early lead. In a third at-bat, Schult was

knocked down again. He grew more agitated as the game got away from his team, and by the seventh inning, he let everyone know of his displeasure.

"I've been on my butt four times already and I haven't seen anybody else knocked down," Schult yelled loudly when entering the dugout, drawing a strong rebuke from a teammate.

"You do the outfield and we'll do the pitching," Judson shot back.

"What did you say?" Schult retorted, turning beet red and proceeding to lose it.

The players started wrestling in the dugout, with Schult grabbing the Rainiers pitcher in a headlock and herding him toward the dugout tunnel before others jumped in and separated them.

"I was going to flush his head in the toilet," Schult said.

Sewell, Schult, Judson, and Brenner were called to Soriano's office to explain things. Fines were levied. Explanations were heard. Nothing was settled. Schult and Judson didn't speak again for the rest of the season.

Things came to a full boil for the Rainiers less than a week later. By August 13, the club had lost nine of ten outings and fallen behind the Angels by twelve and a half games in the standings after losing both ends of a home doubleheader to Vancouver, 15–7 and 3–2. With only a month left in the season and likely sensing trouble for himself, Sewell approached Soriano and demanded that the club announce his contract renewal. Soriano met with Sick twice, and the manager's negotiations went in a much different direction. Sewell was fired and replaced by Brenner. Even though the Rainiers held an admirable 73-57 record at the moment, it was determined that Sewell had lost

Broadcaster Jeff Heath, *left*, is shown with young fans
and Rainiers outfielder Bobby Balcena.

control of the team, though some suggested he never had it in the first place. Interim guys aside, no Rainiers manager had been on the payroll for such a brief time.

"Sewell didn't know what was happening," Schult said. "I think it was because of me that he got fired. I lost my temper. That was my nature. I didn't like losing. I've kind of had a guilty conscience about that ever since."

Sewell wasn't leaving Seattle without taking several shots at his former players. They were overrated. They were crybabies. The infield of first baseman Bill Glynn, second baseman Jack Lohrke, shortstop Leo Righetti and third baseman Milt Smith was the worst he had encountered. Sewell failed to mention that Glynn and Righetti had performed well enough to satisfy Hutchinson the year before.

"When Milt Smith isn't hitting, he isn't worth a damn at third," Sewell told the Post-Intelligencer. "Any ordinary shortstop who can move could beat Leo Righetti out of a job. Second base has been brutal all season. Bill Glynn is a good defensive first baseman, but he has to hit more to be of real value to the club. I'm not trying to put the blast on these boys as individuals, but they just don't have it."

If Sewell and his hot-tempered players didn't supply enough turmoil, there was plenty more in the broadcast booth that season, courtesy of former big leaguer Jeff Heath, a dangerous man with either a bat or a microphone in his hand. A career .293 hitter while in the big leagues, the Seattle resident had played fourteen seasons with four teams at the top level, mostly the Cleveland Indians. Once it was clear that the end was near for him as a big leaguer, a situation hurried along by severely damaged ankle, Heath retreated to his hometown and made an aborted attempt to finish up with the Rainiers in 1950. He batted just .245 with two homers and twenty-four RBI in fifty-seven games, and was done. Six years later, he was back at the ballpark in a working capacity, as a broadcaster for KTVW-TV, which now held the broadcast rights after outbidding KING-TV for them.

A man with rugged looks and a thick build, Heath also had a little Dizzy Dean in him, offering various homespun observations to the listeners. Endearing himself to everyone, he usually took batting practice with Rainiers players before each game. Standing around home plate, Heath was crass and entertaining, often doing a dead-on Babe Ruth impersonation. He would feign staggering up the plate as if hung over, mention something about his lack of sexual prowess the night before, and tap the plate. He had his pants pulled up, shirt out indicating

a bulging waistline, and his hat down, all classic Ruth charac-
teristics. Bar-S Meats, the TV broadcast sponsor, couldn't have
been more thrilled to have this guy in the booth because he had
a Bambino-like appetite, too. In his typical unpolished manner,
Heath would wolf down free Bar-S hotdogs and then, between
belches, tell the audience how great this particular ballpark
concession offering was.

"He was a remarkable person in many respects and a pathetic
person in many respects," Sears said. "Heath was really crude
on TV, but that was part of the appeal. He'd butcher words and
you never knew what he was going to say next."

In July 1956 he unintentionally said the wrong thing on the
air. After an opposing Portland pitcher he disliked was rocked
for a long Rainiers home run, Heath, thinking his microphone
was turned off, remarked impulsively, "Take that, you lousy
bastard." The slip was heard throughout Seattle, causing the
ballclub huge embarrassment, and Heath apologized profusely
for it during the next broadcast, albeit with his typical whimsy.
"Gee kids, I'm sorry about what I said," he said, leaning into
his microphone. "You should never say those kinds of words.
Keep your eye on the ball."

His week of controversy, however, was far from over. A few
nights later at Sicks' Stadium, Heath and Bob Veneman, the
KTVW general manager and vice president, engaged into a nasty
ballpark fight. Heath didn't care for Veneman, who expressed
similar ill feelings toward him by second-guessing everything the
former big leaguer said and did. Hearing one criticism too many,
Heath pushed the TV executive out the door to the broadcast
booth and down a flight of stairs and then bounded after him,
with the two men holding a heated discussion in front of several

fans. As had Heath's on-air obscenity, this episode received a lot of play in the Seattle press and required more apologies from a man now getting into public scrapes as frequently as his comedic inspiration, Babe Ruth.

Once the tumultuous season was over, the Rainiers had finished 91-77 and were well entrenched in second place, an admirable showing considering all of the season-long distractions. Sewell already had left town, an ostracized man who had challenged the team to try and win without him and then watched as it proceeded to capture five of its first six games under Brenner, the interim manager. Schult, who led the Rainiers in hitting at .306 while providing fifteen homers and seventy-five RBI, was sold to the Cincinnati Reds, earning another shot at the big leagues. Heath, a lightning rod for controversy, lost his TV job for good and would have to pay for his own hotdogs now.

The summer of 1956 had proven to be a complicated one, and the Rainiers were now looking for replacements for each of the departed. If there was any good coming out of this rapid turnover, it was probably that job candidates could safely figure on using the isolated ballpark apartment for an overnight stay without fear of walking in on someone in an extra-inning clinch—provided they could wade through all of the baseball equipment now stuffed inside to discourage further temptation. The bad thing was another ballpark vacancy had opened up, one that would perhaps present an even greater challenge to fill than the others. For the first time in nearly two and a half decades, Seattle baseball would need to find a new radio voice.

11. Man behind the Microphone

Everyone knew the sound of his voice, almost no one knew the man. For twenty-five consecutive seasons, Leo Lassen sat behind a microphone and told Seattle everything it wanted to know about baseball. His staccato delivery radiated nonstop from the various pro diamonds located throughout the city. Dugdale Park. Civic Stadium. Sicks' Stadium. While the architecture changed, the description of events did not.

Yet on the eve of the 1957 season, Lassen was unceremoniously dumped from the baseball radio broadcasts. KOL now owned Rainiers broadcasting rights, and there were people at the station who considered him outdated and expendable. Entering contract negotiations, Lassen had held a year-round job and earned $16,500. He was asked to accept $8,500 and work only during the baseball season. Insulted, he said no thanks to the low-ball offer and was replaced by Rod Belcher, a well-known KING-TV and radio sportscaster, but someone different nonetheless.

Leo Lassen had a huge following as the Rainiers' radio broadcaster.

Seattle was undergoing rapid change, with Boeing turning out the nation's first jetliners, Interstate 5 freeway construction cutting through the heart of the city, and new neighborhoods sprouting up throughout the thickly forested suburbs, but silencing Lassen seemed a bit much. For local baseball fans, this man was all they knew when tuning in. He was a Seattle icon, so much a part of everyday life during the spring and summer that midway through the 1956 season the Rainiers had honored him and his broadcast longevity with Leo Lassen Night at Sicks' Stadium. He was given several gifts, including a new Chevrolet car, and former players were brought back to salute him.

"We specifically requested Leo to do our games," said a chagrined Rainiers general manager Dewey Soriano, a lifelong listener himself and powerless to change the executive decision.

"He was more of an institution here than Dave Niehaus,"

pointed out Walt Milroy, briefly a voice for the Rainiers on TV and referring to the longtime radio and television broadcaster for the Seattle Mariners.

It was in 1931, as people fixated on radio as their chief source of home entertainment, when Lassen's nasal, monotone oratory first reached out to a Northwest audience, and he was fully entrenched once the Rainiers were up and running seven years later. He became so popular in Seattle that he reportedly drew more listeners than the national radio show that was unbeatable everywhere else, *Amos 'n Andy*. He drew imitators of all ages, including other announcers who tried to copy him. With his soothing on-air presence, he either kept the city up at night or sent it to bed willingly.

"My mother would have us turn on the radio and turn it to the game," longtime fan Addis Gutmann said. "Lassen's voice used to put her to sleep."

On game night, Lassen could be heard across Seattle. His voice was one of authority and familiarity, and elderly men still repeat certain of his pet phrases to this day, rekindling childhood memories that make everyone feel good all over again.

"It's a high fly back to the left field wall, back, back, back, back, b-a-a-a-a-c-k and it's over!" Lassen would rattle off when Seattle hit a home run, his signature call as an announcer. Other Lassen favorites included "You've never been hit by a foul tip, you don't know what you've missed," which he'd say in a teasing voice, or, "Hang on to those rocking chairs!" an instruction he'd give in an urgent tone when games got tense and complicated. Finally, there was, "Folks, if you're home, go outside the house, look to the south, and there's Mount Rainier, and it looks like a pink ice cream cone," a frequent meteorological touch Lassen added to his broadcasts.

In 1938 Lassen's voice could be heard upstairs as Helen Milroy married Ernie Gustafson on the main floor of her parents' Green Lake home. Milroy's grandmother was bedridden, listening to the Rainiers game as the wedding ceremony took place. Baseball provided unmistakable background noise as the vows were exchanged. After pronouncing them man and wife, the minister turned to the groom and asked urgently, "Did Gyselman get a hit?" The clergyman then turned and hustled upstairs to join grandma and catch the rest of the game.

"He's the one who sold baseball to the town," Rainiers outfielder Edo Vanni said of Lassen. "He had you hanging on every pitch."

Gale Wade was another Rainiers outfielder who grew up listening to Lassen broadcasts as a kid in Bremerton, a waterfront city located opposite Seattle on the other side of Puget Sound, because he was unable to afford or attend the games. Leo's highly detailed radio summations made him feel as if he were there, watching from the seats. "You could sit and look at a blank wall and listen to Leo Lassen and it was like watching television," Wade said. "He was that good."

Briefly playing in the big leagues, Wade counts his most memorable baseball moment as meeting Lassen and then having his hero describe his play for the first time on the radio. He later acquired a vinyl record that contained a collection of classic Lassen play-by-play moments. "I treasure that probably more than anything else," the Rainiers outfielder said.

The man nicknamed "The Great Gabbo" fell into all of this baseball storytelling by accident. He'd always liked baseball but wasn't much of a player. He was cut from the varsity team at Lincoln High School in north Seattle and turned to journalism as an alternative. After holding down various newspaper positions for the *Seattle Post-Intelligencer* and the *Seattle Star*, from office boy to managing editor, he was doing publicity work for the Seattle Indians when opportunity presented itself. KXA radio coverage of the local baseball team had been in place for a year when the regular broadcaster, Ken Stuart, quit before the 1931 season. Several candidates were auditioned without anyone getting hired when Lassen was asked to give it a try.

"Why not you?" Indians owner Bill Klepper said to him. "You know this game, and you could talk the leg off a chair."

From the initial words that came out of his mouth, Lassen was a natural and the obvious choice to bridge a strong connection between Seattle and baseball. There was very little transition period necessary. This was his calling, literally. "I went down to the station, sat down and broadcast my first game," he said. "From the first, it never bothered me a bit."

Lassen described games live in Seattle and recreated the road outings on a delayed basis from a studio, reading reports from wire service copy. He was meticulous in his coverage, explaining the nuances and rules of the game while he rattled off the action. He held nightly baseball seminars for Seattle on the game besides giving the score. He delivered the infield fly rule as if he was reading it out of the book, which he wasn't. "He would recite it exactly the same," Gutmann said. "I could repeat it word for word."

Listeners came to rely on Lassen for the most obscure baseball information and rules interpretations, in almost demanding fashion, swamping him with weekly letters to be read on his pregame show. Among them were the following inquiries or salutations received during the 1950 and 1951 seasons, many of which were answered on the air:

Dear Leo

Are there any other colored players on the Seattle team besides Jackie Albright? He is sure enough a good shortstop. He is sure light for some of us. I am glad we have him on the team. I will be listening to your broadcast every night because we just ain't got the money to go to the games like some of the rich folks have. You sure are a good broadcaster. I guess we will come to town to see you next time and I sure am hoping you will have Jackie down there again. I like that funny [Bill] Schuster. He is so funny when you tell about him. I think you are funny, too. Please mention me when you answer.

Etta Mae Jones
[Editor's note: Jackie Albright was Caucasian]

Leo Lassen,

I want to say thank you for a wonderful season of broadcasting of the ballgames. I have been a ball hound for too many years, back into childhood. Have been shut in this past two years and you will never know how it has helped to hear the games. Thanks again. What about next season? Need votes or cards? Good luck and happy pitching.

A shut-in listener,
Mrs. Cardwell

Leo Lassen:

We are constant users of wonderful Hansen's bread. This card is to let you know how much we enjoy your broadcasting of the baseball games. In our opinion, there is no better announcer in the U.S.A. We turn on TV and the radio so we can hear you. The TV announcer is very poor compared to your splendid style. We are all for you and your wonderful programs.

The Lyon family

Dear Leo,
We heard that Al Lyons is bald-headed. That isn't true, is it? We hope he has as beautiful hair as you do. Mom thinks you are so handsome.

Lita Kieland

Lassen had no qualms about holding up his end as the leading authority on the Rainiers. He reveled in this role. Seattle baseball fan Charles H. Freymueller Jr., who was relocated during World War II to New London, Connecticut, asked the broadcaster in a letter why the team had tailed off so badly by the middle of the 1946 season. An astonished Freymueller received a two-page typed response from the broadcaster, which he hung onto as a keepsake. While there was a complete breakdown of the team enclosed, Lassen could be fairly simplistic in his logic, as the following passage from the letter indicated: "Well, you wanted to know what happened to the Rainiers. There is only one main reason. The other side is getting more runs. Also the league play has sped up about 50 percent, meaning the players are better than the ones during the war."

When the Rainiers were on the road, Lassen went to the station and pulled game updates from a teletype machine. Typically, the message would say nothing more than "Gyselman, ground ball to third base, out." He would dramatize each at-bat, making up balls and strikes and giving the putout imaginary flair. In these instances, most of what he said wasn't true, but nobody knew the difference. Occasionally, his creative work would go for naught. While his made-up broadcast was in progress, with everything supposedly in doubt, occasionally a colleague would break in with a news bulletin and absentmindedly provide a final score. Unlike other announcers, who use all sorts of cozy first-name references or nicknames to describe baseball players, Lassen simply gave out a last name and rarely mentioned the first one.

He could be brutally honest in his assessments, feeling an obligation to point out a player's weaknesses rather than look the other way. A case in point was the slow-footed Heinz Becker, the 1949 Rainiers player with the great fear of earthquakes. "He's a magician with a bat, but he just can't run," the announcer said, on air, of the first baseman and team's leading hitter. "He's the slowest thing to first base that you can imagine."

Lassen did it his way, becoming a huge radio success with no formal training or outside inspiration. He was a detail guy behind the microphone, a trait that served him well with his loyal following. People wanted to hear everything he had to say.

"His description of the games was so different than anyone else," Rainiers batboy Pat Patrick said. "He would tell you that someone was reaching down to flick something off his shoe."

"Leo had no one to pattern himself after," said Belcher, Lassen's replacement. "He developed his own style, which was completely unique."

KRSC-TV found that out when it brought cameras to Sicks' Stadium for the first time in 1949. The station slowly built a viewing audience, but the listening half came at a more begrudging pace. People watched TV out of curiosity. They hung with Lassen out of habit, setting up a radio next to the new set.

"I think people watched it and listened to Leo," said Bill O'Mara, the Rainiers' original TV play-by-play announcer. "That was one of the problems we had, was creating a visual audience for television. With Leo, people who listened to him would completely believe him."

In one instance, O'Mara received a call from a man who had watched the game on the screen but listened to the radio description. Even with visual proof, the fan was convinced the TV broadcast had missed a double play, simply because Lassen had said there was one. In this man's mind, there was no way his chief Rainiers source and certifiable expert on baseball could have been mistaken.

"I said, 'You weren't listening to me, were you?'" O'Mara recalled. "He said, 'Hell, no, I was listening to Leo. Leo said it was a double play and I believe him. You missed the play. I don't even know who you are!' Click."

For fourteen years, while the Indians were turned into Rainiers, Lassen performed a dual media role at the ballpark. Each night, he wrote game stories for the *Post-Intelligencer* after he was done handling his radio chores, supplementing it with a regularly scheduled baseball column. He became a broadcaster exclusively when Seattle's morning newspaper hired Emmett Watson as its beat writer, taking on someone who was Fred Hutchinson's former classmate and baseball teammate at Franklin High, and briefly a Rainiers back-up catcher.

While everyone around town thought they were intimately familiar with Lassen, after inviting him into their homes night after night, all they really knew was the sound of his voice. He was a notoriously shy person. When asked to speak in front of public groups, Lassen did so reluctantly. He was uncomfortable when he was pulled from the protected sanctity of his ballpark or station radio booth. With people eying him, he would become surprisingly nervous, to the point that he would trip over his words. The broadcaster wouldn't permit anyone to take his photo, either. For a lengthy profile about him, the Post-Intelligencer had to rely on a cartoon drawn from a rare outdated image from an old file, with the likeness properly aged, of course.

"He was a complete introvert," O'Mara said. "He wasn't comfortable around anyone. He was just a quiet, retiring man."

Lassen rarely let many people invade his private booth at Sicks' Stadium. He almost never ventured into the clubhouse in later years, either. He preferred to describe the action on the air and on paper strictly from his point of view, while keeping a healthy distance.

"He usually never spoke to a player," said Johnny O'Brien, Rainiers third baseman. "He thought that tainted his broadcast ability. He sent others to talk to the players. That's a purist."

A purist maybe, but he wasn't pure. In the radio booth, Lassen always kept a bottle of bourbon handy and uncapped. He sipped nightly but was careful not to overindulge. He was discovered and told to stop, but only succeeded in doing a better job of hiding it. The bourbon was his only constant companion. Never married, Lassen shared a Wallingford home on Latona Avenue with his mother, Minnie. Catching wind of this arrangement, some Rainiers players felt it was necessary to make rude assessments regarding the broadcaster's sexuality. They knew he grew roses, played the piano, and wrote poetry, which seemed to fuel this idea even more. At a time in the country when the McCarthy hearings were bent on outing Communists and reputations could be easily smeared, the Rainiers assumed Lassen was gay and passed that information around the ballpark. "I was warned by a ballplayer about going up in his booth alone," Patrick said.

Lassen likely was nothing more than a lonely old man. It was usually just the broadcaster, his microphone, and the bourbon. Yet one thing was clear about his existence: people could count on Lassen to show up for work. He didn't miss an inning until laryngitis kept him from a studio game replay in 1940. He didn't miss a home game until the same affliction knocked him off the air in 1954, with his four-game absence drawing headlines and listener concern.

As KOL found out, Lassen wasn't interested in hearing anyone else tell him how to do his job, nor would he consider the possibility that there was any other way of performing his radio duties. He let this be known on more than one occasion, usually talking out loud to no one in particular, as he critiqued the national radio and TV play-by-play announcers.

"He didn't think any other broadcaster he heard was any good," Belcher said. "Guys were doing the World Series and he would let them have it as he listened to them, because he didn't think they knew the rules of baseball. He had a very high opinion of himself."

Belcher learned this firsthand. After taking over the Rainiers' radio responsibilities in 1957, he encountered Lassen alone in a bar. They were well acquainted with each other. Lassen let his replacement know what kind of job he thought Belcher was doing, and it wasn't flattering. "You do a good job on the news and with that rah-rah football and rah-rah basketball," Lassen told him. "But on baseball, you're kind of horseshit."

The Rainiers and Leo Lassen parted ways over a salary squabble.

A little friction between them wasn't a surprise. Well in advance of the Rainiers broadcast booth takeover, they had gone head to head in a most peculiar fashion. Before stepping in for Lassen, Belcher had borrowed liberally from him on the airwaves and made no apologies for it. In 1951 Lassen worked for flagship station KING at the ballpark and Belcher called Rainiers home games for competing KOL without actually watching one of these summertime outings. KING had the broadcast rights, but not the reach to the coastal communities of Aberdeen and Hoquiam. Without opposition, KOL cut a deal to fill the baseball broadcast void.

Belcher sat behind a microphone in a studio with a colleague who listened carefully to what Lassen reported and wrote down everything that happened at Sicks' Stadium and handed over the crib notes. On a delayed basis of several seconds, Belcher recreated games for the grateful listeners more than a hundred miles away. Rather than admit signal limitations, Lassen's Seattle station had chosen to ignore this baseball-crazy region and didn't press the issue when KOL started supplying its own game broadcasts. KOL later outbid KING and became the flagship station and Lassen's employer, reaching all Rainiers listeners.

While handling this job, Belcher had no trouble sitting in a studio rather than the ballpark. As nice as the rest of Sicks' Stadium was, the media facilities were fairly primitive. "It was a great minor-league ballpark, but the broadcast booth was terrible," he said. Nor did adlibbing seem like much of a chore to him. Belcher was good at it. When taking over as the San Francisco 49ers' play-by-play man in 1950, he was informed by the NFL team's beer sponsor, Acme, that his last name was inappropriate in selling its product on the air and he had to change it. He came up with Rod Hughes, adopting a variation of his middle name, Hugh. "I thought I had the perfect name for a beer sponsor," he said. "It meant that you were getting a full-bodied beer."

Pirating games was not a unique practice during this broadcast era. For three years through 1954, Belcher sat in the same studio and recreated big league games from the East Coast to statewide listeners, often competing directly with Lassen and Rainiers broadcasts. As did Lassen when he called Rainiers away games, Belcher would sit back in a chair, first in the Northern Life tower downtown and then on Harbor Island, read the information that came in to KOL on a teletype machine, and let his imagination guide him through each inning. "I broadcast two hundred games that I never saw," Belcher said. "I did day and night games. I wasn't to do more than ten a week."

Lassen also felt threatened by a new kid in town, Keith Jackson, a recent Washington State University graduate who had a crew cut, southern accent, and confident air about him. Jackson joined KOMO-TV and radio in 1954, and worked the next decade in Seattle before becoming best known as the voice of college football for ABC-TV while also calling Monday Night Football, the Olympic Games, and big-league baseball games. Lassen immediately felt uncomfortable around the aggressive newcomer, certain that Jackson was pining for his coveted Rainiers play-by-play position as early as 1957, when Belcher took over instead.

"I was not party to the negotiations with Leo, and I never really knew the man," Jackson said. "All I heard was he hurled accusations around that I was trying to steal his job, which was a bunch of nonsense. I found him to be considerably complicated."

Lassen sat out the 1957 and 1958 seasons before he was coaxed back for two more, and then he was dumped from the radio booth permanently. Another salary dispute was used as an excuse to make another change, and his earlier fears came true. He was replaced by Jackson. Bitter over his second expulsion, Lassen never attended another baseball game. He became a recluse at his north-end home, in which he now resided alone. He didn't want to see anyone and turned down most interview requests. He remained a martyr, as far removed from the baseball world as he once had been totally consumed by it.

On the air, he had signed off every game broadcast with the following words: "Uh, this is Leo Lassen speaking. I hope you enjoyed it." Now he was a man in exile, forever unplugged from his hometown. Television was partly responsible for putting him there, forcing electronic media broadcasters across the country to provide a schtick, to ham it up in the booth, to readily compete for an audience now given far more entertainment choices than ever. Lassen was old style and wasn't budging, and Seattle reluctantly let go of its legend. There actually was a positive surrounding his departure from the Rainiers radio booth. The first time he was pushed away, Lassen didn't have to sit there and watch firsthand the disheartening breakup of the Pacific Coast League as he knew it.

12. Major Intrusion

Emil Sick was a sick and agitated man entering the 1957 baseball season. Now sixty-three, he suffered from emphysema and was under doctor's orders to chew on rubber cigars rather than the real thing. Celebrating his twentieth anniversary in business with the Rainiers, he couldn't even light up a stogie to com-memorate this milestone. All he could see around him was the greed of others potentially tearing apart his solidly constructed baseball franchise. He felt he deserved better. After all, his Seattle teams had topped all minor-league entries in collective home attendance during his ownership, drawing 6,600,965 fans since 1938, a figure superior to those in the two flagship cities that were set to flee the Pacific Coast League: population-rich Los Angeles, which had waved 6,310,970 inside during this period, and San Francisco, which had rung up 6,041,570. Even with the disruption of World War II, Sick had made a profit on baseball. He owned the ballpark his team played in and the facility, which had been remodeled once, was debt free. He had created a model franchise, and his fiscal prudence now was under harsh attack.

The Major Leagues were moving in fast to take over the coveted and untapped California territories. Two months into the 1957 season, everything was set into motion when a National League vote gave its blessing to the Brooklyn Dodgers and New York Giants, encouraging them to change addresses the following year if they desired. At the same meeting, the Cincinnati Reds were denied the right to move to New York.

The courtship of Los Angeles had been a persistent one, dating back before World War II and involving several suitors. On December 8, 1941, a meeting had been set up to facilitate a possible St. Louis Browns move to Southern California, but the tragic events of the previous day in Hawaii made any baseball business seem trite: the gathering was canceled and further discussion was effectively tabled for the near future. Twelve years later, the Browns again made noise about relocating to the West, as did the Philadelphia Athletics, Philadelphia Phillies, and Cincinnati Reds, with each of these franchises looking to move elsewhere after struggling to maintain a strong fan base. Los Angeles was equally guilty of fanning interest its way, actively pursuing the Major Leagues. Still on the outside in 1955, Los Angeles city leaders attended the New York Yankees–Brooklyn Dodgers World Series and began earnest discussions with the Washington Senators. All along, though, the Dodgers seemed like a likelier candidate to shake things up, having already revolutionized the game once before by breaking the color line with Jackie Robinson.

What disturbed people on the West Coast the most was

watching everyone mess with longstanding tradition. For eighteen consecutive seasons after Sick had created the Rainiers, there hadn't been a lineup change in the eight-team PCL, a baseball creature of habit. The first sign of decay for the league didn't turn up until 1956, when the Oakland Acorns, rich in history after celebrating the antics and following the lead of noted baseball personalities Casey Stengel and Billy Martin but forever scrambling for fans in the East Bay, were forced to disband and replaced by a Canadian team, the Vancouver Mounties. The league all of a sudden had turned international but would quickly become less cosmopolitan. The thought of the PCL losing its two largest metropolitan areas—both California cities boasted more than 2 million residents, compared to Seattle's 550,000—was unsettling to Sick, whose success had left him in a unique and highly defensive position. He was one of the few in the West who could afford to sustain a big-league franchise, though he was unwilling to randomly open up his checkbook again and lay down a greater investment for baseball than he had in 1937. "I think it is fair to state that we in Seattle have the most at stake," he said.

Frail health or not, there was a hard-line businessman still lurking inside the Rainiers' owner. Sick was ready to fight with every resource available to him, and he led virtually a one-man campaign to preserve PCL interests as best he could, presiding over meetings and handing out marching orders. He met and argued with baseball commissioner Ford Frick. Sick suggested rather cryptically that people should boycott league games still being played in Los Angeles, and was roundly criticized for it by a California press corps that eagerly awaited the arrival of the Dodgers and Giants. At a time when UFO sightings were the norm, particularly in the Northwest, the Seattle man sarcastically referred to the Dodgers' owner Walter O'Malley and his Giants counterpart Horace Stoneham "as the Majors invaders."

In anticipation of this moment, the Seattle owner had suggested two years earlier, in a letter to retiring PCL president Clarence Rowland, that it was inevitable that the big leagues would come and great change would follow, maybe even the shift of the Rainiers to some sort of Northwest league. Yet in his next sentence, the brash Sick made it clear that he had no intention of going that route, short of being dragged kicking and screaming. Slyly attempting to align political power, he proposed that his vice president, Torchy Torrance, replace Rowland as league president.

As reality set in, Sick scoffed at the considerable outside horse-trading needed to pull off the California takeover and the disingenuous liaisons formed. O'Malley traded his Double-A Texas League franchise in Fort Worth and accompanying ballpark lease for the Los Angeles Angels holdings and that city's Wrigley Field, temporarily making the wealthy real estate man a PCL owner and colleague of Sick—though he never once attended a meeting—and O'Malley then handed over his newly acquired LA ballpark to the city in exchange for land to build Dodger Stadium. Stoneham eventually swapped his Triple-A Minneapolis franchise in the American Association and its ballpark lease for the San Francisco Seals and Seals Stadium lease, and he, too, had instant league membership. The PCL was now fully infiltrated by people with questionable motives.

Sick wasn't foolhardy enough to think he could stop progress, but he was adamant that these carpetbaggers were going to pay a hefty price for their West Coast acquisitions and his potential lost business. In late August, the Rainiers owner announced that he and the rest of the league planned to sue everyone for damages. The Dodgers. The Giants. The National League. The franchise moves wouldn't be made official until October, but Sick was on the offensive. With threats and counterthreats in place, all parties met after the season in Sacramento, with Stoneham in attendance but O'Malley arrogantly sending club president Emil "Buzzy" Bavasi in his place. It took two days to hammer out an agreement, with powerful baseball people locking horns. "The meeting in Sacramento with Mr. Stoneham and Mr. Bavasi present was one of the most dramatic business meetings I have ever attended," Sick said. Almost gloating over his backroom victory, Sick sent a conciliatory letter on November 5 to the absent O'Malley in Brooklyn: "I'm sorry you did not make the meeting in Sacramento. You were well represented, although you were missed personally. I hope that something can be worked out to settle all pressing matters."

A month later at the winter baseball meetings in Colorado Springs, Colorado, the Dodgers and Giants revealed they had begrudgingly agreed to a $900,000 settlement, allocating $150,000 to each of the surviving six PCL franchises over the next three years by taking 10 cents off every admission. They also agreed to pay for any costs incurred in securing replacement teams, such as upgrading ballparks, and for disrupting the operations of any other affected minor league. The PCL actually lost three teams when the Hollywood Stars were forced to move because they were considered an infringement on Los Angeles's big-league territorial rights. Phoenix, Salt Lake City, and Spokane were brought in as replacements, though Phoenix lasted just two extreme seasons in the reorganized Triple-A league—capturing the pennant in 1958 but finishing last and pulling in a meager 79,106 season attendance in 1959.

Once everything had been realigned, it was clear why baseball leaders had been eager to add Los Angeles and San Francisco and resistant to elevating the entire PCL to Major League status. The first big-league game played in Los Angeles in 1958 drew 78,672 people—432 fewer fans than what Phoenix managed for the entire season a year later—with everyone converging on a Dodgers–Giants game played on a Friday afternoon at the Los Angeles Memorial Coliseum for a contest won by the home team, 6–5. This collection of enthusiastic baseball humanity set a big-league record for a regular-season outing and was part of a three-game series with San Francisco that attracted a hefty 167,209 to the gate—a figure nearly matching or exceeding the total attendance for half of the PCL teams in 1958.

Gale Wade played that final season for the Los Angeles Angels and then was traded from Spokane to the Rainiers the next year after the PCL had undergone its forced makeover. Things were different and there was no getting around it. For starters, owing to the drop in its population base, the league was no longer considered an "open classification," which resulted in the loss of its elevated minor-league status and corresponding player protections. More than anything, things simply felt watered down.

"When it changed, it wasn't the same," said Wade, who had listened to those Leo Lassen radio broadcasts of the PCL before playing in it. "When they broke it up, there was the feeling that something was missing. It wasn't that bad, but it didn't seem like the same place or have the same importance it once had."

As the big-league invasion was well under way, the Rainiers

The 1957 Seattle Rainiers roster included, *from left*, coach Edo Vanni, manager Lefty O'Doul, Ray Orteig, Hal Bevan, Jim Dyck, Leo Righetti, Joe Taylor, Juan Delis, Maury Wills, and Bobby Balcena.

were operating with a curious mix of personnel in 1957. They had a new manager, Frank Joseph "Lefty" O'Doul, considered a San Francisco icon even then, and trotted out a speedy young infielder named Maury Wills, who, within three years, would become a household name throughout big-league baseball for the Los Angeles Dodgers.

Following the Luke Sewell debacle, O'Doul was a welcome and familiar face to Seattle. He was now managing in his twenty-third consecutive season in the PCL and working for his fifth team among the eight member franchises. Most people in the league had played for or against him. He made things fun on the field and comfortable in the clubhouse. He had a Rainiers second baseman named Eddie Basinski, an accomplished violin player who once played in the Buffalo symphony orchestra and was nicknamed "The Fiddler," and the lighthearted O'Doul used to give him the hit-and-run sign by mimicking playing his instrument of choice. However, the manager was a short-timer in Seattle, already leaning toward retirement when he showed up. After improving things in 1957, guiding the Rainiers to an 87-80 record and fifth-place finish, he was done with managing. After working the bench in San Francisco, San Diego, Oakland, Vancouver, and Seattle, he retired and walked away with a 2,094-1,970 PCL managerial record.

The situation with the Rainiers wasn't overly stressful for the front office, but interest in the team was lagging, and the talent pool was mediocre. With the big leagues and TV severely cutting into the take at the gate, revenues were down and money for new players was limited. O'Doul wasn't given much to work with, and he had to scramble for talent. His best starting pitcher, thirty-five-year-old Duane "Dee" Pillette, had called up the manager and asked for a job after the season had started, after being considered damaged goods elsewhere.

Coming off an arm injury, Pillette had been released by the Baltimore Orioles and then the PCL's San Francisco Seals. He repaid the manager's faith in him with a 16-8 season and 3.16 ERA, using an arm that now defied previous medical opinions and was never idle long. The starting pitcher had been in Seattle for just a few days, sitting in the dugout with O'Doul, when another Rainiers pitcher was forced out of a game in the first inning with an arm injury, and he was pointed to the mound for long relief.

Pillette's unplanned Seattle debut went well as he took a 1–1 tie into the bottom of the ninth inning. Scheduled to bat with two outs and the winning run on base, he waited for a pinch-hitter to replace him and received his second surprise of the night. O'Doul informed him, since the game conceivably could go on for an extended time and he was short of available arms, Pillette was to bat for himself and stay on the mound. The manager got half of it right when the pitcher lined a game-winning single into the outfield. "You know, you're worth the bonus money," O'Doul kidded the veteran.

Pillette felt a strong connection with the city. His father, Herm, had pitched for the Seattle Indians in 1933 and 1934, and at the age of twelve, Pillette was an Indians batboy during his dad's second tour of the city. The California native found great comfort in the Northwest. "Seattle was always a good baseball town," he said. "Since my father played there, I always liked Seattle and I liked the way they treated you. They didn't treat you like a jock. The fans were really good to you. You were a Coast League guy."

Maury Wills thrived under this atmosphere, too. He had never seen the West Coast until the Rainiers acquired him from the Brooklyn Dodgers organization. A Washington DC native, he hadn't been much of anywhere, struggling to get out of the lower minors. Considered a weak-hitting and slick-fielding player, and shifting between shortstop and second base, Wills had to prove himself to O'Doul, whose first impression of him in spring training wasn't flattering. "The kid can't hit," O'Doul offered bluntly. "He runs with the speed of a rocket through space, but the fact is unchallenged. You can't steal first base."

Wills proved to be a better player than his manager envisioned. In 147 games for Seattle, usually hitting seventh in the lineup, he batted .267, though demonstrating no power at all, going homerless for the season. His strength would be his disruptive ability on the base paths. He led the club with twenty-one stolen bases, and he won a late-season game by advancing from first to third on a bunt. He became a confident player with a bit of a swagger, rescued from the edge of baseball obscurity.

"My dream of going to the big leagues was just about over then," Wills said. "I had to rise to the occasion with the Rainiers. Seattle was good for my career because it was the first time I got to play with a lot of hardened, veteran players."

One of his mentors was the pitcher Joe Black. The twenty-four-year-old Wills was so thrilled to be around him, a man nine years older, that during spring training in San Bernardino, California, he offered to drive Black to the golf course every day after practice. Wills had a car; Black didn't. Wills didn't play golf, either. He initially sat in his small vehicle and waited for the older teammate to finish his eighteen holes. After several trips to the course, Wills tired of this routine and finally suggested that he give the game a try. He was a natural, shooting 85 the first time out, leaving Black feeling certain he had been scammed. "He was all over me because he felt he had been set up," the infielder said.

Wills had grown up in the projects of the nation's capital, and was such a skilled athlete that Ohio State, Syracuse, and several black universities offered him football scholarships to play quarterback. He decided on baseball for two reasons: all the adults in his neighborhood talked about a black man who had played for the Brooklyn Dodgers and broken the game's color line, and Wills's stated goal thereafter was to line up alongside Jackie Robinson. Just as important, a big-league player named Jerry Priddy, later the Rainiers' manager and second baseman, had singled him out at a DC baseball clinic and made him feel special.

After his summer in Seattle, however, Wills was reclaimed by the California-bound Dodgers, and he panicked. He thought it was the worst possible thing that could happen to him and he didn't want to go back. He had only bad memories from his prior experiences in the Brooklyn organization and was convinced that staying in Seattle was his best ticket to the big leagues. It didn't matter that he wasn't going far, that he wasn't leaving the PCL, that the Dodgers were merely shipping him across the state to their new Triple-A affiliate in Spokane. Wills voiced his strong objections in a letter addressed to club general manager Dewey Soriano and published in the *Seattle Times*:

During my brief stay with the Rainiers, I reacquired the faith I had in baseball that I once had. I'm very grateful to you for giving me the chance to play open classification ball. The Seattle Rainiers treated me swell. Now you have sold me back to the organization that I've given six hard years of my career and they haven't paid me more than $500 a month or given me a chance to play Triple-A ball. Dewey, you have torn down everything that I built up this past season. Is there no hope in baseball for a player who wants to play baseball?

Wills vividly remembers that disenchantment, his fears of taking a step back with his baseball career. "Playing with the Rainiers and playing in Sicks' Stadium, that was probably my springboard to getting to the big leagues," he said. "I was very disappointed. I wanted to stay. I was dejected." Of course, Wills's passionate argument proved moot. Within a year and a half, he was a finished product in the big leagues, playing solidly for the Dodgers in Los Angeles, and by 1962 he would be the talk of baseball with a big-league record 104 stolen bases, one of six times he led the National League in that category.

Wills never forgot what the Rainiers did for his baseball career, which decades later would lead to his return to the Northwest for a brief and unsuccessful stint as manager of the big-league Seattle Mariners after he had failed to land the same job with the expansionist Seattle Pilots. There was no question the city had maintained a firm grip on him. "If I didn't have a chance to play for the Seattle Rainiers, there wouldn't be a Maury Wills stealing 104 bases, the captain of the Dodgers, an MVP," he said. "It turned my life around."

Midway though that 1957 season, the Rainiers tried to do the same for another raw baseball talent, ironically someone else who hailed from Washington DC and would soon be bound for Los Angeles and athletic greatness, though in another pro sport. One morning, Sicks' Stadium was locked down tight, with just a few people allowed inside for an individual tryout that was held in top secrecy. O'Doul, Soriano, a couple of Cincinnati Reds executives, a batting practice pitcher, and batboy Pat Patrick eagerly watched as Elgin Baylor pulled on a Rainiers baseball uniform and was put through an intense ballpark inspection.

Baylor was Seattle University's All-America basketball player, a 29.7-point scorer and the nation's leading rebounder at 20.3 per outing as only a sophomore, and a superb athlete in many ways. He played basketball and mulled going out for football at the College of Idaho, now Albertson's College, but transferred out when it became clear his talents were better suited for a bigger school. Now he was giving pro baseball a few random moments of his time.

Occasionally, Baylor had turned up at Seattle U baseball practices to take a few swings and crush balls at Broadway Field, leaving people mesmerized by his untapped ability. "I'm not sure how well he would have hit the curve, but, yes, Elgin may have missed his calling," said Jim Harney, a Chieftains basketball teammate of Baylor's and one of the school's repeatedly dumbfounded baseball players.

In the Sicks' Stadium workout, Baylor demonstrated uncanny ability, though he hadn't played organized baseball since high school. He hit the ball hard. He hit it to the opposite field. The graceful 6-foot-5 athlete flawlessly took grounders and throws at first base. Those in attendance wanted to sign Baylor on the spot, but he declined the offer. This encounter was no different for him than joining the Seattle U baseball players at practice; it was a lark. Basketball was his stated vocation, which he would prove over and over again while playing fourteen N BA seasons with the Minneapolis and Los Angeles Lakers. Widely considered the Michael Jordan of his time, Baylor averaged 27.4 points per game in his pro career and made eleven appearances in the All-Star Game.

"He was an absolute natural but he had no interest," said Patrick, the only living witness to this brief encounter between Baylor and pro baseball. "They were talking to him and ready to talk lots of money."

Five decades later, Baylor—now an elderly man and the Los Angeles Clippers' general manager—responded to queries about his brief flirtation with the Rainiers from his seat in a college arena where he and a colleague were scouting players. After all those years, the moment didn't register, though the idea of it made him lean back and smile and request that the details be repeated to him again, so he could further digest a moment apparently lost in time. "I don't remember that, though that doesn't mean it didn't happen," Baylor said, before turning to the man seated next to him and remarking, "Can you believe that?"

As the 1957 season wound down and PCL baseball was losing its grip everywhere, Sicks' Stadium suddenly had the look of a multipurpose venue. Besides the discreet Baylor workout, two unforgettable, high-profile events were held within ten days inside the ballpark. On August 22, 16,961 people jammed inside to witness world heavyweight boxing champion Floyd Patterson trade punches with Olympic gold medalist Pete Rademacher in a ring erected over home plate, with Patterson knocking out the challenger in the sixth round. On September 1, on a Sunday night on Labor Day weekend several hours after the Rainiers had lost to the lame-duck Los Angeles Angels, 6–3, Elvis Presley strode out onto a stage set up over second base wearing a trademark gold jacket and a smirk, sending a crowd of fifteen thousand mostly squealing teenagers into a frenzy in his first Seattle appearance before driving off in a Cadillac that went out through a gate in the right-field fence.

Otherwise, there was an air of great uncertainty hovering over the Seattle ballpark. Maybe if Baylor had been signed and put on the Rainiers roster, O'Doul might have stuck around Seattle longer. Yet the Pacific Coast League was changing, and it was probably a good time for O'Doul to move on. His next destination, however, didn't make anyone feel any better about his departure. Mentioning that he might open a restaurant, which he did and which still exists, O'Doul headed back to San Francisco, taking up residence in a new big-league city emerging at Seattle's expense and joining the newly moved Giants as batting coach.

Weakened PCL aside, the 1958 season was as miserable as any for the Rainiers. As part of its working agreement with the Cincinnati Reds, the team agreed to move its training camp from California to the U.S.-Mexican border town of Laredo, Texas, which proved to be a harsh and overheated baseball setting. It might as well have been Mars. The weather was unbearable, the field was in horrible condition, and new manager and former big leaguer Connie Ryan and several players were frequently ill with intestinal problems after drinking the water. The Rainiers were housed in a gym, sleeping on army cots in one big room, sharing limited restroom facilities.

"It reminded me of prison," Basinski said of his spring confinement. "It was rough. I'd never seen cockroaches as big as I did in Laredo, Texas. They were all over the place. You'd go to a restaurant and they'd be crawling all over the place and they'd just knock them away."

To fill out their exhibition schedule, the Rainiers were forced to play a series of games south of the border against Mexican League teams. They rode a bus through mountain passes without guard rails, entrusting their safety to a carefree driver often steering with one hand and gesturing with the other while sitting sideways, chattering away at his passengers, oblivious to the fact that they were clutching their seats in fear. In Monterrey, Seattle players watched wide-eyed as fans tossed snakes around the stands, scattering entire sections. Two four-foot-long reptiles, allegedly not poisonous, were flung onto the field one night. One snake landed precariously close to first-base coach Edo Vanni, who became so terrified he took off running and didn't return to the field for the final three innings.

Apparently, the Rainiers never recovered from this spring ordeal. Ryan's team finished in eighth and last place with a miserable 68-86 record. These guys lost fourteen consecutive games and threatened to break a long-running PCL record, falling three setbacks shy of Sacramento's 1925 standard for league futility with an 8–4 victory over the Phoenix Giants at home in

Rainiers center fielder Vada Pinson hit .343 and stole thirty-seven bases in 1958.

mid-August. The big-league working agreement with Cincinnati was not working out well for the Rainiers. In a midseason deal, the Reds acquired veteran pitcher Don Newcombe from the now Los Angeles Dodgers and for payment pulled starting pitchers Art Fowler and Charlie Rabe out of Seattle and shipped them to the Dodgers' Triple-A teams in Spokane and St. Paul, thus gutting the Rainiers' rotation.

To the Reds' credit, they sent Vada Pinson to Seattle. An

electrifying nineteen-year-old center fielder who was projected as the next big thing in Cincinnati, he played the first month and a half of the 1958 season in the big leagues with the Reds, and was placed with the Rainiers when he slumped a bit. Seasoning in the PCL was good for Pinson, who hit .343 with eleven homers and seventy-seven RBI, and led the league in stolen bases with thirty-seven. Shortly after his arrival, he showed precisely what he could do to shake things up by stealing home in the eighth inning and providing the winning run in a 5–4 victory over the San Diego Padres. He singled to center, moved to second when a teammate walked and advanced to third on a fielder's choice, and was nearly all the way home before opposing pitcher Bob Alexander realized what was happening and could react and throw to the plate.

Pinson also turned up in Seattle with a big-league attitude that didn't go over well initially. Spotting the newcomer mistreat a clubhouse boy, Rainiers veteran catcher Hal Bevan grabbed the young outfielder by the neck and said sternly, "Pick on him once more, and I don't care if you're the second coming of God, I will lay you out." The words must have sunk in. Years later, in his second stint in Seattle for baseball, serving this time as the Mariners' batting coach, Pinson was a quiet, unassuming personality in the clubhouse.

While Pinson batted third and supplied repeated heroics, Gale Wade, the cleanup hitter for the team, generated a Rainiers game to remember. A Bremerton High alumnus who had fancied himself as more of a football player and had pined for a Notre Dame scholarship that never came, Wade joined the Rainiers while the 1958 season was in progress. He had played briefly in the big leagues with the Chicago Cubs, and his career was winding down. On July 31, he hit two doubles and a grand-slam homer while driving in eight runs during a 10–3 victory over the Salt Lake City Bees in the second game of a doubleheader at Sicks' Stadium. His hitting was music to everyone's ears: that day, the team was handing out transistor radios to players who met certain offensive incentives.

"I won all nine of them," said Wade, a right fielder. "It was something I couldn't believe. It was a lot of fun that night, something I had never experienced before. But I gave all those transistors away in the clubhouse except one. I only needed one."

Outside of Wade's single-night heroics and Pinson's overall play, there wasn't much else to get enthused about that season. The club was so desperate for fans that one of its marketing schemes was to have employees place vouchers for free tickets on cars downtown that had accumulated parking tickets. Seattle season attendance dipped precariously that season to 142,499. Ryan was fired. He left town bitterly complaining of the limited budgetary resources available to him. The Rainiers needed a boost and turned to a familiar face. They hired Hutch again.

Hutchinson's three-year stint with the St. Louis Cardinals was so uneven that it earned him National League manager of the year honors in 1957 and got him fired in 1958. Always welcome in Seattle, Hutch was hired on the rebound by Sick as the 1959 Rainiers manager and also as general manager, agreeing to a three-year contract worth $30,000 annually. With the aging owner's health more in question and the PCL baseball landscape less appealing because of the increased Major League presence in the area, there was considerable speculation about Hutch's third tour of duty with the franchise. The suggestion was made that Sick might turn the franchise over to a consolidated own-ership group headed by Hutchinson, Soriano, and other local businessmen. "I can't confirm that," Sick said at the time. "But we're willing to set him up pretty well. If anybody can revive interest in baseball here, Hutch can do it."

Unfortunately, that wasn't the case. At spring training in El Centro, California, a big improvement over Laredo, Hutchinson took a long look at the roster and made an honest assessment. "It doesn't look too promising," he told Rainiers beat writers. As for assuming all operations, he didn't even stick around long enough to celebrate another birthday bash at the ballpark. Quite possibly, Hutch was worn out by the Seattle job this time, especially in early May, when on consecutive nights his team played fourteen-inning and twenty-one-inning games against the Phoenix Giants, winning them both, 5–4 and 6–5. The latter contest lasted five hours and fifty-six minutes. It wiped out the back end of a proposed doubleheader, though the marathon lasted five innings longer than the two games combined that were originally scheduled. As the team stumbled through a 74-80 season he wouldn't finish, Hutchinson simmered with each setback. He still took out his frustration in anger, yet now did so in private rather than in the company of his players. Still, the loud, crashing sounds were hard to ignore.

"I got along fine with him, because I was a competitive per-son," Rainiers pitcher Dave Stenhouse said. "I hated to be in his way when he got angry. Sometimes it was funny, because he hit anything that got in front of him, but I respected the man a lot and his need to be alone."

On July 8, 1959, a month before his fortieth birthday, Hutchin-son agreed to a sudden promotion, returning to the big leagues once again as the Cincinnati manager. The move certainly didn't do anything to promote the Reds' working agreement with Seattle, though this arrangement would be renewed for yet another season. When Hutch left the club this time, the Rainiers were in last place with a 38-46 record, and Alan Strange, a former Seattle shortstop and a much less demanding personality, became the interim manager. Hutchinson and Strange had been Rainiers teammates in 1938.

Hutchinson wasn't gone three weeks when an announcement was made in New York that a third Major League, the Continental League, had been planned for the 1961 season, two years out, sending the city into a temporary baseball frenzy. The cities of New York, Houston, Toronto, Denver, and Minneapolis–St. Paul were awarded franchises, and Seattle was mentioned as a possibility for one of the three remaining teams, but Rainiers and league officials shot the idea down.

"Actually, I can't take this story too seriously," Sick told the *Seattle Post-Intelligencer*. "I'd first have to see some money behind these statements from the cities mentioned. Furthermore, many of the cities mentioned, including Seattle, don't have ballpark facilities which could accommodate Major League baseball, and it takes money to get these facilities."

The third league was never formed. Only New York and Houston moved forward with plans to operate franchises and joined the National League in 1961 with expansion teams called the Mets and Colt .45s. (The latter would later be renamed the Astros after the gun company that was its namesake complained.) In Seattle the Hutch-less Rainiers turned their attention to escaping the cellar, but couldn't get any higher than seventh place even after winning fourteen of fifteen games late, including eleven in a row, and Mark Freeman had thrown a no-hitter, beating Vancouver, 3–0, on the road in August—the sixth and last hit-less game turned in by a Rainiers pitcher.

Future Dodgers ace Claude Osteen pitched for the Rainiers that season, while outfielder Lou Skizas, a former big-leaguer nicknamed "The Nervous Greek," was on his way down, a mid-season acquisition from the Reds. Skizas was another showman, rattling off an eighteen-game hitting streak while entertaining fans with a batter's box routine that would include covering his bat with dirt, wiping it off between his legs, and kissing it before sticking one hand in his back pocket and taking practice swings. It didn't get much mention at the time, but reserve catcher Roger Jongewaard was sold by the Rainiers to the Salt Lake City Bees in early May, the ballclub parting ways with a man who later would return to the city and spend several seasons as the Seattle Mariners' player personnel director, drafting the likes of Ken Griffey Jr. and Alex Rodriguez.

The 1959 season had held much promise with Hutchinson back for a third tour of duty but was as deflating as any when the man entrusted with reinvigorating Seattle baseball was unable to resist a return to the Majors. Baseball's highest level couldn't keep its hands off anybody or anything out west: Hutch, the cities of Los Angeles and San Francisco, even the neighborhood kid raking the infield and doing anything else the Rainiers asked of him.

To be inside Sicks' Stadium, Ron Santo had only to leave his family duplex, cross an empty lot, and make his way through the parking lot of the venue. The trip took five minutes, tops. For four summers, the kid next door handled every menial job for the Rainiers, from batboy to grounds-crew member to press

Ron Santo, shown in his Franklin High School senior photo, was a Rainiers clubhouse attendant and groundskeeper.

box attendant to clubhouse attendant. He delivered hotdogs to sportswriters, shined Vada Pinson's baseball shoes on a daily basis though he was just eighteen months younger than the center fielder, and was a Hutchinson favorite. He gladly did whatever was asked of him, relishing every minute of his early pro baseball exposure. "I was in my glory when I was in that ballpark," Santo said.

One humiliating afternoon was a notable exception. In 1958 the Cincinnati Reds arrived in Seattle to play their annual exhibition game against the Rainiers, their top farm club, and front-office executives asked if Santo, a budding baseball prospect at nearby Franklin High School, would be willing to take some batting practice swings alongside the big leaguers. They wanted to see the high school senior up close, as did every other organization, because the word was out the kid could hit. "I said OK," Santo said. "I was really excited about it."

The teenager grabbed his 31-ounce bat and stepped into the cage to face pitcher Don Newcombe, now trying to rebound from arm trouble after coming over in the convoluted trade that earlier had disrupted the Rainiers pitching staff. Santo admittedly was nervous just looking at the veteran. He had reason to be uneasy when Newcombe's first pitch ran in on him and broke the kid's bat in half. Santo just stood there helpless, not sure what to do next. Reds catcher Ed Bailey instinctively tossed him his bat. The thing weighed 38 ounces, but it felt like 38 pounds. Santo flailed away, impressing no one. His nerves, made worse by the unfamiliar equipment, had worked against him. He handed the heavy bat back to Bailey, politely thanked the veteran for letting him use it, and received a snide remark in return. "That bat separates the men from the boys," Bailey told him mockingly. The ultracompetitive Santo walked away simmering, vowing he would never forget the insult, determined to someday clear his name.

Overcoming his forgettable audition, the Sicks' Stadium apprentice made it to the big leagues midway through the 1960 season with the Chicago Cubs. His best signing bonus offer was $75,000, most were $50,000, and he signed with Chicago for $25,000, more concerned with opportunity than cash flow. All sixteen big-league teams wanted him, but he was loyal to a Seattle-based scout, Dave Kosher, the onetime Hornsby protégé who had helped steer Santo through this process, and joined the Cubs organization because it felt right to him. "It paid off," Santo said. "In a year, I was in the big leagues."

Santo would spend fifteen seasons as a third baseman in Chicago, the last one playing across town for the White Sox. He was selected as an All-Star nine times, received the golden glove award five times, and hit 342 home runs. He had a Hall of Fame career, though he's still waiting on induction. By a comfortable margin, he remains Seattle's greatest homegrown baseball talent in terms of big-league performance. He always had the ability to make it to the Majors, and hanging out at Sicks' Stadium as a teenager reinforced the idea. He got a taste of pro ball and all he had to do was walk a couple of blocks for it.

"I lived so close and I so looked forward to that," Santo said. "In those days Triple-A baseball was like Major League baseball, with doubleheaders on Sunday and teams coming in for a week. A lot of the Rainiers went up and came back, and you knew those guys. I loved it."

Santo watched everything the players did, even the bad stuff, and took mental notes. He saw a few Rainiers regularly snub the usual collection of five to six kids waiting outside the clubhouse for autographs, looking away as they came out the door, getting in their cars, and slamming the door. "They walked right by them, and I said to myself, 'They're not even in the big leagues and they're not signing autographs,'" he recalled. "I knew right then, that no matter what happened to me, I was going to sign autographs."

Santo was good at every sport he played, and he played all of them. Quarterbacking the Franklin football team, he led the league in passing, was a first-team all-city selection, and was offered and turned down a University of Washington football scholarship. He was a starting guard in basketball, the team playmaker. He hit .512 for the Quakers baseball team as a senior, was selected as the all-city catcher while playing out of position (a teammate was injured), and shared in three league championships. He also was named most valuable player of the annual City-State high school baseball all-star doubleheader in Seattle, which earned him a trip to the Hearst national all-star game in New York. However, adversity would soon head for him, much like a Newcombe fastball in on the hands.

Shortly after signing with the Cubs, Santo was diagnosed with diabetes. Failing to swing that 38-ounce bat was nothing compared to this burden. Fearful that if those in pro baseball knew of his condition his career would be hampered, he hid the news from the team. Each day for a month, he went to Seattle's Providence Hospital to learn how to manage the disease, though the treatment back then was crude at best. He initially refused to take insulin, concerned he might have a negative reaction. In the Majors, Santo once administered a shot to himself, and a Chicago teammate saw him do it and said nothing. When Santo went out and collected a couple of hits that day, the other player pulled him aside and said, "Whatever it is you're taking, I want some of it, too."

After spending just a season and a half in the minors with teams in San Antonio and Houston, Santo was called up to the

Majors. In his Cubs debut, he batted sixth in the order and went 3-for-7 with five RBI in a doubleheader sweep of the Pittsburgh Pirates. "I knew I had a gift," Santo said. "It's what you make of that gift. Players don't always have God-given talent but make themselves what they are. I was given God-given talent to hit and throw a ball. The one thing I didn't have was speed. Everything was easy for me."

Santo was both pleased and annoyed to play against Cincinnati early in his first big-league season. The Reds were managed by his Seattle mentor, Hutchinson, someone he idolized and respected so much he used to tell everyone he was from Hutch's hometown. In his first at-bat, Santo also noticed that Ed Bailey was still doing the catching. The same guy who had lent him the big bat. The same mouthy guy who had given him the humiliating parting shot two years earlier at Sicks' Stadium. The Cubs rookie stepped in and out of the batter's box, and then he turned to the man behind the plate and reintroduced himself.

"I don't know if you remember me, but I was in Seattle, working out, and you handed me a bat," Santo said with purpose, the former Rainiers groundskeeper and clubhouse kid about to settle at least one outstanding score with the big leagues for his hometown. "You said this bat separates the men from the boys. I'm a man now."

13. Joltin' Joe

One of the advantages of playing baseball for a brewery owner was that everyone was given ample opportunity to sample the boss's product. Emil Sick had two cases of Rainier beer delivered to the clubhouse after each night game at home, three cases after a Sunday doubleheader. Sad thing was, outfielder Joe Taylor usually didn't wait for the postgame beverages to arrive.

Taylor was a gifted power hitter who had been through Seattle before, playing for the ballclub in 1956 and 1957, on his way to the big leagues each time. However, the Alabama native returned to the Rainiers in 1960 after using up all of his chances at the next level. The Philadelphia Athletics, Cincinnati Reds, St. Louis Cardinals, and Baltimore Orioles each brought him up for a look, but those four teams collectively needed just 105 at-bats to figure him out and pass on him. Taylor had enough skills to stay in the big show, but not the willpower.

"He had incredible talent," said pitcher Dick Fitzgerald, a

Joe Taylor was an enigma, unable to stay sober long for the Rainiers.

teammate of Taylor's in Seattle and Vancouver. "He could have been a hall of famer."

"Joe Taylor should have been a superstar in the big leagues," said Rainiers infielder Maury Wills, who became one with the Los Angeles Dodgers.

"He could have been another Babe Ruth," said second baseman Eddie Basinski, a teammate of Taylor's in Portland, Vancouver, and Seattle, in all sincerity.

Taylor's problem was he couldn't stay sober. He drank more than Babe Ruth, which was a lot. Often he sipped gin or vodka all day before reporting to the ballpark. Fitzgerald spent a season with Taylor playing winter baseball in Nicaragua and almost never saw him sober. Teammates used to watch the slugger stagger up to home plate and wonder if he could remain upright. Players joked that Taylor always saw two balls coming at him whenever he batted, and his challenge simply was picking out the right one to swing at. When he could connect, he was ox strong; overly developed in his upper torso, he had a short, compact swing that made him explosive at the plate.

On opening day for Portland in 1955, Taylor launched three long home runs. Two years later during an opening day double-header for the Rainiers, he pounded three more homers in a sweep of the San Francisco Seals, driving in nine runs. The last long ball reportedly traveled more than five hundred feet over the left center-field fence and is believed to be the longest homer hit out of Sicks' Stadium. Others left people equally awestruck, in particular one that left the park in 1960. "He hit one out dead center, over the wall, which was pretty high," said Larry Ellingsen, a Rainiers batboy and clubhouse attendant. "I'd never seen anyone do that." Taylor actually would be one of three players to pull off that feat, joining Seattle outfielder Al Lyons in 1950 and joined by Hawaii outfielder Dick Simpson in 1964, each needing to drive one considerably longer than the 415-foot distance listed to clear everything in straightaway center.

Taylor, however, had to have a few belts before and after each belt. He considered this standard practice for his baseball career. "Joe Taylor used to say in the clubhouse that when the game was finished one of my jobs was to bring him a beer," said the batboy Pat Patrick. Charlie Metro, the wartime Rainiers outfielder, was manager of the Vancouver Mounties for the 1959 season and had

With his classic swing, Joe Taylor could hit the ball as far as anyone.
(Bob Peterson photo)

Taylor on his roster. On a trip to Seattle that season, the rocket-fueled power hitter lined one off the center-field wall against the Rainiers for a triple. When he pulled into third, Metro, who was coaching the bag, caught an extra-strong whiff of his player. "I patted him on the shoulder and said, 'Nice going, Joe,'" he said. "I almost passed out from the booze."

Some nights were tougher than others for Taylor. On one occasion, he showed up falling-down drunk for a Mounties game in Vancouver and quickly was ushered to the showers. Taylor put on his uniform, but Metro told the trainer to confine the wobbly player to the clubhouse. Taylor kept ignoring this directive and turning up in the dugout. He was a likeable guy, just not very bright at times. As a close game wound down, Taylor chirped at Metro, repeating a steady refrain: "Put me in Charlie. I'll break this game open for you." In the ninth inning, with the Mounties now in need of some runs, Metro gave in. The manager figured if Taylor could chatter on like that, maybe he could swing a bat, but Metro was wrong. The unsteady slugger watched three strikes down the middle zip past him. He didn't wave at one of them. Heading for the clubhouse after the game was over, Taylor spotted his manager and ill-advisedly shouted, "Charlie, you dumb shit, why did you put me in?"

Metro couldn't get mad at Taylor. He just used the alcoholic player whenever he could, praying the man wouldn't hurt himself. The manager looked the other way, especially when he heard about the time the slugger showed up in a foggy state at a San Diego airport, having missed the Mounties team flight to Hawaii, and asked the gate attendant when the next train to the islands was leaving. "I loved the guy," Metro said. "He played his heart out, to the best of his ability. He could hit. He could have been fabulous. But I just don't know if anybody in the big leagues would have put up with him long."

Playing for Portland in 1955, Taylor was sleeping off a hangover in the left-field bullpen during a game when Basinski lined one in that direction for a sure double. The outfielder woke up with a start when he heard the pitchers scramble, reached out, and reflexively grabbed the ball. Interference was called and Basinski was waved out while standing at second base. The enraged Portland manager, Clay Hopper, a Mississippi native not partial to African American players to begin with, rushed out of the dugout, screaming at Taylor, "Get your black ass back here and get in the clubhouse where you can't hurt us anymore." Taylor was through in Portland following that episode. Elsewhere, others went to great lengths to protect him.

In 1957 Rainiers manager Lefty O'Doul advised his players to deal with Taylor as best they could as the man stumbled through another season. O'Doul often told the outfielder to sit out batting practice, hoping he would straighten up by game time. Even in a constantly inebriated state that year, Taylor batted .305 with 22 home runs and 72 RBI over 115 games for Seattle before finishing that season in the big leagues with the Reds. In one Rainiers game, Taylor cracked a homer and three doubles, and O'Doul remarked, "That's what happens when a guy sobers up."

Yet Taylor hardly went anywhere without a good buzz on. Dressing next to first base coach Edo Vanni in the Rainiers clubhouse, he often grew frustrated, repeatedly putting his foot in the wrong shoe. When you're drunk, nothing ever fits. "He didn't always know what town he was in," Vanni said. "He was always out at night. He didn't know there was a clock. He never went to bed."

People weren't nearly as patient with Taylor the last time he came through Seattle. A month into the 1960 season, he went on a bender in Rainier Valley after a game. Coming out of a tavern, he climbed into someone else's car. It looked like his—same make, model, and color—but it wasn't his. Since everything was fairly standard in auto production back then, his key fit into the ignition, the engine turned over, and he was off on a perilous ride. Before his outing was over, Taylor had rammed this "borrowed" vehicle into another and was arrested for drunken and negligent driving, though luckily escaping auto theft charges. The Rainiers briefly suspended him, giving him a second chance, but things would get worse for the slugger.

Six weeks later, Taylor showed up drunk to Sicks' Stadium and was pulled out of a game against the Portland Beavers in the fourth inning. He was hit by a pitch and headed for first base, only to trip over the bag and fall down. An indignant Rainiers manager Dick Sisler suspended him, telling reporters sternly,

"I'm fully aware of Joe's past and I'm certainly not going to put up with it. The game of baseball is bigger than Joe Taylor." Taylor was unrepentant, separately informing a *Seattle Times* reporter, "Once you get a reputation like I've got, every little thing you do is wrong. They said I was drunk. I didn't feel drunk."

Taylor, who alternated between left field and right, was likeable and immensely talented but had no self-control whatsoever. To illustrate this weakness, players liked to tell the following story they swore was true: Taylor once got dressed in his Sunday best and was walking to church with good intentions when a carefree teammate pulled alongside him in a car and suggested that they go to a red-light district establishment together before the doubleheader that day. According to the story, Taylor shrugged and got in. "He got away with everything," Patrick said. "He didn't worry about anything."

Temptations were everywhere for Taylor, a married man with two children. After one game, Patrick encountered Taylor leaving the ballpark in a hurry, dressed in a fancy suit and headed for a woman waiting in a pink Cadillac idling nearby. When the batboy asked where he was headed, Taylor said, "Not now, son. I'm just going to pitch and putt down at the stockyards."

Taylor's career in Seattle appeared to be over after Sisler suspended him. Although general manager Cedric Tallis was fully prepared to release Taylor, something of an obstacle prevented the Rainiers from placing him in baseball purgatory: the team was still in the pennant race. With Taylor near the top of the league's home run leaders, Rainiers players were convinced they couldn't win the championship without him and his big bat. Giving a pair of impassioned clubhouse speeches to the other players behind closed doors, third baseman Johnny O'Brien and Vanni strongly suggested that Taylor needed their help, not banishment. Making their case for Taylor's reinstatement, the two men argued that everyone in the room had been stumbling drunk at some time in their baseball careers, and no one protested.

O'Brien, finishing up his pro baseball career in Seattle after playing for three big-league teams, came up with a creative solution: He proposed that their troubled teammate breathe on Rainiers trainer Freddie Frederico each day upon arrival at the ballpark to demonstrate his sobriety. If there were intoxicants detectable, Taylor couldn't play. Otherwise, he would take his usual place in the lineup. For a short-term penalty to settle his most recent infraction, Taylor wouldn't be allowed to play in the PCL All-Star Game held in Spokane.

This appeared to be a workable solution until Taylor stepped in the batter's box again. He was totally lost without alcoholic inspiration of any kind percolating through his system. Cold turkey, he went through a disastrous 6-for-50 spell, with no long balls. Teammates could barely stand to watch this once-dangerous hitter now flail away in such a helpless and haphazard manner, and a concerned O'Brien realized that his plan had backfired. He went back to the Rainiers general manager with yet another solution, concluding that Taylor desperately needed something to get his swing back.

O'Brien proposed giving Taylor a shot of vodka before each game. He carefully told Tallis that while his teammate wasn't any help to the Rainiers in a seriously drunken state, nor was he worth a damn without a drop of alcohol in his system, either. How about meeting somewhere in the middle? The GM protested when he first heard this idea, but practically in the next sentence, the exasperated team executive agreed. Tallis had made a big investment in Taylor's abilities before the season started, moving home plate fifteen feet to shorten the fences for his slugger, and wanted to see this work. The general manager asked only that everyone wait until the team went back on the road before lubricating the home-run hitter, holding off until the team reached Portland before giving Taylor his needed liquid assistance, and that they mix the needed alcohol boost with soft drinks. "They also used to give it to him in milkshakes," *Post-Intelligencer* beat writer Paul Rossi recalled. Said O'Brien, who played bartender as well as infielder thereafter, "Every day it was, 'Joe, I've got your medicine.'"

The vodka worked wonders. Properly fueled, Taylor hit four home runs in the next five games. He finished with thirty homers, which was a career best for him at any level and the most by a Rainiers player. He finished second in long balls in the PCL that season and also provided a robust .291 batting average and ninety-four RBI. The magic clubhouse brew didn't bring a pennant, though, as the Rainiers finished 77-75 and in fourth place, fourteen and a half games behind Spokane.

When the season ended, everyone on the ballclub headed for home the following day. Fitzgerald, who was from Philadelphia, ran into Taylor, a Pittsburgh resident, at the airport. Both were flying to Pennsylvania. At that particular moment, they were teammates, yet total strangers. "He was in bad shape," Fitzgerald said. "He didn't recognize me."

While Taylor supplied a large chunk of the offense and plenty of histrionics during the 1960 season, former Major Leaguer Don Rudolph was the Rainiers' pitching ace. The left-hander finished as the PCL's earned run average leader at 2.42 while compiling a 13-10 record. He was a confident but laid-back personality on the mound. He also was accompanied everywhere by his wife, Patricia, a plain-looking woman whose best-known attributes were well hidden during the baseball season. In the winter, she was a popular stripper in the Los Angeles area, answering to the whimsical stage name "Patti Waggin," and Rudolph was her manager. This dark-haired woman sat alone during games at Sicks' Stadium because other players' wives were too squeamish about her unconventional occupation to make friends and keep her company. After his brief stint in Seattle, Rudolph returned to the Majors, where the family business was treated in a lighthearted fashion. "Alas, the wrong Rudolph had the great curves," Chicago White Sox owner Bill Veeck quipped after trading the pitcher to the Cincinnati Reds.

If the 1960 season wasn't challenging enough for the Rainiers, with all the drink orders that needed filling and the potential for table dances, the team then had to face significant changes in the local baseball lineup. Dormant for fifty-five years, a Seattle-Tacoma baseball series was revived when the southern Puget Sound city replaced a faltering Phoenix franchise as a Pacific Coast League entry. On April 22 a crowd of 4,101 patiently sat through a fifty-five-minute rain delay at Tacoma's Cheney Stadium to watch the newly formed Giants take a historic, 3–2 victory over the Rainiers, with high-kicking, hard-throwing Juan Marichal, not long for the minors, outdueling Rudolph on the mound. Yet while Tacoma took out a new membership in the PCL, a long line of other people turned theirs in.

O'Brien, after setting up shots of vodka in the Seattle clubhouse for the good of the team, retired from pro baseball that winter. The Rainiers asked him to come back for the 1961 season, offering to let him play in home games only, but injuries had taken a considerable toll on the versatile athlete, a consensus All-America basketball player for Seattle University well before Elgin Baylor assumed that role, and he declined. The Rainiers had tried to sign O'Brien and his twin brother, Ed, to contracts when they came out of college in 1953, but lost a bidding war to the Pittsburgh Pirates, who obtained the siblings in a package deal worth $70,000 to $80,000. Johnny O'Brien, an infielder and part-time pitcher, would play just one season for the Rainiers before turning to politics, becoming King County commissioner for several terms, and later the Kingdome's top administrator. Eddie O'Brien, an outfielder and starting pitcher, drifted from the big leagues to the Salt Lake City Bees, losing his first PCL game to the Rainiers in 1958. He would spend a full season in uniform at Sicks' Stadium in 1969, as bullpen coach for the Seattle Pilots, a big-league expansion team.

Leo Lassen, the beloved yet tired voice of Seattle baseball for twenty-seven seasons, was next to go. This parting was not amicable, as KOMO radio practically shamed Lassen into leaving by making him a ridiculously low salary offer. For the second time in his career, he understood the message behind the meager paycheck numbers and said no thanks, and this time he wasn't coming back.

The biggest change for the Rainiers came at the top. The man who started it all, the baseball savior with all of those beer resources, Emil Sick, was done, too. After twenty-three seasons as owner, he sold his team holdings to the Boston Red Sox once the 1960 season ended. Sick's exit was highly emotional but hardly unexpected. As a lifetime smoker now fighting emphysema, asthma, and heart problems, he was in poor health and needed to get out of the game. After magically building a baseball empire and watching World War II tear it down, then rebuilding it again and witnessing another ebb in business, the beer baron finally gave in to a changing world. The encroachment of television everywhere and of the big leagues into the Los Angeles and San Francisco markets had watered down his product, as had the revitalization of University of Washington football across town with the team making appearances in consecutive Rose Bowls. The changes in the baseball landscape and in the sport's relationship with the media left Sick with a flat and foamless product, and once he received his final payment from the Dodgers and Giants for disrupting the PCL, his financial reserves began to run dry as well.

"He wasn't even in it for the money," Dewey Soriano told the *Post-Intelligencer*. "Even in the years when the team made money, it was all plowed back into the ballclub. He was a man of courage and foresight. He hung on and kept investing in baseball long after it was obvious there was no chance to do anything but lose money."

Gone was the familiar sight of Sick in an expensive, neatly pressed suit and straw hat standing at home plate for each home opener, greeting fans in a proud and polished manner while welcoming in the new season over the ballpark public-address system. The owner kept the ballpark in order to lease it out, promised to provide broadcast sponsorship, and negotiated assurances that the team would still be called the Rainiers in his absence.

Sick told in newspaper interviews of how the franchise had become too difficult to operate, that he had lost all enjoyment trying to keep it afloat. Later it was revealed that the ballclub actually hadn't been sold, that Sick simply gave it away to the Red Sox, his return nothing more than the dollar needed to make the transaction legal and the knowledge that his once prized possession would be in better hands. Either way, the manner in which baseball was presented in Seattle had changed dramatically.

"When Emil Sick sold the franchise to the Red Sox, you could feel it and see clearly that the glory days were gone," said Keith Jackson, Lassen's able replacement in the radio booth.

Even more succinct was the reaction of Diana Ingman, one of Sick's daughters, who was raised on the Rainiers and nights spent at the ballpark: "It got disheartening the last year. We weren't Major League anymore."

By 1961 anything less than a big-league attitude in Seattle, in any endeavor, wouldn't cut it. The Space Needle would rise up out of hallowed baseball ground like some sort of exaggerated right-field foul pole, built next to the downtown site that had once housed the well-worn Civic Stadium, the Seattle Indians, and, if only temporarily, the earliest rendition of Sick's Rainiers, to become the city's most recognizable landmark. This beacon of the World's Fair and a permanent addition to the skyline was a symbol of the city's increasingly progressive attitudes, though the flying saucer–like restaurant top also, unintentionally, paid homage to the region's somewhat loony, UFO-crazed past.

Seattle wanted to be noticed and taken more seriously in the worst way, and the Century 21 World's Fair, with its futuristic theme and thought-provoking exhibitions, gave it a huge platform. Global attention was an instant byproduct, as were ten million visitors, who included plenty of dignitaries and celebrities, most notably England's Prince Philip and future presidents Lyndon Johnson and Richard Nixon; future presidential candidate Bobby Kennedy; astronaut John Glenn and cosmonaut Gherman Titov; and Walt Disney, John Wayne, Jack Lemmon, Elvis Presley, and Sammy Davis Jr. from the entertainment world. Already a forward-thinking place, with Boeing supplying much of the nation's commercial air travel needs after working overtime to support a mammoth war aviation effort, the city had world trade opportunities multiply several times over after hosting the nation's first World's Fair in two decades. Seattle no longer considered itself a minor-league town, and that included its place in the sporting world.

The city secured a regular PGA Tour stop in 1960, and by the second year, Jack Nicklaus had collected his second career victory at Broadmoor Golf Club. Heavyweight boxing contender Sonny Liston fought and beat Eddie Machen at Sicks' Stadium in 1960, following Floyd Patterson's lead in picking up a fight in Seattle. The city remained ever diligent in its pursuit of a National Football League franchise, regularly hosting an exhibition game each summer at Husky Stadium, and now the newly created American Football League was casting furtive looks its way. There was no shortage of sporting opportunities. "They did come," said Gordon Clinton, Seattle mayor in 1956–64. "I think that was recognized as part of the impetus for having the Fair."

Yet while his mayoral peers in Los Angeles and San Francisco took active roles in negotiating sweet deals to land big-league baseball teams for their cities, Clinton did not see this as part of his job description. He was a contemporary of past Rainiers headliners Fred Hutchinson and Edo Vanni, graduating from

Seattle's Roosevelt High School in 1937, the same year the others had received their diplomas at Franklin and Queen Anne, respectively. Yet advancing the summertime game was not in his best political interest. "That wasn't my legacy," Clinton said. "I was more concerned with getting the Opera House built, the Space Needle built and the other floating bridge over to the East Side built. I never had too much activity with sports, except playing squash at the YMCA and going to the sports banquets. I wasn't too knowledgeable in activities tied to sports."

Without a strong political ally interceding, Seattle watched in dismay as the big leagues expanded without it. In 1960 the American League put more teams in Los Angeles and Washington DC, while another Washington franchise was moved to Minnesota. A year later, the National League set up new clubs in New York and Houston. The addition of four new big-league teams also put a drain on available manpower, systematically watering down the talent now available to the Rainiers and the rest of the minor leagues. The city was next in line to receive a Major League baseball team, but the wait would be long. Sick's timing had been perfect when he jumped into baseball, but time had run out on him as big-league expansion afforded new opportunities.

"Had Emil been young enough, he would have been right in the forefront of getting a Major League franchise," said Bill Sears, former Rainiers publicist. "I know he and Dewey Soriano talked about it, about the Major Leagues ultimately coming here. But he was getting pretty old then. Obviously, he didn't have a stadium."

While people were sad to see Sick go, others welcomed the hands-on assistance Boston would provide the Rainiers, hoping

Johnny Pesky managed the Rainiers for two seasons after the
Boston Red Sox took over franchise operations. (Bob Peterson photo)

that the moribund franchise would receive a needed boost. In
a suggestion that recalled the intrigue caused by Babe Ruth's
dugout dalliance with the Rainiers years ago, Red Sox Hall of
Famer Ted Williams was briefly mentioned as a possible Seattle
managerial candidate, but this did not come to pass. Instead,
Williams agreed to work with Rainiers players as a hitting instructor during spring training in DeLand, Florida, and to conduct a
midsummer check-up of the hitters at Sicks' Stadium, and the
bench job went to Johnny Pesky for the next two seasons.

The Rainiers finished 86-68 and in third place, eleven games
behind Tacoma, but attendance was flat all season. Everyone's
attention was fixated on the dramas playing out in the big leagues.
Roger Maris led a season-long assault on Ruth's sacred home
run record of sixty in a season, with one New York Yankees
slugger feverishly chasing another before Maris broke the mark
on the final day, and Seattle's own Fred Hutchinson guided the

Satchel Paige of the Portland Beavers was greeted by boxer
Eddie Cotton, left, and others on a 1961 visit to Seattle.

Cincinnati Reds into the World Series to take on Maris and his
teammates, ultimately losing the Fall Classic in five games.

At Sicks' Stadium, there was nothing nearly as compelling going
on, though there was stuff worth watching. On August 27, 1961,
just 4,763 fans showed up for the Rainiers' doubleheader sweep
of the Portland Beavers and a true baseball novelty act. On the
mound for the visitors that day in the seven-inning second game
was Satchel Paige, who, before getting lifted for a pinch-hitter,
tossed four frames, gave up a pair of runs on three hits, struck
out two, and walked two, receiving no decision in a 3–2 loss to
Seattle. Paige supposedly was fifty-five years old, and although the
figure was roundly disputed, the legendary one was as resistant
as ever to unraveling the ongoing mystery. "I'm between 50 and
60, and I'll say no more than that," the pitcher allowed when
pressed by a *Seattle Times* reporter in the clubhouse.

Rainiers outfielder Dave Mann concentrates on the pitcher. (Bob Peterson photo)

Rainiers outfielder Dave Mann, who led the PCL in stolen bases that season with thirty-three, had roomed with Paige five years earlier when both were with the Triple-A Miami Marlins of the International League. According to his answers in Seattle, Paige hadn't aged any since then. Mann and Paige shared hotel accommodations but not birthday secrets, not even when the fun-loving Paige started cracking open the three or four bottles of scotch he always kept on hand.

"People were always asking how old he was and it was a different answer in every city," Mann said. "Everywhere he'd go, he'd tell a different lie. Satchel was always like a hired gun and I was quite sure he was fifty-something back then, but he was a darn good fifty-something. No, he never told me how old he was."

The guys wearing Rainiers uniforms were a lot younger than that as Boston started running its best prospects through the Northwest, players such as future big leaguers Earl Wilson, Dick Radatz, Galen Cisco, Lou Clinton, Don Schwall, and Jay Ritchie. Younger still was Stew MacDonald, an eighteen-year-old pitcher signed in June for $100,000 after graduating from Seattle's Roosevelt High School and immediately asked to pitch for the Rainiers in an exhibition game against the Red Sox.

Before a sellout crowd of 13,506 at Sicks' Stadium, MacDonald received a shock to his baseball system, walking five and giving up a grand-slam homer to big leaguer Gary Geiger in one rugged inning of a 5–4 loss. The teen spent most of the summer in Texas, at Class D Alpine, before returning and finishing the season with the Rainiers. Once back, he threw four innings of scoreless relief before drawing his first starting assignment in a doubleheader on the final day of the 1961 season, registering only zeroes again. Everyone in the Red Sox organization was impressed when he fired a five-hit shutout, beating Spokane 4–0.

Nothing changed for MacDonald between the end of that season and the start of the next one. In an opening day double-header in 1962, the young right-hander stopped the Vancouver Mounties 2–1, striking out twelve batters. A more seasoned Seattle starter, Elmer Singleton, won the other game, giving the Rainiers something old and new and unusual on the mound that day: Singleton was forty-one years old, MacDonald was nineteen. "Twin Victories, Stew-pendous" read the *Seattle Post-Intelligencer* headline the following morning.

A month into that 1962 season, MacDonald was the league leader in strikeouts and anticipating a quick promotion to Boston, but he turned up in a San Diego hospital instead after taking a liner off the knee from former Rainiers catcher Jesse Gonder, a ball hit so hard it ricocheted into the Seattle dugout and was ruled a ground-rule double. Things would get only worse for the young pitcher thereafter. "I couldn't bend my leg," MacDonald said. He was told it was only a bruise and to take the mound for his next start. MacDonald went eight innings in a 1–0 loss to Spokane at home, gutting it out and striking out eight batters, but he paid a steep price for it. "I chipped a bone in my shoulder doing that," he said.

MacDonald wasn't nearly as effective on the mound, but he pushed on. He was credited with his fifth victory in eleven decisions, defeating Salt Lake City at home, 6–3, but wasn't around for the finish. Nursing a 3–0 lead into the sixth inning, MacDonald slugged a towering two-run home run off future big leaguer Jim Brewer, sending the ball high over the left-field light standards. When he came up in the eighth inning, MacDonald was asked to bunt against Bees reliever Don Prince. The first pitch nearly hit him in the legs. The act was clearly intentional, but the umpire did nothing other than tell the young Rainiers pitcher to quit complaining and get back in the batter's box. The next pitch hit MacDonald squarely in the jaw, fracturing it and dropping him to the ground. "I pitched ten days later with a sponge in my mouth," he said.

The Red Sox finally shut down the battered MacDonald in July with a 5-8 record and a 3.31 earned run average, and brought him to Boston to have his right arm examined. A career-threatening calcium deposit was discovered just below his armpit. He pitched infrequently the next four seasons, mostly in the lower minors. He lost velocity and tried throwing a knuckleball. He appeared in just one more game for the Rainiers, pitching two innings in 1963, enough for then-manager Mel Parnell to reach a negative conclusion.

"When I got him, he was this big bonus kid and they expected a lot out of him, but I had to call Boston and tell them, 'He can't pitch, he's got a bad arm,'" Parnell recalled. "He was the nicest kid in the world. The kid wanted to be successful, but he had an egg under his armpit and he just couldn't do it."

Yet after a long layoff, MacDonald's arm felt loose and strong again and he threw for Red Sox scouts, who were encouraged enough to recommend that he start the 1967 season at Triple-A Toronto of the International League. He never made it. Two weeks from reporting, he had more bad luck. During a trip to pick up Chinese takeout food in suburban Bellevue, MacDonald's car was broadsided by a female drunk driver, a collision that sent his vehicle careening over a twelve-foot embankment and left him with severe back injuries that would take ten years to fully heal. He later would play professional golf briefly as a middle-aged man on the Champions Tour, but his sporting highlight should have been a dozen years or more in the big leagues. "Whenever I walked out on the mound, I felt very confident," MacDonald said. "I was given this talent for a reason. I really felt it was a gift from God. I knew I had the stuff to do it."

Restocking the roster for the 1962 season, the Rainiers went back in time, signing outfielder Jim Rivera to a midseason contract. Jungle Jim was in town again after an eleven-year absence, though forty now and well past his baseball prime. He had a two-homer game, but his second coming wasn't enough to fill many more seats. He hung around for the last half of that season and the first half of 1963 before drawing his release and making a classy departure on his way to the Mexican League. "I hate to leave," Rivera told reporters while packing up. "Everything I have I owe to baseball, and particularly to the baseball team in Seattle that backed me so well."

The Rainiers' season and the World's Fair opened almost simultaneously in 1962, and it was painfully clear Seattle didn't have much interest in local baseball. Sicks' Stadium crowds were smaller than the worst days of World War II, with just 136,156 visiting the ballpark, or barely 2,000 per game. When pitcher Tracy Stallard was sent from Boston to the Rainiers in May, team and World's Fair promoters saw a chance for widespread publicity. Stallard was infamous for serving up Maris's record-breaking home run the previous season. The Fair announced that it was flying in the Brooklyn kid, Sal Durante, who'd caught number sixty-one in the Yankee Stadium stands and offered him $1,000 if he could glove a ball dropped from the Space Needle by Stallard. When advised how dangerous this was, the publicists huddled and then asked the nineteen-year-old Durante to catch a Stallard ball tossed from a nearby Ferris wheel. The kid snagged five warm-up throws from the Rainiers pitcher and then dropped the ball that counted, but was given the money anyway. "What's the matter, Sal?" Stallard kidded after the muff. "Too many butterflies? It was right to you."

While Durante cashed in, Seattle players had a dependable cash source permanently dry up in 1962. Charles E. Sullivan, the generous local florist who handed out $10 on the spot to anyone in a Rainiers uniform launching a home run or pitching a shutout, died in November.

In 1963 the World's Fair was over, and Seattle's baseball fortunes continued to plummet. Parnell was the new manager, replacing Pesky, who was brought up to run the Red Sox and left at just the right time. Parnell made the Rainiers a one-year job after suffering through a 68-90 season, finishing thirty games out in a newly aligned ten-team, two-division PCL. Oklahoma City, Denver, and Dallas had been added, and Vancouver was dropped. Equally distressing, Rainiers attendance reached an all-time franchise low of 132,769, or 1,794 fans per game.

"Seattle definitely was a big-league city and I'm sure the fans had that on their minds," Parnell said. "Seeing those other teams go to the Major Leagues I'm sure had an effect on them, too, and that had an effect on our ballclub. The Red Sox wanted me to come back the next year, but I told them I had had enough."

Low on talent at most positions that season, the Rainiers either had too many Smiths or not enough—there were four on the roster. On May 7 at Oklahoma City, the Rainiers used all of them in a game for the first and only time, with each one making an important contribution. Pete Smith was the starting pitcher, and he worked eight innings, striking out eight batters. Robert Smith threw three scoreless innings in relief of Pete Smith. Paul Smith, pinch-hitting for Pete Smith in the eighth, homered to tie the game at 2. Starting outfielder Bobby Gene Smith came up with a game-winning single in the eleventh inning, capping Seattle's 3–2 victory. If that wasn't confusing enough, Oklahoma City had a Hal Smith at catcher. Seattle's quartet of Smiths was together on the roster for just a month before Paul Smith was released and picked up by Tacoma.

There was only one Billy Spanswick, and he was sensational for the Rainiers amid the season-long despair. The left-handed pitcher compiled a 14-8 record with a 3.16 earned run average, striking out 209 batters in 185 innings, including 15 on a brisk April night against the Denver Bears. Typical of those disinterested times at Sick's Stadium, just 565 fans witnessed Spanswick's single-game strikeout mastery.

The 1963 season would be Joe Taylor's last one in pro baseball. After leaving Seattle three years earlier, he had wandered aimlessly through the PCL, playing for Vancouver, Hawaii, and San Diego, somehow slugging 26 home runs for the Padres in 1961 before getting shuttled off to Puebla in the Mexican League. He hit 19 homers south of the border in his farewell season, no doubt fueling his long-ball efforts with frequent shots of tequila. He finished with 272 homers in his thirteen pro seasons, just 8 coming in the big leagues, gathering his wits long enough on the big stage to unload 2 in a 1957 game for the Reds and provide a 3–2 victory over the Brooklyn Dodgers.

The man had so much more to offer the game, but his personal demons had a tighter grip on him than he did his bats.

In truth, Taylor and the Rainiers were a lot alike. After experiencing moments of greatness, flirting with the big leagues, and being continually surrounded by alcohol, the slugger and the franchise both seemed resigned to accepting a much less glamorous baseball fate.

14. Last At-Bat

As the Seattle Rainiers entered 1964 they were in their twenty-seventh season of operation, a figure matching the number of outs in a regulation ballgame and perhaps suggesting they were down to their final swings. Midway through that summer, another baseball solution was offered to the Northwest: the Seattle Indians. But hadn't that been tried before with minimal success? This was not the return of Seattle's old minor-league team, but a possible move for the Cleveland Indians, rich in World Series appearances and Hall of Fame players. In June, the team refused to renew its lease at Cleveland Stadium and considered relocating to another city.

Seattle, mulling this Indians to Rainiers to Indians transformation, eagerly started another money grab, only this time without badges and sirens and well away from the ballpark. With a big league team for hire and a post–World's Fair civic mentality that said go for it, city leaders asked people to buy

The Rainiers' marquee draws an audience.

tickets in support of a Seattle baseball team that didn't exist.
Coupons were printed on the sports pages of the *Post-Intelligencer*
and *Times* each day asking for donations to the "Citizens' Committee for Major League Baseball," listing a local address and
phone number.

As a show of good faith to those wayward Indians, 1,927

As a hitting instructor, Ted Williams, *second from left*, meets with Rainiers personnel Earl Johnson, *left*, Dick Bee, Edo Vanni, and Johnny Pesky.

Northwest baseball fans wrote checks totaling $596,128. People patted themselves on the back for this while conveniently forgetting that the only venue they had to offer was Sicks' Stadium, which still wasn't big enough for the big leagues. After a couple months of courtship, Cleveland baseball executives Gabe Paul and William Daley toured Seattle and its ballpark, which seemed a little silly, considering that Paul previously had worked for the Cincinnati Reds when that team had a player-working agreement in place with the Rainiers and he likely wasn't seeing anything new. Imagine trying to operate an existing team in this confusing baseball environment, with people ignoring you and waving cash at someone else.

"I guess I more or less understood the motivation behind that, but there wasn't a whole lot we could do except hang in there," Rainiers general manager Dick Bee said. "My primary concern was working closely with the Boston Red Sox and keeping baseball alive."

On October 17, with the World Series playing out between the New York Yankees and St. Louis Cardinals, and the Pacific Coast League season over for a month, the Indians, after entertaining relocation offers from Atlanta, Dallas, Oakland, and Seattle, surprised no one in baseball's inner circles by announcing they had renegotiated a new deal with Cleveland and were staying put. It was against this backdrop that the Rainiers played their final Triple-A season in Seattle, retiring the trademark name and burying some of the franchise's biggest names before stepping aside for a different brand of pro baseball in its place and later for the eventual arrival of the Major Leagues.

No one said 1964 was the last season for the Rainiers, but there were clues everywhere. Chests puffed out since wowing everyone with the World's Fair, city leaders started pushing for stadium bond issues and feverishly discussing the need to obtain big-league teams in all sports. The new manager was Edo Vanni, an original member of the Rainiers whose hiring had allowed him to come full circle with the franchise yet smacked of little more than a convenient stopgap. And on May 5, Sicks' Stadium welcomed just 388 people inside on a frigid night to watch the Salt Lake City Bees defeat the home team, 4–2, setting a franchise-low for attendance and leaving the concessions virtually untouched.

Amid all the commotion, a baseball season was played out, overseen by Vanni, who had worked the previous three years in the Rainiers' publicity department, keeping a low profile. Not many have followed this particular career path, going from baseball huckster to baseball manager, but Vanni was a capable man. Throughout his career, he had combined his ballpark savvy with natural salesmanship skills and could offer plenty of references. While managing Class A Wenatchee in 1955, a blindfolded Vanni agreed to participate in a pregame promotion in Salem, Oregon. When the locals trotted out a black bear for him to wrestle, he didn't protest or back off. As long as he wasn't dealing with snakes, he was fine. To everyone's delight, Vanni pulled on a catcher's mask and rolled around some with the animal at home plate, getting swatted on the leg but otherwise surviving the moment intact. "I couldn't stand the garlic breath that bear had," he wisecracked. On another occasion in Wenatchee, Vanni observed how the ballpark was nearly empty for the first game of a series, pulled his players together, and instructed them to start a nasty brawl and keep the punches flying as long as possible. After word of the mayhem, reportedly five separate fights going at once, was circulated around town by the radio broadcasters for the game, the seats were full the next night.

The Rainiers needed a boost of something in 1964. The franchise now drew only a fraction of the fans that once had come out to see Vanni play, and maybe even a decimal point when factoring in that May 5 near no-show. Besides the big-league attitudes put forth, the Seattle ballclub now had to contend with hydroplane racing and the increasing lure of recreational pursuits such as fishing, boating, and mountaineering in the Northwest, with the climbing sport given a huge boost when Seattle's Jim Whitaker in 1963 became the first American to reach the summit of Mount Everest.

To celebrate his good fortune in becoming Seattle's manager,

Vanni and former Rainiers teammate and boyhood chum Fred Hutchinson were headed for the outdoors themselves. They had arranged to go on a winter hunting trip near Yakima, just two pro baseball managers and some guns alone in the eastern Washington wilderness. Those vacation plans would be scrapped by something that would prove to be even bigger news than the Cleveland Indians' half-hearted flirtation with the city.

Discovering a lump below his right collarbone, Hutchinson flew home and went directly to Swedish Hospital, accompanied by Vanni. The career baseball man came through a back entrance and used an assumed name to prevent the public from learning about his serious health concerns until it was absolutely necessary. Dr. Bill Hutchinson, the man's brother, and another physician, a specialist, performed a biopsy on him and, on New Year's Eve, Fred Hutchinson, a lifelong smoker, learned of an awful fate that would shock the baseball world from Seattle to Cincinnati. The tumor was malignant and he had terminal lung cancer.

After receiving this prognosis, a shaken Hutchinson wandered alone into Vito's Restaurant at Ninth Avenue and Madison Street, not far from the cluster of hospitals overlooking Seattle. He grabbed an open bar stool, which by chance sat him next to Bill Sears, his former Rainiers public relations director, and ordered a drink. Sears would never forget the ensuing conversation, able to recite it line by line several decades later.

"What are you doing here? Everything all right?" a surprised Sears asked, scanning the blank look on the other man's face.

"No," Hutchinson said firmly.

"What?" Sears stammered.

"I've got cancer and it's serious," the baseball man said.

"Hutch, are you serious?" Sears replied, unsure what else to say.

"Damn right, I am," Hutchinson said. "There's a chance I could make it, but it's very slim."

Four days later, at a news conference held in the Seattle office of his old schoolmate Dewey Soriano, now the Pacific Coast League president, Hutchinson hauntingly would tell the rest of the world that he was sick with cancer. His battle with this disease would become so public that he would implore kids not to smoke in a front-page newspaper article in the Post-Intelligencer; each of his ensuing health setbacks would be publicized nationwide; and his brother years later would establish an internationally recognized cancer center that sprawls along the shoreline of Seattle's Union Bay and prominently bears Fred Hutchinson's name.

"It's like having the rug jerked out from under you," said Hutchinson, who planned to keep managing the Reds as long as he could while traveling back and forth to Seattle and submitting to radiation treatments. "You're feeling fine, and then somebody tells you that you have cancer."

Jolted by his friend's life-threatening illness, Vanni headed for spring training in DeLand, Florida. He was holding down a job that twice belonged to Hutchinson, determined to be as tough and old school in approach as his boyhood friend. Once Vanni gathered his players together, he made the following observation: while Boston had given him sufficient talent to work with, many of these bright, young Red Sox prospects were pampered and soft, certainly not as disciplined as they should be. To no surprise, the manager butted heads with several players.

Under Vanni's direction, the Rainiers started on a positive note, sweeping their opening three-game series at Indianapolis, a new league member of the now twelve-team PCL. However, the season wasn't eleven days old when Vanni tossed hothead outfielder Pete Jernigan off the team in Denver. Jernigan's transgressions were multiple: failing to run out a grounder, misplaying a ball that fell for a double, angrily tossing a helmet into the stands after being lifted for a pinch-hitter, and using profanity that could be heard by fans. "I told him he was selfish," the manager said. "I'm running a ballclub here, not a country club." Jernigan, twenty-two, was a given a reprieve, but Vanni ran him off again for good in June. This time, Jernigan told a fan who asked him for a ball—Richard Hunt, a twelve-year-old kid from Spokane who happened to suffer from rheumatic fever—that he would first have to chew Beechnut tobacco to get it. When the boy complied, he became violently ill. Jernigan was banished to Albuquerque and the Rainiers were served with a sheriff's complaint over the incident the next time they visited Spokane.

Jim Lonborg, a rookie pitcher on the fast track to the big leagues, knew all about the residual effects of chewing for the first time. Having joined the Rainiers in late May, the innocent newcomer was seated in the bullpen when a veteran pitcher offered him a tobacco plug, goading him to try it by saying, "Hey, rookie, if you're going to be a big-league ballplayer, you've got to try this stuff." The twenty-one-year-old right-hander indulged in the foreign substance and regretted it immensely. "Seattle was the first place I tried chewing tobacco and I puked my guts out," said Lonborg, whose vomiting career with the Rainiers would not be limited to that initiation process.

Vanni was returning from dinner and lengthy personnel discussions with Neil Mahoney, Red Sox minor-league director,

Rico Petrocelli, Rainiers shortstop, had a few run-ins with manager Edo Vanni.

when the visiting executive pointed to someone walking past and asked a pointed question: "Isn't that your starting pitcher tomorrow?" It was 3 a.m. and Lonborg had been caught breaking curfew. He was ordered to report to the ballpark in four hours for a personal workout during which Vanni made the pitcher run until he threw up. "I see you had Chinese food last night," the manager said, showing no compassion. Said Lonborg, who won five of twelve decisions in his single Seattle season, "Edo was a very interesting man."

Rico Petrocelli locked horns with the Rainiers manager, too. In July, the nineteen-year-old shortstop asked to sit out a game in Tacoma, citing a groin injury. Vanni told him to tape it and play. Petrocelli argued back that he had been hobbled with injuries for a month and wasn't getting any better. Vanni stubbornly refused to budge on his lineup card. The infielder stormed out of the clubhouse, grabbed a bus back to Seattle, and later returned home to Brooklyn for two weeks. "I sent him home," Vanni recalled. "I said, 'Come back when you want to play baseball.' When he came back, he apologized." Three years later, after making it to the World Series with Boston, Petrocelli called Vanni and thanked him for his part in making it happen.

"I learned a lot from him," said Petrocelli, who would hit ten homers for the Rainiers five seasons before slugging forty for Boston. "Instead of the easy way, I learned the hard way. He was trying to toughen me up. He was trying to get me ready for the big leagues. It was the wrong thing for me to do and I apologized to him. I don't think we'll see another man like him in baseball again."

No question, Vanni liked to argue. He was ejected several times that season, once while bringing the lineup card out to umpire Russ Goetz and kicking dirt all over the plate. Wisely, Vanni had a punching bag installed in the dugout, an anger outlet similar to Hutchinson's and one covered with printed words offering the following warning: "Belt me, I'm free; helmets are $150."

On May 16 Vanni couldn't get tossed quick enough in the first game of a doubleheader against Indianapolis at Sicks' Stadium. The Rainiers allowed fifteen first-inning runs and lost 18–0. The contest was called early, making it a mercy killing. Eleven runs were scored before an out was registered. Seattle reliever Billy McLeod was charged with ten runs and optioned to Double-A Reading after the game, if not during it. The Indians' Marv Staehle batted three times in that extended first inning, walking twice and making the final out. The Indianapolis team had been a late arrival to the ballpark, forced to skip batting practice and seemingly unprepared to inflict so much damage.

Providing a calming effect for this team was another Earl Averill, doing what his Hall of Fame father had done before World War II, which was finish up his pro baseball career at home after the big leagues had determined his skills were on the downside. Dad actually was christened Howard Earl Averill; this one was Earl Douglas Averill. Father and son were at the ballpark every day on home stands, with the retired Averill adhering to a daily regimen that never wavered. Calling and making sure he had game tickets waiting at the ballpark, he left his house in Snohomish, some forty-five miles from Sicks' Stadium, and drove to a suburban Lynnwood restaurant and ordered a milkshake and a roast beef sandwich, always eating at a designated hour, always eating the same thing. Continuing on to the ballpark in Rainier Valley, he took in batting practice and then the game, witnessing his son enjoy a most valuable player season for the Rainiers with a .316 average, fourteen homers, and sixty runs batted in. "That was his routine and you could set your clock by it, though he didn't eat that much," the younger Averill said. "He got a chance to go to every game and he was always there."

Even with Vanni's tough-love antics and the Averill family moments, the 1964 Rainiers finished 81-75, nine games back of the San Diego Padres, and settled for fourth place. Coincidentally,

Rainiers owner Emil Sick addresses the Sicks' Stadium crowd.

the ballclub started to fade from contention in August at the same time Hutchinson's health slipped noticeably in Cincinnati, forcing the ailing man to hand over his Reds duties on an interim basis to Dick Sisler, one former Rainiers manager replacing another, before officially giving up his job to Sisler almost two months later.

On September 13 the Rainiers unknowingly played the franchise's final games with a Sunday doubleheader split across the state in Spokane. Seattle won the opener, 1–0, on future big leaguer Wilbur Wood's fourth shutout of the season and lost the nightcap, 4–3, on an eighth-inning home run by the Indians' Dick Nen. Making the final game breezy and fun, Vanni handed over the managing chores to veteran outfielder Felix Maldonado, let pitcher Merlin Nippert play right field, and sat back and watched. After four seasons, Boston had said nothing about making any changes in its operation of the Rainiers franchise. If there were no sense of finality on closing day, it would come soon enough.

Confined to a hospital oxygen tent, a failing Emil Sick, his lungs destroyed by emphysema, gestured to family members for a cigarette. The weakened man knew his time was running out. This request went unfulfilled, a relative gasping that he could blow up everyone if he were allowed to light up. With so many of his organs shutting down, it might have been the only way he could be certain what ultimately did him in. On November 10, while having surgery at Swedish Hospital, Sick, seventy, suffered a stroke and died. The papers said a civic leader, tycoon, and baseball patron had met his end. Mainly he was a man who had quenched the city's thirst in many different ways; besides brewing a favorite beverage, he had made summers fun and people proud by giving them a team to rally around and championships to celebrate, in the process unifying the city like no other man after a decade of Depression-era hardships. He wouldn't live to see big league baseball expand to thirty teams, twelve west of St. Louis, including six from the PCL territory he so passionately fought for—Seattle, San Francisco, San Diego, Oakland, and two entries from Los Angeles—with only Portland and Sacramento remaining as Triple-A cities, having attempted and failed to join the others.

Forty-eight hours after Sick's passing, Hutchinson, his lungs also decimated by cancer, was gone, too. He died at a Bradenton, Florida, hospital, having been rushed by ambulance from his Anna Maria Island home after he had deteriorated rapidly with family members gathered around him over the weekend. Hutchinson, forty-five, lived just eleven months after finding something wrong with his chest. No doctor could save the doctor's kid. In Seattle, people mourned the loss of the Rainiers' teenaged pitcher and championship manager; everywhere else, homage was paid to a respected big-league man. A Saturday memorial service in Florida drew two hundred people, among them baseball executives, fellow big-league managers, and Hall of Fame players Luke Appling and Hank Greenberg. Hutchinson's body was flown home and seven hundred attended his Monday funeral at Rainier Beach Presbyterian Church. A mile-long procession accompanied his flag-draped casket to Renton's Mount Olivet Cemetery for burial, the baseball man given full military honors for his wartime Navy service.

Two weeks later in November, the Red Sox, now eager to cut ties with a forgotten franchise and operate a Triple-A team closer to home, pulled out of Seattle. They forged a deal with Toronto to make it the organization's top feeder team and sold their Rainiers holdings to the Los Angeles Angels. Three days before Christmas came the symbolic kicker, if not a complete break: the new California owners announced they were changing the team nickname to Angels, same as the parent club. It was another death in the family for Seattle, now putting the Rainiers to rest alongside the franchise's fallen leaders. Minor-league baseball would survive in the city, but it wouldn't be the same at all. Seattle teams used to battle the Angels, and now they would have to be them, an ironic twist of events for the longtime local baseball fan.

"There were always concerns on the part of Boston that we were a whole continent away and the time element was bad," Bee said. "They were shuttling players back and forth, especially pitching. It wasn't easy being three thousand miles apart."

It was three up and three down in a matter of weeks, and the Rainiers had been retired in order. Considering their deep-rooted investment in the franchise, it was probably fitting that Sick and Hutchinson were spared from witnessing the removal of their favorite baseball brand name.

In the aftermath, baseball wasn't done in Seattle, just Emil Sick's Rainiers. The beer man's name remained emblazoned across the front of the ballpark, keeping his memory alive and eventually allowing him to partake in the big leagues in absentia, if only briefly. In 1965 there were remnants of the old franchise in uniform, and in the front office for the Seattle Angels, the newly installed Triple-A club: Vanni was hired as general manager and former Rainiers Earl Averill, Bobby Gene Smith, Hal Kolstad, and Fred Holmes had crossed over as players. Sicks' Stadium's new tenant would stick around for four years, still not big league, still struggling for fans, but the Angels would win another PCL pennant for the city in 1966 and keep the grass cut and infield raked.

Two months after that league championship was secured in 1966, a man who had shared in three of them for the Rainiers prior to World War II, "Kewpie Dick" Barrett, died in his sleep in Seattle. He was sixty. The pitcher had stayed out of trouble, out of jail, but he was never a great picture of health, outside of that sturdy right arm of his, battling alcoholism, diabetes, and assorted other ailments for years.

Twenty-two years after suggesting it was worthy of the Major Leagues, and eleven seasons after Los Angeles and San Francisco had fled the PCL, Seattle got its big baseball break, landing an American League expansion franchise. Dewey Soriano, former Rainiers pitcher and general manager, was the architect of this deal, arranging to have Sicks' Stadium doubled in size to twenty-five thousand and promising to keep pushing for a dome stadium with big-league specifications. "Rainiers" was considered among the many nickname candidates, but "Pilots" won out, not too alarming since Soriano formerly had served as a ship's pilot. Vanni was hired in the front office to sell group tickets and promote the club, though bear wrestling was not on the program. On April 11, 1969, the first big-league game was played in Seattle and the Pilots beat the Chicago White Sox, 7–0. The good baseball feelings wouldn't last. Twelve months later, the franchise was bankrupt and sold and moved to Milwaukee.

The Pilots had not been Seattle's first Major League franchise, either, arriving two years after the Seattle SuperSonics of the National Basketball Association went into operation.

Without a baseball paycheck for the first time in three decades, since Emil Sick had paid half his salary while Edo was at war, Vanni decided it was time to cash in the Rainier beer stock he'd negotiated for when he was a sought-after teenager signing his first pro baseball contract. Originally worth 35 cents a share, the stock had split four times. He pocketed $180,000 and turned around and used that money, plus $5,000 more, to build a Queen Anne apartment building, which he would manage not far from his brick home looking out on the city.

On December 5, 1975, Rainiers radio broadcaster Leo Lassen, seventy-six, died at Ballard Community Hospital, a bitter old man disconnected from the game that had once consumed him. He had no known family members and few close friends. Yet his memorial service was well attended by strangers, or people who considered him a valued acquaintance, if only through the airwaves. "He taught me to love baseball," Rainiers fan Addis Gutmann said. "We never met, but I went to his funeral." Lassen was honored posthumously when Gutmann and other supporters raised the necessary funds to install a plaque with his image at Lower Woodland Park, where several fields also bear his name.

It was not a good seventy-two hours for the Rainiers' broadcast booth. On December 8, 1975, at the same time Lassen was being eulogized across town, another baseball voice was silenced. Jeff Heath, the accomplished Babe Ruth impersonator and ousted Rainiers TV commentator, visited with his Queen Anne neighbor Mike Budnick, a former Rainiers and big-league pitcher, walked five blocks briskly to his house, went inside, and suffered a fatal heart attack. He was sixty.

Sicks' Stadium would remain a lonely place until a Class A team took up residence there from 1972 to 1976, calling itself the Seattle Rainiers. It was just a name now, with no connection whatsoever to the previous team's glory. The players were mostly teenagers, the seats empty, and the press box unused and full of pigeons. In 1977 the city unveiled a second big-league expansion franchise, the Mariners, after once again having considered "Rainiers" as a possible nickname; the new team's home was the recently constructed Kingdome, built for baseball and multipurpose use. In Rainier Valley, Sicks' Stadium sat idle, owned by the city and overgrown with weeds, and was finally torn down two years later and eventually replaced with a couple of tenants, the latest a national chain hardware store, keeping only home plate in place and a plaque on the corner of Rainier Avenue South and South McClellan Street.

"The last time I was in it after the Pilots fiasco, there was that single A team called the Rainiers playing there, and the place smelled of urine and you could tell it was not going to be around long," said Sean Sheehan, Sick's grandson.

Jerry Priddy, the former Rainiers player-manager who wouldn't back away from a good fight, turned out to be one of baseball's most bizarre stories. After an aborted attempt at a PGA Tour career, the eleven-year big leaguer was arrested by the FBI in Los Angeles in 1973 and charged with attempting to extort $250,000 from a cruise line by threatening to blow up one of its ships. He went to prison and went bankrupt. In 1980, after serving his time, Priddy, now sixty, stood up after having breakfast and then dropped to the floor with a fatal heart attack.

After failing to catch on with the Rainiers, showboating softball pitcher Bob Fesler was released by minor-league teams in Denver and Visalia, California, before reluctantly returning to his other sport and reclaiming his amateur status after a two-year layoff. A Boeing plumber and pipefitter on the side, he remained a dominant softball pitcher until he reached middle age, earning hall of fame status in his sport although unable to let go of the dream of playing pro baseball once again. Fesler also was a hard-living man who drank way too much, and his lifestyle finally caught up with him in 1983, when he was fifty-four and died in Seattle from complications during surgery.

"He was a great athlete but he was a piece of work," said Sears, the publicist responsible for giving Fesler his brief taste of Rainiers baseball. "He should have been playing back in the old days, with Ruth and those guys, when the rules were a little more thin."

Most people would have thought it would be the last thing in him to go, but Jo Jo White's heart gave out on him on October 9, 1986. The former Rainiers outfielder and manager was seventy-seven when he died in Tacoma from complications following heart surgery. He retired from baseball in 1969 after forty-two seasons in the game, stepping down as a coach for the Kansas City Royals, and he had moved back to the Northwest. White spent his last years attending, but barely watching, Mariners home games, instead milling around the Kingdome and bantering with adoring fans who still remembered him.

Whimsy was lost when White departed, but ballpark belly laughs disappeared when resident Rainiers shortstop and funny man Bill Schuster died at the age of seventy-four on June 6, 1987, in El Monte, California. Living in a mobile home park, he suffered a fatal heart attack after returning from dinner out with his wife and friends, his last meal said to have been a typically cheerful occasion.

Among all the great players who pulled on a Rainiers uniform, two Seattle players were selected when it was time to pick the thirteen-player PCL All-Century team. Barrett, chalking up twenty-win seasons with ease, was a no-brainer selection as a pitcher. The other guy singled out was third baseman Dick Gyselman, maybe a surprise to some, but he was no less worthy. After all, his name was lumped together now with players such as Joe DiMaggio, Gene Mauch, Steve Bilko, and Ernie Lombardi. Seattle's Hutchinson and Rivera weren't listed anywhere. But no one in minor-league history had played more games at third than Gyselman, who logged roughly 2,500. When he died of bone cancer in Seattle in 1990, at eighty-two, he had lived a full life, a full baseball life.

Joe Taylor went home to Pittsburgh and spent much of his free time seated on a bar stool at a favorite hangout, keeping his glass filled and having his mail sent only to this address. People said he took a job as an ambulance driver, which seemed a bit ironic considering his shaky record behind the wheel. Taking into account the alcohol abuse he heaped on himself, the former Rainiers slugger lived far longer than anyone might have imagined. He died on March 18, 1993, sixteen days after his sixty-seventh birthday.

The former Patricia Hartwig also passed away in 1993. People knew her better as the wife of one-time Rainiers and big-league pitcher Don Rudolph. They knew her best as Los Angeles stripper Patti Waggin. She outlived her husband by twenty-five years, losing him to a California truck accident shortly after he left baseball and started a construction business. She remains the only stripper to have her caricature turn up on the back of a Topps baseball card, on Rudolph's, of course.

Four members of the Rainiers' earliest championship years went out practically together. Second baseman Al Niemiec, a proud World War II veteran to the end, died in Kirkland, Washington, in 1995; pitcher Hal Turpin and center fielder Bill Lawrence died in 1997 in Roseburg, Oregon, and Redwood City, California, respectively; and first baseman George Archie followed them in death in 2001 in Nashville, Tennessee. All of these guys were good for extra innings: Turpin lived to be ninety-four, Lawrence ninety-one, Archie eighty-seven and Niemiec eighty-four.

Soriano, the man who hired Hutchinson as the Rainiers' manager and brought the first big-league baseball team to Seattle,

Edo Vanni and Fred Hutchinson, shown at 1955 spring training, were Rainiers legends.

was seventy-eight when he died in 1998. He departed during the last full year the Mariners played in the Kingdome, just as they were preparing to move across the street to newly built Safeco Field. He was remembered at both ballparks, though under different circumstances. To honor Soriano, the Kingdome hosted its first and only wake. Keeping him close to the game in Seattle, a friend casually and without detection dropped some of Soriano's ashes around home plate during Safeco's Opening Night ceremonies.

Vanni was the last man standing from the Rainiers' original lineup, a fact he ruefully noted. He never made it to the big leagues, World War II made sure of that, but no one in Seattle had been associated with baseball longer and in so many different capacities—and this was a badge of honor no one else could hold up. He played parts of eighteen pro seasons, all in the Northwest except for a half season spent in Birmingham, Alabama. Vanni served in every baseball capacity imaginable, from clubhouse attendant to general manager, and was acquainted with Babe Ruth, Lou Gehrig, Connie Mack, and all the other baseball luminaries who had come through his hometown. He was affiliated with every pro baseball team in Seattle that had been in operation since 1920, except the Mariners, and the modern-day franchise was so respectful of his place in the local baseball world that it offered him a lifetime pass to all home games at Safeco. His basement was a baseball shrine piled high with scrapbooks, photos, uniforms, and autographs, with Babe Ruth's smooth handwriting mounted on the wall at the center of it all.

He could be annoying and overbearing to teammates and prospects who played for him, wanting more than they were willing to offer and demanding it in an unrelenting fashion. Or in later years, while watching the game veer off in directions that he didn't approve, he could be politically incorrect on a massive scale in venting his displeasure, after a certain Mariners center fielder felt compelled to publicly criticize the direction of the franchise. "Ichiro pulled a Pearl Harbor on us!" the former World War II veteran once shouted into the phone to a Seattle sportswriter.

Like the Rainiers, Vanni had much more good than bad in him. The man and the team had made Seattle feel important on a national scale for the first time, urging the city to stand up and be counted and demand to be Major League—or at least be recognized as the close facsimile that it was. He had helped turn it into one of the most successful minor-league franchises found anywhere, his teams at times surpassing the larger and more smug Los Angeles and San Francisco for crowd count, civic connection, and pure ballpark joy. The weight of his baseball contribution couldn't have been made more clear than when, after this eighty-nine-year-old man died of congestive heart failure on April 30, 2007, a moment of silence was held for him the following night before the Mariners–Chicago White Sox game at Safeco Field, and a church full of people gathered in north Seattle to pay their respects the following Saturday afternoon.

Though the funeral was Catholic and heavy on ceremony and tradition, those entering the sanctuary were handed brightly colored baseball cards of Vanni made special for the solemn occasion, and a red Rainiers hat was hung up front, sharing space with the presiding priest, someone who confided that he had visited Sicks' Stadium as a kid and already was familiar with the man he was about to eulogize. Former Rainiers Johnny O'Brien, Len Tran, and Bob Duretto were among the mourners, as were former broadcaster Rod Belcher and Bill Sears the publicist, the franchise dwindling in ranks more than ever by now.

Baseball would continue in Seattle, but the last original member of a golden era was gone, leaving only memories and those musty scrapbooks behind. After all of the words of praise and tearful remembrance had been delivered on Vanni's behalf, a baseball taps was played, sending the right fielder off in an appropriate manner, one that would have met his full approval though he liked to argue about everything. Off to the side, a church pianist deliberately and skillfully played "Take Me Out to the Ballgame," which is what Vanni and the Rainiers did.

Acknowledgments

Before I run off the field one last time with the Seattle Rainiers, it's time for a traditional baseball victory celebration. This would of course involve a lot of infield back-slapping, head-rubbing, and high-fives, capped off by an enthusiastic dog-pile of players in the middle of it all, with me at the bottom of this mass of happy humanity, lying prone and flashing a 1995 Ken Griffey Jr. smile.

I'd like to thank the 150-plus players, managers, club executives, batboys, broadcasters, writers, politicians, and fans who contributed their Rainiers memories, especially those people who did not live to see the final written result. A moment of silence goes out for Tommy Byrne, K Chorlton, Marv Grissom, Addis Gutmann, Buddy Hancken, Larry Jansen, Vern Kindsfather, Lou Kretlow, Hillis Layne, Bill O'Mara, Paul Rossi, Bob Stagg, and Edo Vanni.

Others who contributed their vast knowledge, opinions,

arguments, statistics, negatives, perspective, or general support include Randy Adamack, Mark Armour, Rod Belcher, Russ Dille, Michael Duckworth, Clay Eals, Dave Eskenazi, Dick Fitzgerald, J Michael Kenyon, David McCumber, Marsha Milroy, Walt Milroy, Pat Patrick, Dwight Perry, Nick Rousso, Eric Sallee, Lytton Smith, Gerry Spratt, Rob Taylor, and Art Thiel.

Finally, I have to pay tribute to my understanding wife, Nancy, and daughters, Dani and Mikayla, who allowed me to spend way too much time with a sporting passion that could be seen either as a mature love of Seattle baseball history, or a pursuit not all that different from collecting grown-up trading cards.

Appendix All-Time Roster

Personal information for some Rainiers players is incomplete because records are not readily available or do not exist, particularly for those individuals who played briefly during World War II and before, and did not play in the Major Leagues.

Name, Nickname	Years with Rainiers	POS	B	T	HT	WT	Date and Place of Birth	Date and Place of Death	Years in Major Leagues
Adams, Robert Henry, "Bobby"	1959	2B, 3B	R	R	5-10	170	12/14/1921 Tuolumne CA	2/13/1997 Gig Harbor WA	1946-59
Albright, Harold John, "Jack"	1949-51	SS, 3B, 2B	R	R	5-9	175	6/30/1921 St. Petersburg FL	7/22/1991 San Diego CA	1947
Aleno, Charles, "Chuck"	1945-46	3B, UTIL	R	R	6-0	215	2/19/1917 St. Louis MO	2/10/2003 Deland FL	1941-44
Amaya, Frank	1959	UTIL	R	R	5-11	150	1935		None
Anderson, Harold V., "Hunk"	1946	P	R	R	6-1	200	7/14/1919 Seattle WA	4/1/2002 Mountlake Terrace WA	None
Anderson, Herbert J., "Herb"	1955-57	1B	R	L	6-0	178	7/5/1936 Everett WA		None
Archie, George Albert	1939-40	1B	R	R	6-0	170	4/27/1914 Nashville TN	9/20/2001 Nashville TN	1938, 41, 46
Ardizoia, Rinaldo Joseph, "Rugger"	1949-50	P	R	R	5-11	180	11/20/1919 Oleggio, Italy		1947
Atkins, Arnold Truman, "Arnie"	1956	P	R	R	5-10	185	11/21/1925 Muscatine IA	6/11/2010 Ashford AL	None
Atkins, Ralph	1950	1B	L	L	6-1	180	3/30/1925 Los Angeles CA	11/13/2000 Los Angeles CA	None
Averill, Earl Douglas	1964	3B, OF, C	R	R	5-10	190	9/9/1931 Cleveland OH		1956, 58-63
Averill, Howard Earl, "Earl"	1941	OF	L	R	5-9	172	5/21/1902 Snohomish WA	8/16/1983 Everett WA	1929-41
Aylward, Richard John, "Dick"	1956-58	C	R	R	6-0	190	6/4/1925 Baltimore MD	6/11/1983 Spring Valley CA	1953
Babe, Loren Rolland	1958	3B	L	R	5-10	180	1/11/1928 Pisgah IA	2/14/1984 Omaha NE	1952-53
Babich, John Charles, "Johnny"	1943-44	P, OF	R	R	6-1	195	5/14/1913 Albion CA	1/19/2001 Richmond CA	1934-36, 40-41
Baczewski, Frederic John, "Fred"	1956	P	L	L	6-3	200	5/15/1926 St. Paul MN	11/14/1976 Culver City CA	1953-55
Baer, Robert	1939	2B	L	R	5-10	165	4/16/1916 Glasgow MT	8/8/1998 Vancouver WA	None
Bailey, Wesley L., "Wes"	1952	P	L	R	6-2	183	12/7/1922 Logan UT	2/22/2010 Alamo CA	None
Balcena, Robert Rudolph, "Bobby"	1955-58	OF	R	L	5-7	160	8/1/1925 San Pedro CA	1/4/1990 San Pedro CA	1956
Barrett, Tracy Souter, "Dick"	1938-42, 47-49	P	R	R	5-9	175	9/28/1906 Montoursville PA	10/30/1966 Seattle WA	1933-34, 43-45
Bartalini, Robert	1955	P	R	R	5-11	172	11/20/1936 Mendocino Co. CA	7/3/1998 Sonoma Co. CA	None
Basgall, Romanus Montgomery, "Monty"	1955	2B, 3B	R	R	5-10	185	2/8/1922 Pfeifer KS	9/22/2005 Sierra Vista AZ	1948-49, 51
Basinski, Edwin Frank, "Eddie"	1957-58	2B, 3B	R	R	6-1	172	11/4/1922 Buffalo NY		1944-45, 47
Bauer, Calix S., "Cal"	1957-59	2B, OF	R	R	5-9	175	9/10/1934 Mankato MN		None

Beamon, Charles Alfonzo, Sr., "Charlie"	1960	P	R	R	5-11	195	12/25/1934	Oakland CA			1956-58
Beard, William E., "Bill"	1942, 46	C, OF	R	L	5-10	185	11/12/1916	Oregon City OR	9/15/2000	Salem OR	None
Bearden, Henry Eugene, "Gene"	1954	P	L	L	6-3	204	9/5/1920	Lexa AR	3/18/2004	Alexander City AL	1947-53
Beasley, Andrew A. M. A. L., "Bud"	1947-48	P	L	L	5-8	170	12/8/1910	Melrose NM	7/17/2004	Reno NV	None
Beck, Walter William, "Boom-Boom"	1938	P	R	R	6-2	200	10/16/1904	Decatur IL	5/7/1987	Champaign IL	1924, 27-28, 33-34, 39-45
Becker, Heinz Reinhard	1949	1B	B	R	6-2	200	8/26/1915	Berlin, Germany	11/11/1991	Dallas TX	1943, 45-47
Beers, Clarence Scott	1952	P	R	R	6-0	175	12/9/1918	El Dorado KS	12/6/2002	Tucson AZ	1948
Berger, Louis William, "Boze"	1941	2B, 3B, SS, OF	R	R	6-2	180	5/13/1910	Baltimore MD	11/3/1992	Bethesda MD	1932, 35-39
Besse, Herman A., "Herm"	1947-49	P, 1B	L	L	6-2	190	8/16/1911	St. Louis MO	8/13/1972	Los Angeles CA	1940-43, 46
Bestudik, Joseph, "Joe"	1948	OF	R	R	5-11	185	12/25/1917	Springfield IL	11/30/1990	Lakewood CA	None
Bevan, Harold Joseph, "Hal"	1957-60	3B, 1B, C	R	R	6-2	198	11/15/1930	New Orleans LA	10/5/1968	New Orleans LA	1952, 55, 61
Bevens, Floyd Clifford, "Bill"	1942, 49	P	R	R	6-3	210	10/21/1916	Hubbard OR	10/26/1991	Salem OR	1944-47
Bickhaus, Ernest Richard, "Ernie"	1950	P	R	R	5-11	170	12/2/1921	Quincy IL	10/6/2007	Hettick IL	None
Birkofer, Ralph Joseph	1956	P	L	R	5-11	213	11/5/1908	Cincinnati OH	3/16/1971	Cincinnati OH	1933-37
Black, Joseph, "Joe"	1957	P	R	R	6-2	220	2/8/1924	Plainfield NJ	5/17/2002	Scottsdale AZ	1952-57
Blackwell, Ewell	1955	P	R	R	6-6	195	10/23/1922	Fresno CA	10/29/1996	Hendersonville NC	1942, 46-53, 55
Bloomfield, Gordon Leigh, "Jack"	1958-59	3B, SS, 2B	L	L	6-2	175	8/7/1932	Monti Alto TX			None
Bonetti, Henry Raymond	1938	OF	L	L	6-0	184	8/31/1911	Santa Barbara CA	2/24/1989	Santa Maria CA	None
Bonnell, Arthur B., "Art"	1946	PR	R	R	6-0	180	2/11/1920	Los Angeles CA	10/4/2007	Coto de Caza CA	None
Borland, Thomas Bruce, "Tom"	1961	P	L	L	6-3	172	2/13/1933	El Dorado KS			1960-61
Boyce, William J., Jr., "Bill"	1949	OF	R	R	6-0	190	2/1/1923	Brighton MA	3/2/1994	Watertown MA	None
Boyd, Robert Richard, "Bob"	1952	1B, OF	L	L	5-10	170	10/1/1919	Potts Camp MS	9/7/2002	Wichita KS	1951, 53-54, 56-61
Boyle, John Clifford	1963-64	P	L	L	6-1	180	2/2/1942				None
Brenner, William W., "Bill"	1955-56	P, MGR	R	R	6-1	205	10/30/1920	Tumwater WA	5/19/1979	Portland OR	None
Bridges, Thomas J. D., "Tommy"	1950	P	R	R	5-10	155	12/28/1906	Gordonsville TN	4/19/1968	Nashville TN	1930-43, 45-46

continued

Name, Nickname	Years with Rainiers	POS	B	T	HT	WT	Date and Place of Birth	Date and Place of Death	Years in Major Leagues
Briskey, Richard Michael, "Dick"	1945	INF, P	R	R	5-11	175	10/12/1927 Yakima WA		None
Brown, Hector Harold, "Hal"	1950-51	P	R	R	6-2	182	12/11/1924 Greensboro NC		1951-64
Brown, Lloyd Andrew	1941	P, 1B	L	L	5-9	170	12/25/1904 Beeville TX	1/14/1974 Opa-Locka FL	1925, 28-37, 40
Brunswick, Gordon Fred, "Gordy"	1951-53	OF, 1B	R	R	6-2	205	1/12/1927 Tacoma WA	1/6/1988 Tacoma WA	None
Budnick, Michael Joe, "Mike"	1939, 42, 50	P	R	R	6-1	200	9/15/1919 Astoria OR	12/2/1999 Seattle WA	1946-47
Bukowatz, Jack	1954-55	2B, SS, 3B	R	R	5-9	155	11/4/1930 Butte MT		None
Buonarigo, Nickolas Thomas, "Nick"	1943-44	C	R	R	5-10	180	1/26/1921 Detroit MI	8/20/1994 Van Nuys CA	None
Busby, David Barton	1963	P	R	R	6-2	203	4/20/1941		None
Buzas, Joseph John, "Joe"	1946-47	1B, 2B, 3B	R	R	6-1	180	10/2/1919 Alpha NJ	3/19/2003 Salt Lake City UT	1945
Byrne, Thomas Joseph, "Tommy"	1954	P, 1B, 3B	L	L	6-1	182	12/31/1919 Baltimore MD	12/20/2007 Wake Forest NC	1943, 46-57
Calvert, Paul Leo Emile	1951-52	P	R	R	6-0	185	10/6/1917 Montreal, Quebec	2/1/1999 Sherbrooke, Quebec	1942-45, 49-51
Campbell, Robert Stuard, "Bob"	1957, 60	3B	R	R	6-2	190	9/15/1936 Los Angeles CA		None
Campbell, William Gilthorpe, "Gilly"	1939-41	C, 1B	L	R	5-7	182	2/13/1908 Kansas City KS	2/21/1973 Los Angeles CA	1933, 35-38
Carlson, Vance Walter	1952	P	R	R	6-0	180	11/14/1925 Falun KS		None
Carnett, Edwin Elliott, "Eddie"	1942-43, 46	OF, P, 1B	L	L	6-0	185	10/21/1916 Springfield MO		1944-45
Carpenter, John M.	1945	P	L	R	6-3	210	1917		None
Carpenter, Paul Nagle	1944-45, 47	OF	R	R	6-0	175	2/9/1914 Norwalk CT	2/24/1993 Whittier CA	None
Carter, Leon Eugene	1959	3B	R	R	5-11	180	1931		None
Castro, Dominic Frank	1945	C	R	R	5-10	190	11/5/1914 Los Angeles CA	7/11/1996 Whittier CA	None
Cecil, Rex Rolston	1947	P	L	R	6-3	195	10/8/1916 Lindsay OK	10/30/1966 Long Beach CA	1944-45
Chorlton, K Byron	1949-53	OF, SS	R	R	6-3	185	10/26/1928 Seattle WA	3/17/2009 Bellevue WA	None
Christie, Claude Tyler	1951-53	C	R	R	6-0	185	9/14/1926 San Francisco CA	3/24/2003 Twainhart CA	None
Christman, Marquette Joseph, "Mark"	1950	3B	R	R	5-11	180	10/21/1913 Maplewood MO	10/9/1976 St. Louis MO	1938-39, 43-49
Christopher, Lloyd Eugene	1943-44	OF	R	R	6-2	190	12/31/1919 Richmond CA	9/5/1991 Richmond CA	1945, 47

Name		Pos	B	T	Ht	Wt	Born	Birthplace	Died	Death Place	
Chum, Clarence Nottingham, "Chuck"	1958-59	P	R	R	6-3	205	2/1/1930	Bridgetown VA			1957-59
Cisco, Galen Bernard	1961	P	R	R	5-11	215	3/7/1936	St. Marys OH	1/25/1996	Camden NJ	1961-65, 67, 69
Clark, Michael John, "Mike"	1951	P	R	R	6-4	190	2/12/1922	Camden NJ	12/6/1997	Wichita KS	1952-53
Clinton, Luciean Louis, "Lou"	1961	OF	R	R	6-1	185	10/13/1937	Ponca City OK	10/6/1999	Limestone AL	1960-67
Coggin, Clifford, "Cliff"	1953	P	R	R	6-0	199	11/3/1924	Athens AR			None
Cole, Edward William, "Ed"	1941	P	R	R	5-11	170	3/22/1909	Wilkes-Barre PA	7/28/1999	Nashville TN	1938-39
Coleman, Gordon Calvin, "Gordy"	1960	1B	L	R	6-2	218	7/5/1934	Rockville MD	3/12/1994	Cincinnati OH	1959-67
Coleman, Soloman Hampton, "Hank"	1949	P	R	R	6-2	175	2/12/1928	Red Springs NC			None
Collins, Robert Joseph, "Rip"	1941-42	C	R	R	5-11	176	9/18/1909	Pittsburgh PA	4/19/1969	Pittsburgh PA	1940, 44
Collins, Wayne	1946	P	R	R	5-11	186	8/27/1927	Seattle WA			None
Colman, Frank Lloyd	1949-50	1B, OF	L	L	5-11	188	3/2/1918	London, Ontario	2/19/1883	London, Ontario	1942-47
Combs, Merrill Russell, "Merl"	1953-54	INF	L	R	6-0	172	12/11/1919	Los Angeles CA	7/8/1981	Riverside CA	1947, 49-52
Conatser, Astor Clinton, "Clint"	1947	OF	R	R	5-11	182	7/24/1921	Los Angeles CA			1948-49
Coscarart, Joseph Marvin, "Joe"	1939-40, 43	2B, 3B, SS	R	R	6-0	185	11/18/1909	Escondido CA	4/5/1993	Sequim WA	1935-36
Coughtry, James Marian, "Marlan"	1961	3B, SS	L	R	6-1	170	9/11/1934	Hollywood CA			1960, 62
Craddock, Walter Anderson, "Walt"	1960	P	R	L	6-0	176	3/25/1932	Pax WV	7/6/1980	Parma Heights OH	1955-56, 58
Cramer, Roger Maxwell, "Doc"	1950	PH	L	R	6-2	185	7/22/1905	Beach Haven NJ	9/9/1990	Manahawkin NJ	1929-48
Creeden, Cornelius Stephen, "Connie"	1944	OF, 1B	L	L	6-1	200	7/21/1915	Danvers MA	11/30/1969	Santa Ana CA	1943
Criscola, Anthony Paul, "Tony"	1947	OF	L	R	5-11	180	7/9/1915	Walla Walla WA	7/10/2001	La Jolla CA	1942-44
Cronin, Peter James	1961	C	L	R	6-1	195	10/7/1937				None
Cullen, Timothy Leo, "Tim"	1964	3B	R	R	6-1	185	2/16/1942	San Francisco CA			1966-72
Davis, Gerald Lee, "Gerry"	1956, 58	P	L	L	6-1	175	7/21/1932	Kansas City KS	3/12/2004	Bedford TX	None
Davis, Howard	1944	OF	L	R	5-7	155	3/20/1926				None
Davis, James Bennett, "Jim"	1950-54, 58	P	B	L	6-0	180	9/15/1924	Red Bluff CA	11/30/1995	San Mateo CA	1954-57
Davis, Oran Percy	1950	3B	L	R	6-0	185	4/22/1925	Alice TX	11/23/2006	Temple TX	None

continued

Name, Nickname	Years with Rainiers	POS	B	T	HT	WT	Date and Place of Birth	Date and Place of Death	Years in Major Leagues
Davis, Thomas Oscar, "Tod"	1950	2B	R	R	6-2	190	7/24/1924 Los Angeles CA	12/31/1978 West Covina CA	1949, 51
Debus, Ronald Frank	1963	3B	L	R	5-11	185	7/2/1937		None
DeCarlo, William	1938	C	R	R	6-0	185	10/12/1916 N. Hollywood CA	11/16/1992 Sherman Oaks CA	None
Del Duca, Arthur James, "Art"	1951-53	P	R	R	6-0	175	6/2/1927 Methuen MA		None
Del Guerico, Thaddeus, "Ted"	1949	1B	R	R	6-2	195	12/29/1927 Newark NJ	11/23/2006 Newark NJ	None
Delis, Juan Francisco	1957-58	OF, 3B	R	R	5-11	170	2/20/1928 Santiago, Cuba	7/23/2003 Havana, Cuba	1957
Demoran, Joseph Louis, "Joe"	1943-46	P	B	B	5-11	185	10/29/1914 Biloxi MS	4/26/1998 Biloxi MS	None
Derflinger, William Dennis, "Bill"	1944	OF	R	R			1/21/1920 Seattle WA	11/2/1991 Campbell CA	None
Dickey, Lloyd Joseph	1956	P	L	L	6-1	170	9/18/1929 San Francisco CA	1/17/1998 San Bruno CA	None
Dittmer, John Douglas, "Jack"	1959	2B	L	R	6-1	175	1/10/1928 Elkader IA		1952-57
DiTusa, Domenick Richard	1958	OF	R	R	6-1	190	8/29/1935 Chicago IL		None
Dixon, Sherwin Cody	1956	2B, SS	R	R	6-0	170	11/4/1930 Lynchburg VA		None
Dobbins, Joseph C., "Joe"	1943-46	INF, OF	R	R	5-10	170	5/5/1913 Farmington MO		None
Dodge, Ronald W.	1959	UTIL	L	R	6-1	170	1936		None
Dotterer, Henry John, "Dutch"	1958	C	R	R	6-0	209	11/11/1931 Syracuse NY	10/9/1999 Syracuse NY	1957-61
Dotterer, Thomas Bradshaw	1960	3B	L	R	6-1	185	12/19/1936 Syracuse NY		None
Dreisewerd, Clemens Johann, "Clem"	1949	P	L	L	6-1	195	1/24/1916 Old Monroe MO	9/11/2001 Ocean Springs MS	1944-46, 48
Drummond, Charles	1958	P	R	R	6-0	190	7/3/1930 Parksly VA	11/22/2004 Galloway Township NJ	None
Dubiel, Walter John, "Monk"	1947	P	R	R	6-0	190	2/12/1918 Hartford CT	10/23/1969 Hartford CT	1944-45, 48-52
Duren, Rinold George, Jr., "Ryne"	1955	P	R	R	6-1	195	2/22/1929 Cazenovia WI		1954, 57-65
Duretto, Robert John, "Bob"	1955-56	3B, C	L	R	5-9	170	9/17/1927 Los Angeles CA		None
Dumbaugh, Robert Eugene, "Bobby"	1957	SS	R	R	5-8	170	1/15/1933 Dayton OH		1957
Dyck, James Robert, "Jim"	1956-59	3B, OF, 1B	R	R	6-2	205	2/3/1922 Omaha NE	1/11/1999 Cheney WA	1951-56
Earley, Arnold Carl	1961	P	L	L	6-1	200	6/4/1933 Lincoln Park MI	9/29/1999 Flint MI	1960-67

Name	Years	Pos	B	T	Ht	Wt	Birth date	Birthplace	Death date	Death place	MLB
Elliott, Herbert Glenn, "Glenn"	1943-46	P	R	R	5-10	170	11/11/1919	Sapulpa OK	7/27/1969	Portland OR	1947-49
Endress, Ernest, "Ernie"	1942	2B, 3B, OF	R	R	6-4	205	9/15/1919	Seattle WA	11/29/1992	Poulsbo WA	None
Erautt, Joseph Michael, "Joe"	1951-52, 54	C	R	R	5-9	175	9/1/1921	Vibank, Saskatchewan	10/6/1976	Portland OR	1950-51
Evans, William Lawrence, "Bill"	1953-54	P	R	R	6-2	180	3/25/1919	Quanah TX	11/30/1983	Grand Junction CO	1949, 51
Fallon, Charles Grover	1941	C, 3B	R	R	6-0	165	10/16/1914	Quincy MA	3/31/1978	Quincy MA	None
Farrell, George E.	1940-41	OF, C, 3B	R	R	6-0	180	12/10/1916	Escalon CA	7/28/2002	Rockville MD	None
Federoff, Alfred, "Al"	1957-58	2B	R	R	5-10	165	7/11/1924	Bairdford PA			1951-52
Ferguson, Robert Lester, "Bob"	1946	P	R	R	6-1	180	4/18/1919	Birmingham AL	5/23/2008	Wetumpka AL	1944
Fernandes, Edward Paul, "Ed"	1938	C, UTIL	B	R	5-9	185	3/11/1918	Oakland CA	11/27/1968	Hayward CA	1940, 46
Fernandez, Froilan, "Nanny"	1952-54	2B, 3B, SS, OF	R	R	5-9	170	10/25/1918	Wilmington CA	9/19/1996	Lomita CA	1942, 46-47, 50
Fernandez, Humberto, "Chico"	1963	SS	R	R	6-0	170	3/2/1932	Havana, Cuba			1956-63
Fesler, Robert Clelland, "Bob"	1955	P	R	R	6-0	180	8/21/1929	Nampa ID	8/29/1983	Seattle WA	None
Finley, Robert Edward, "Bob"	1945-46	C, 1B	R	R	6-1	200	11/25/1915	Ennis TX	1/2/1986	West Covina CA	1943-44
Fischer, Charles William, "Carl"	1942-46	P	R	L	6-0	180	11/5/1905	Medina NY	12/10/1963	Medina NY	1930-35, 37
Fitzgerald, Richard Edward, "Dick"	1960	P	L	L	6-0	185	6/16/1935	Philadelphia PA			None
Fletcher, Alfred Vanoide, "Van"	1952, 54-55	P	R	R	6-2	185	8/6/1924	East Bend NC	3/17/2010	Yackinville TN	1955
Fletcher, Guy William	1947-50	P	R	R	6-1	189	8/23/1910	East Bend NC	4/1974	East Bend NC	None
Foisy, Ronald Douglas, "Ron"	1956	SS	R	R	5-9	165	8/30/1933	Bremerton WA			None
Fondy, Dee Virgil	1959	1B, OF	L	L	6-3	196	10/31/1924	Slaton TX	8/19/1999	Redlands CA	1951-58
Ford, Douglas	1947	P	R	R	6-1	210	7/6/1921	Seattle WA			None
Foster, Larry Lynn	1963	P	L	R	6-0	185	12/24/1937	Lansing MI			1963
Fowler, John Arthur, "Art"	1958	P	R	R	5-11	180	7/3/1922	Converse SC	1/29/2007	Spartanburg SC	1954-57, 59, 61-64
Foy, Joseph Anthony, "Joe"	1964	3B	R	R	6-0	215	2/21/1943	New York NY	10/12/1989	Bronx NY	1966-71
Fracchia, Donald Anthony, "Don"	1956	P	R	R	6-0	190	2/1/1931	Richmond CA			None
Frazier, Keith F.	1945	P, 1B	L	L	6-0	178	5/18/1913	Peetz CO	6/17/1992	Irvine CA	None

continued

Name, Nickname	Years with Rainiers	POS	B	T	HT	WT	Date and Place of Birth	Date and Place of Death	Years in Major Leagues
Freeman, Mark Price	1959	P	R	R	6-4	220	12/7/1930 Memphis TN	2/21/2006 Rancho Mirage CA	1959-60
Frey, Linus Reinhard, "Lonny"	1950	3B, 2B	L	R	5-10	160	8/23/1910 St. Louis MO	9/13/2009 Coeur 'd Alene ID	1933-43, 46-48
Fricano, Marion John	1957-58	P	R	R	6-0	170	7/15/1923 Brant NY	5/18/1976 Tijuana, Mexico	1952-55
Furnaro, Vincent J., "Vince"	1943	SS	L	R	5-11	175	1918		None
Gabrielson, Leonard Hilbourne, "Len"	1938, 43, 46	1B	L	L	6-3	210	9/8/1915 Oakland CA	11/14/2000 E. Palo Alto CA	1939
Galehouse, Dennis Ward, "Denny"	1949-50	P	R	R	6-1	195	12/7/1911 Marshallville OH	10/14/1998 Doylestown OH	1934-44, 46-49
Garber, Robert Mitchell, "Bob"	1958	P	R	R	6-1	190	9/10/1928 Hunker PA	6/7/1999 Redwood City CA	1956
Garbowski, Alexander, "Alex"	1951-53	SS, 1B, 3B	R	R	6-1	185	6/25/1925 Yonkers NY	6/27/2008 Putnams Valley NY	1952
Gardner, William Frederick, "Billy"	1964	2B	R	R	6-0	180	7/19/1927 Waterford CT		1954-63
Gatto, Phillip, "Phil"	1944-45	PH	L	R	5-10	158	11/11/1927 Portland OR	6/14/1984 Portland OR	None
Gay, Frederick Leonard, "Fred"	1946	P	L	L	6-2	180	1/14/1914 Savannah GA	8/23/1989 Plano TX	None
Gerheauser, Albert, "Al"	1950	P	L	L	6-3	190	6/24/1917 St. Louis MO	5/28/1972 Springfield MO	1943-46, 48
Gibson, John Russell, "Russ"	1963-64	C	R	R	6-1	195	5/6/1939 Fall River MA	7/27/2008 Swansea MA	1967-72
Gibson, Thomas Ervin, "Tom"	1957-59	P	R	R	6-4	215	10/4/1936 Yakima WA	10/30/2009 Houston TX	None
Gil, Tomas Gustavo, "Gus"	1960	INF	R	R	5-10	180	4/19/1939 Caracas, Venezuela		1967, 69-71
Gilbert, Drew Edward, "Buddy"	1960	OF	L	R	6-3	195	7/26/1935 Knoxville TN		1959
Gilday, James, "Jim"	1943	SS	R	R	5-11	170	9/26/1920	3/1959	None
Gile, Donald Loren, "Don"	1961, 63	1B, C, OF	R	R	6-6	220	4/19/1935 Modesto CA		1959-62
Gill, John Wesley, "Johnny"	1945	OF, 1B	L	R	6-2	190	3/27/1905 Nashville TN	12/26/1984 Nashville TN	1927-28, 31, 34-36
Ginsberg, Myron Nathan, "Joe"	1955	C	L	R	5-11	180	10/11/1926 New York NY		1948, 50-54, 56-62
Glynn, William Vincent, "Bill"	1955-57	1B, OF	L	L	6-0	190	7/30/1925 Sussex NJ		1949, 52-54
Goldman, Louis H., "Lou"	1941	P	L	L	6-2	170	4/12/1918 Dallas TX	2/2/2003 Irving TX	None
Goldsberry, Gordon Frederick	1951, 53	1B	L	L	6-0	170	8/30/1927 Sacramento CA	2/23/1996 Laguna Hills CA	1949-52
Gonder, Jesse Lemar	1958	C	L	R	5-10	190	1/20/1936 Monticello AR	11/14/2004 Oakland CA	1960-67

Name	Years	Position	Bats	Throws	Height	Weight	Birth date	Birthplace	Date	Location	Majors
Gorbould, Robert Clarence, "Bobby"	1944-46	2B, SS, 1B, OF	R	R	5-10	190	11/19/1920	Alberta, Canada	12/23/2003	Long Beach CA	None
Gorsica, John Joseph Perry, "Johnny"	1948	P	R	R	6-2	180	3/29/1915	Bayonne NJ	12/16/1998	Charlottesville VA	1940-44, 46-47
Grasso, Newton Michael, "Mickey"	1948-49	C, OF	R	R	6-0	195	5/10/1920	Newark NJ	10/15/1975	Miami FL	1946, 50-55
Gray, Robert Stanley, "Stan"	1943-44	INF	L	R	5-11	170	11/13/1918	Pasadena CA	3/30/2000	Pasadena CA	None
Gregory, Paul Edwin	1938-41, 46	P	R	R	6-2	180	6/9/1908	Tomnolen MS	9/16/1999	Southaven MS	1932-33
Grilli, Guido John	1961, 63-64	P	L	L	6-0	188	1/9/1939	Memphis TN			1966
Grissom, Marvin Edward, "Marv"	1951	P	R	R	6-3	195	3/31/1918	Los Molinos CA	9/18/2005	Red Bluff CA	1946, 49, 52-59
Guay, Lawrence Edward, "Larry"	1942, 46	P	R	R	6-1	180	8/13/1918	Montana	8/21/1992	Oakland CA	None
Guindon, Robert Joseph, "Bobby"	1964	1B	L	L	6-2	185	9/4/1943	Brookline MA			1964
Guldborg, John Burton, "Bud"	1951	P	L	R	6-1	185	1/13/1924	Palo Alto CA	1/15/2002	San Leandro CA	None
Gyselman, Richard Renald, "Dick," "The Needle"	1938-44, 47	3B	R	R	6-2	170	4/6/1908	San Francisco CA	9/20/1990	Seattle WA	1933-34
Haefner, Milton Arnold, "Mickey"	1951	P	L	L	5-8	160	10/9/1912	Lenzburg IL	1/3/1995	New Athens IL	1943-50
Hair, William Edward	1960	SS, 3B, 2B	R	R	6-3	195	1/9/1934	St. Louis MO			None
Hall, Robert Louis, "Bob"	1946-48, 51-52, 54	P	R	R	6-2	195	12/22/1923	Swissvale PA	3/12/1983	St. Petersburg FL	1949-50, 53
Hall, Roy David	1962-63	1B, 3B	R	R	6-0	180	12/4/1940				None
Hallett, Thomas Samuel	1962	P	R	R	6-2	195	11/30/1935				None
Hamner, Wesley Garvin, "Wes"	1951	2B, SS	R	R	5-11	172	3/18/1924	Richmond VA	12/15/2003	Richmond VA	1945
Hancken, Morris Medlock, "Buddy"	1939	C	R	R	6-1	175	8/30/1914	Birmingham AL	2/15/2007	Orange TX	1940
Hanlon, Richard Charles, "Dick"	1959	P	R	R	5-10	175	2/9/1933	San Francisco CA	9/27/2003	Milbrae CA	None
Hardy, Carroll William	1959	OF	R	R	6-0	185	5/18/1933	Sturgis SD			1958-64, 67
Harrell, William, "Billy"	1962-64	OF, 3B, 2B, SS	R	R	6-1	180	7/18/1928	Norristown PA			1955, 57-58, 61
Harris, Anthony Spencer, "Spencer"	1940-42	OF, 1B	L	L	5-9	145	8/12/1900	Duluth MN	7/3/1982	Minneapolis MN	1925-26, 29-30
Hawkins, Francis Xavier, "Frankie"	1943	2B, 1B	R	R	5-11	176	5/5/1915	San Francisco CA	11/16/1978	Gold Beach OR	None
Hawkins, John Thomas	1964	P	R	L	6-0	185	2/28/1943				None
Hayden, Eugene Franklin, "Lefty"	1955-57	P	L	L	6-2	175	4/14/1935	San Francisco CA	6/13/2003	Lodi CA	1958

continued

Name, Nickname	Years with Rainiers	POS	B	T	HT	WT	Date and Place of Birth	Date and Place of Death	Years in Major Leagues
Heard, Jehosie, "Jay"	1955	P	L	L	5-7	155	1/17/1920 Athens GA	11/18/1999 Birmingham AL	1954
Hearn, Richard H., "Dick"	1945	P	R	R	6-2	185	1918 St. Augustine FL		None
Heath, John Geoffrey, "Jeff"	1950	OF	L	R	5-11	200	4/1/1915 Fort William, Ontario	12/9/1975 Seattle WA	1936-49
Hedgecock, James E., "Jim"	1948	P	L	L	6-0	175	7/2/1921 Pueblo CO	6/7/1970 Alameda Co. CA	None
Heffner, Robert Frederic, "Bob"	1961, 63	P	R	R	6-4	205	9/13/1938 Allentown PA		1963-66, 68
Heltzel, William Wade, "Heinie"	1946	SS	R	R	5-10	150	12/21/1913 York PA	5/1/1998 York PA	1943-44
Hemsley, Ralston Burdett, "Rollie"	1947-48	C	R	R	5-10	170	6/24/1907 Syracuse OH	7/31/1972 Washington DC	1928-44, 46-47
Henrich, Robert Edward, "Bobby"	1959	SS	R	R	6-1	185	12/24/1938 Lawrence KS		1957-59
Hernandez, Peter, "Pete"	1952, 54	P	R	R	6-0	178	7/18/1929 Hayward CA	6/23/1987 Hayward CA	None
Higbe, Walter Kirby, "Kirby"	1950	P	R	R	5-11	190	4/8/1915 Columbia SC	5/6/1985 Columbia SC	1937-43, 46-50
Hill, James Wesley, "Jim"	1947	C	R	R	6-1	195	12/31/1919 Yuma AZ	6/9/1981 Calabasas CA	None
Hjelmaa, Harold L., "Bud"	1949	3B	R	R	5-11	167	8/23/1927 Seattle WA	8/18/2005 Seattle WA	None
Hoffman, Harold E.	1943-44	C	R	R	6-0	195	1916		None
Hofmann, John William	1949-51	P	L	R	6-3	215	11/30/1923 Buffalo NY		None
Holmes, Frederick Thomas	1964	P	R	R	6-5	225	5/22/1942		None
Holt, Eugene G., "Gene"	1944	P	L	L			1921		None
Hook, James Wesley, "Jay"	1959	P	L	R	6-2	182	11/18/1936 Waukegan IL		1957-64
Hopke, Frederick Lawrence	1960	1B	L	L	6-3	225	1/25/1937		None
Hopper, James McDaniel, "Jim"	1947	P	R	R	6-1	175	9/1/1919 Charlotte NC	1/23/1982 Charlotte NC	1946
Hornsby, Rogers	1951	MGR	R	R	5-11	175	4/27/1896 Winters TX	1/5/1963 Chicago IL	1915-37, 52-53
Howell, Edwin Lee	1962	OF	R	R	6-2	185	11/5/1936 Detroit MI		None
Hughes, James Albert, "Jim"	1962	SS	R	R	6-3	185	10/21/1934		None
Humphreys, Calvin S.H., "Cal"	1953, 55-56	P	R	R	6-1	200	1/15/1934 Seattle WA		None
Hunt, Arthur Leland, "Mike"	1938-39	OF	R	R	6-3	205	10/12/1907 Santa Clara CA	11/25/1997 Federal Way WA	None

Name	Years	Pos.	B	T	Ht.	Wt.	Born	Birthplace	Died	Death Place	Major League
Hutchinson, Frederick Charles, "Fred"	1938, 55, 59	P, MGR	L	R	6-2	200	8/12/1919	Seattle WA	11/12/1964	Bradenton FL	1939-40, 46-54, 56-64
Hutchinson, Ira Kendall	1946	P	R	R	5-10	180	8/31/1910	Chicago IL	8/21/1973	Chicago IL	1933, 37-41, 44-45
Hutson, Eulas D., "Bud"	1952	OF	R	R	6-0	185	2/6/1926	Atkins AR	7/1993	St. Paul MN	None
Isringhaus, Glenn A.	1956-57	P	R	R	6-0	170	10/1/1933	St. Louis MO			None
Jakucki, Sigmund, "Sig"	1947	P	R	R	6-2	198	8/20/1909	Camden NJ	5/28/1979	Galveston TX	1936, 44-45
Jansen, Lawrence Joseph, "Larry"	1955-57	P	R	R	6-2	190	7/16/1920	Verboort OR	10/10/2009	Verboort OR	1947-54, 56
Jeffcoat, Harold Bentley, "Hal"	1960	P	R	R	5-11	185	9/6/1924	West Columbia SC	8/30/2007	Tampa FL	1948-59
Jenkins, Wilburn Ray, "Jake"	1959	C	R	R	5-11	180	5/9/1929				None
Jenney, Lloyd P.	1954	C, OF	L	R	6-0	185	2/17/1929	Astoria L.I. NY	10/11/1981	Virginia	None
Jenson, John Curtis, "Curt"	1961-62	SS	R	R	6-1	170	2/6/1935	Logan UT			None
Jernigan, Paul Douglas	1962-64	OF	R	R	6-0	190	5/5/1941				None
Jewell, James Augustus, "Jim"	1943	INF	R	R	6-0	185	1/2/1919	Washington	4/21/1985	Hawthorne CA	None
Johnson, Chester Lillis, "Chet"	1945	P	L	L	6-0	175	8/1/1917	Redmond WA	4/10/1983	Seattle WA	1946
Johnson, Earl Douglas	1951-52	P	L	L	6-3	190	4/2/1919	Redmond WA	12/3/1994	Seattle WA	1940-41, 46-51
Johnson, Robert Lee, "Bob"	1947-48	OF, 1B, 2B	R	R	6-0	180	11/26/1905	Pryor OK	7/6/1982	Tacoma WA	1933-45
Johnson, Roy Cleveland	1944-45	OF, 3B	L	R	5-9	175	2/23/1903	Pryor OK	9/10/1973	Tacoma WA	1929-38
Johnson, Stanley Lucius, "Stan"	1963-64	OF	L	L	5-10	180	2/12/1937	Dallas TX			1960-61
Johnson, Sylvester W., "Syl"	1941-45	P	R	R	5-11	180	12/31/1900	Portland OR	2/20/1985	Portland OR	1922-40
Jonas, Wilfred R., "Pete"	1938, 43, 46-47	P	L	R	5-6	170	6/4/1916	Walla Walla WA	10/1/2005	Spokane WA	None
Jones, James Dalton, "Dalton"	1963	2B	L	R	6-1	180	12/10/1943	McComb MS			1964-72
Jones, James Joseph, "Jim"	1957	P	B	L	6-1	190	3/4/1938	Tacoma WA	12/1/2007	Welton AZ	None
Jongewaard, Roger E.	1959	C	L	R	6-1	195	1936	Long Beach CA			None
Joshua, Joseph, "Joe"	1954	OF, SS, 3B	R	R	5-11	202	6/10/1922	San Antonio TX	10/11/1998	Los Angeles CA	None
Judnich, Walter Franklin, "Wally"	1950-53	OF, 1B	L	L	6-1	205	1/24/1917	San Francisco CA	7/12/1971	Glendale CA	1940-42, 46-49
Judson, Howard Kolls, "Howie"	1955-57	P	R	R	6-1	195	2/16/1926	Hebron IL			1948-54

continued

Name, Nickname	Years with Rainiers	POS	B	T	HT	WT	Date and Place of Birth	Date and Place of Death	Years in Major Leagues
Kahle, Robert Wayne, "Bob"	1946-47	3B, 2B	R	R	6-0	170	11/23/1915 New Castle IN	12/16/1988 Inglewood CA	1938
Kaney, Joseph Allen, "Joe"	1947	SS, 2B, OF	R	R	5-11	160	3/3/1927 Alameda CA	1/12/1990 Sacramento Co. CA	None
Karpel, Herbert, "Herb"	1948-50	P	L	L	5-9	180	12/27/1917 Brooklyn NY	1/24/1995 San Diego CA	1946
Kats, William G., "Bill"	1943-45	OF	R	R	6-0	175	2/18/1912 Pocatello ID	8/1984 Pocatello ID	None
Kazak, Edward Terrance, "Eddie"	1958-59	3B	R	R	6-0	175	7/18/1920 Steubenville OH	12/15/1999 Austin TX	1948-52
Kearse, Paul Edward, "Eddie"	1940, 42	C	R	R	6-1	195	2/23/1916 San Francisco CA	7/15/1968 Eureka CA	1942
Keating, James Joseph, "Buck"	1947-48, 50	P, OF	R	R	6-2	196	11/27/1921 San Francisco CA	9/5/1988 San Rafael CA	None
Keesey, James Ward, "Jim"	1944	1B	R	R	6-0	170	10/27/1902 Perryville MD	9/5/1951 Boise ID	1925, 30
Kelleher, Francis Eugene, "Frankie"	1940	OF, 3B	R	R	6-1	195	8/22/1916 San Francisco CA	4/13/1979 Stockton CA	1942-43
Kellert, Frank William	1959	1B	R	R	6-2	185	7/6/1924 Oklahoma City OK	11/19/1976 Oklahoma City OK	1953-56
Kelly, Robert Edward, "Bob"	1955	P	R	R	6-0	180	10/4/1927 Cleveland OH		1951-53, 58
Kennedy, William Aulton, "Bill"	1955-60	P	L	L	6-2	195	3/14/1921 Carnesville GA	4/9/1983 Seattle WA	1948-53, 56-57
Keriazakos, Constantine Nicholas, "Gus"	1952	P	R	R	6-3	187	7/28/1931 West Orange NJ	5/4/1996 Hilton Head SC	1950, 54-55
Kimball, Kenneth Richard, "Ken"	1949	P	R	R	6-1	180	5/4/1925 Salt Lake City UT	6/19/1997 San Francisco CA	None
Kindsfather, Jacob Vernon, "Vern"	1950-55	P	R	R	5-11	176	12/12/1926 Vancouver WA	12/21/2008 Vancouver WA	None
King, Lynn Paul	1941-43	OF, 3B, 2B	L	R	5-9	165	11/28/1907 Villisca IA	5/11/1972 Atlantic IA	1935-36, 39
Kohlwes, William F.	1959	P	R	R	6-1	185	1938		None
Kolstad, Harold Everette, "Hal"	1961, 63-64	P	R	R	5-9	190	6/1/1935 Rice Lake WI		1962-63
Kretchmar, Albert A., "Al"	1942, 46	2B, 3B	R	R	5-11	175	11/3/1921 Seattle WA	4/10/2006 Yakima WA	None
Kretlow, Louis Henry, "Lou"	1955, 57	P	R	R	6-2	185	6/27/1921 Apache OK	9/12/2007 Enid OK	1946, 48-56
Kropiewnicki, Robert	1958	P	R	R	6-0	200	8/5/1938		None
Krsnich, Rocco Peter, "Rocky"	1951-52, 55	3B, SS	R	R	6-1	174	8/5/1927 West Allis WI		1949, 52-53
Krueger, William L., "Bill"	1944	SS, 3B	R	R	6-1	175	5/23/1922 Hickory NC	4/26/1961 Cincinnati OH	None
Kuehl, Karl Otto	1957	1B	L	R	5-11	175	9/5/1937 Monterey Park CA	8/6/2008 Scottsdale AZ	1976

continued

Name	Years	Pos	B	T	Ht	Wt	Birth date	Birth place	Death date	Death place	Majors
Kunley, Joseph, "Joe"	1945	2B	R	R							None
Kutyna, Marion John, "Marty"	1958	P	R	R	6-0	190	11/14/1932	Philadelphia PA			1959-62
Lains, Joseph	1963	P	L	L	5-11	185	1938				None
Lamanno, Raymond Simond, "Ray"	1950	C	R	R	6-0	185	11/17/1919	Oakland CA	2/9/1994	Berkeley CA	1941-42, 46-48
Lawrence, Leigh	1960	P	R	R	6-3	200	11/1/1933	Godfrey IL			None
Lawrence, Robert Earl	1962	1B	L	L	6-4	215	7/10/1938				None
Lawrence, William Henry, "Bill"	1938-43, 49	OF, MGR	R	R	6-4	194	3/11/1906	San Mateo CA	6/15/1997	Redwood City CA	1932
Layne, Ivoria Hillis, "Hillis"	1947-50	3B, OF	L	R	6-0	170	2/23/1918	Whitwell TN	1/12/2010	Chattanooga TN	1941, 44-45
Lehner, Paul Eugene	1952	OF	L	L	5-9	165	7/11/1920	Dolomite AL	12/27/1967	Birmingham AL	1946-52
Leishman, Edwin W., "Eddie"	1938	INF	R	R	5-9	155	12/20/1910	Oakland CA	12/28/1972	San Diego CA	None
Leivelt, John Frank, "Jack"	1938-40	MGR	L	L	5-11	175	11/14/1885	Chicago IL	1/20/1941	Seattle WA	1909-14
Lewis, Kermit D.	1946	OF	R	R	6-1	170	1/29/1914	Linn Creek MO	1/24/1997	Camdenton MO	None
Libke, Albert Walter, "Al"	1942, 44	P, 1B, OF	L	R	6-4	215	9/12/1918	Tacoma WA	3/7/2003	Wenatchee WA	1945-46
Lohrke, Jack Wayne	1956-57	UTIL	R	R	6-0	180	2/25/1924	Los Angeles CA	4/29/2009	San Jose CA	1947-53
Lombardi, Victor Alvin, "Vic"	1955-56	P	L	L	5-7	158	9/20/1922	Reedley CA	12/7/1997	Fresno CA	1945-50
Lonborg, James Reynold, "Jim"	1964	P	R	R	6-5	210	4/16/1942	Santa Maria CA			1965-79
Lovrich, Thomas Michael, "Tom"	1952-54	P	R	R	6-6	165	3/17/1930	Los Angeles CA			None
Lowrey, Harry Lee, "Peanuts"	1959	2B	R	R	5-9	170	8/27/1917	Culver City CA	7/2/1986	Inglewood CA	1942-43, 45-55
Lundberg, Donald Merritt, "Don"	1952	C	R	R	6-1	195	1/13/1930	Seattle WA			None
Luttrell, Lyle Kenneth	1957	INF, P	R	R	6-0	180	2/22/1930	Bloomington IL	7/11/1984	Chattanooga TN	1956-57
Lybeck, Charles August, "Chuck"	1957	P	B	R	6-1	180	10/31/1934	Kent WA			None
Lyman, William Neal, "Bill"	1944-45	SS, 2B, 3B	R	R	5-11	162	3/4/1914	Lynn MA	5/28/1986	Santa Ana CA	None
Lyons, Alfred Harold, Jr., "Al"	1949-52	OF, P	R	R	6-2	195	7/18/1918	St. Joseph MO	12/20/1965	Inglewood CA	1944, 46-48
Mabe, Robert Lee, "Bob"	1959	P	R	R	5-11	165	10/8/1929	Danville VA	1/9/2005	Danville VA	1958-60
MacDonald, Stewart	1961-62, 64	P	R	R	6-1	190	1/18/1943	Seattle WA			None
MacLeod, William Daniel, "Billy"	1962-64	P	L	L	6-2	190	5/13/1942	Gloucester MA			1962

Name, Nickname	Years with Rainiers	POS	B	T	HT	WT	Date and Place of Birth	Date and Place of Death	Years in Major Leagues
Maddern, Clarence James	1952-54	OF, 1B	R	R	6-1	185	9/26/1921 Lowell AZ	8/9/1986 Tucson AZ	1946, 48-49, 51
Maldonado, Felix Juan	1963-64	OF	R	R	5-10	165	5/24/1938 Ponce, Puerto Rico		None
Mallott, Donald Earl, "Don"	1954	INF	R	R	6-1	180	11/23/1929 Los Angeles CA		None
Malmberg, Harry William	1959-62	SS, 2B, 3B	R	R	6-1	170	7/31/1925 Fairfield AL	10/29/1976 San Francisco CA	1955
Mann, Ben Garth, "Garth"	1946-47	P	R	R	6-0	155	11/16/1915 Brandon TX	9/11/1980 Italy TX	1944
Mann, Wolferin David, "Dave"	1961-62	OF	B	R	6-2	190	6/2/1932 Berkeley CA		None
Manno, Donald D., "Don"	1947	OF	R	R	6-1	190	5/4/1915 Williamsport PA	3/11/1995 Williamsport PA	1940-41
Mapes, Clifford Franklin, "Cliff"	1946	OF	L	R	6-3	205	3/13/1922 Sutherland NE	12/5/1996 Pryor OK	1948-52
Marchand, Albert J., "Chink"	1938	OF	L	R	6-0	192	9/21/1911 St. Louis MO	11/8/1995 Florissant MO	None
Marshall, Clarence Westly, "Cuddles"	1944	P	R	R	6-3	200	4/28/1925 Bellingham WA	12/14/2007 Santa Clarita CA	1946, 48-50
Marshall, John Delmer	1943	P	R	R	6-2	200	2/24/1923 Bellingham WA	3/1980 Bremerton WA	None
Martin, John Darrell, "Darrell"	1958-62	P	R	R	6-2	175	10/5/1935 Prague OK		None
Martin, Raymond Joseph, "Ray"	1951	P	R	R	6-2	177	3/13/1925 Norwood MA		1943, 47-48
Martinez, Henry	1939	3B, SS, 2B	R	R	5-11	168	11/7/1916 Honolulu HI	1944 In Pacific War combat	None
Martinich, John Anthony, "Tony"	1955	PH	R	R	6-0	190	10/5/1931 New York NY		None
Martyn, Robert Gordon, "Bob"	1960	OF	L	R	6-0	176	8/15/1930 Weiser ID		1957-59
Marvier, Phillip Donald, "Phil"	1955	OF	L	L	5-11	160	9/14/1935 San Francisco CA		None
Matheson, Willard Francis, "Bill"	1941-46	OF, INF	R	R	5-11	185	7/9/1914 Oakland CA	4/5/1985 Los Angeles Co. CA	None
Mauro, Carmen Louis	1954-58	OF	L	R	6-0	167	11/10/1926 St. Paul MN	12/19/2003 Carmichael CA	1948, 50-51, 53
McAnany, James, " Jim"	1963	OF	R	R	5-10	196	9/4/1936 Los Angeles CA		1958-62
McCall, John William, "Windy"	1949, 59	P	L	L	6-0	180	7/18/1925 San Francisco CA		1948-50, 54-57
McClure, John, " Jack"	1944	P	R	R	6-2	210	4/7/1918 Modesto CA	11/21/1951 Birmingham AL	None
McCormack, Levi W.	1938	OF	R	R	6-1	186	6/11/1913 Lapwai ID	9/4/1974 Spokane WA	None
McDonald, George Thomas	1945-46, 48	1B	L	L	6-0	195	4/12/1917 Seattle WA		None

Name	Year(s)	Position	B	T	Ht	Wt	Birthdate	Birthplace	Death date	Death place	Service
McGhee, Warren Edward, "Ed"	1951	OF	R	R	5-11	170	9/29/1924	Perry AR	2/13/1986	Memphis TN	1950, 53-55
McGinnis, Paul B.	1939-40	SS, 2B, 3B	R	R	5-10	165	11/14/1914	Portland OR	3/26/2000	Colorado Springs CO	None
McLaughlin, Patrick Elmer, "Pat"	1945	P	R	R	6-2	175	8/17/1910	Taylor TX	11/1/1999	Houston TX	1937, 40, 45
McManus, James Michael, "Jim"	1958	1B	L	L	6-4	215	7/20/1936	Brookline MA			1960
Meister, John H.	1947	P	R	R	6-4	205	1929	Seattle WA			None
Metro, Charles, "Charlie"	1946	OF, INF	R	R	6-0	178	4/28/1919	Nanty Glo PA			1943-45, 62, 70
Meyer, Russell Charles, "Russ"	1957	P	B	R	6-1	185	10/25/1923	Peru IL	11/16/1998	Oglesby IL	1946-57, 59
Michael, Herman Henry	1938	1B	R	R	6-1	190	3/26/1912	Artois CA	7/7/1958	Willows CA	None
Michal, George	1957	P	R	R	6-0	185	2/8/1936	Buckley WA			None
Mierkowicz, Edward Frank, "Ed"	1948	1B	R	R	6-4	205	3/6/1924	Wyandotte MI			1945, 47-48, 50
Modrell, Gary W.	1964	P	R	R	6-1	195	1936				None
Moffett, Raymond, "Ray"	1939	P	L	L	6-1	175	1916	Oakley CA			None
Mohr, Leon Leonard, "Lee"	1947-50	OF, INF	B	R	5-10	162	10/8/1920	The Dalles OR	1/21/1978	Contra Costa Co. CA	None
Molitar, Robert B. "Bob"	1943	P	R	R	6-1	163	10/21/1919	Spokane WA	7/14/2009	Spokane WA	None
Monaco, Blas	1946	2B, 1B	B	R	5-11	170	11/16/1915	San Antonio TX	2/10/2000	San Antonio TX	1937, 46
Montalvo, Jose Enrique, " Joe"	1951	C, 1B	R	R	6-4	210	6/6/1926	New York NY	10/20/2009	Kissimmee FL	None
Montgomery, Robert Edward, "Bob"	1964	C	R	R	6-1	203	4/16/1944	Nashville TN			1970-79
Moore, Edward	1958	OF	R	R	6-1	195	9/21/1929	Fort Worth TX			None
Moore, James Wirt, " Jim"	1955	2B, SS	R	R	5-11	170	3/26/1931	Salem OR			None
Moran, Cyril M., "Butch"	1948	1B	R	R	5-11	175	5/12/1917	San Francisco CA	11/12/1978	Los Angeles CA	None
Moran, James A., "Jimmy"	1956	2B	R	R	6-1	185	4/19/1924	Oakland CA			None
Morehead, David Michael, "Dave"	1962	P	R	R	6-1	185	9/5/1942	San Diego CA			1963-70
Morrissey, Joseph Anselm, "Jo Jo"	1939	2B, SS, 1B	R	R	6-1	178	1/16/1904	Warren RI	5/2/1950	Worcester MA	1932-33, 36
Moyer, Robert Raymond, "Bobby"	1948	1B	R	R	6-2	210	7/3/1925	New Ringgold PA	4/10/1997	Southfield MI	None
Muffett, Billy Arnold	1962	P	R	R	6-1	198	9/21/1930	Hammond IN	6/15/2008	Monroe LA	1957-62
Mullen, Ford Parker, "Moon"	1942-43	2B, 3B, SS, C	L	R	5-9	165	2/9/1917	Olympia WA			1944

continued

Name, Nickname	Years with Rainiers	POS	B	T	HT	WT	Date and Place of Birth	Date and Place of Death	Years in Major Leagues
Mullens, Frank A.	1947-48	OF	R	L	5-9	165	3/3/1922 Los Angeles Co. CA	10/20/1976 Davis CA	None
Muller, Frederick William, "Freddie"	1938	2B	R	R	5-10	170	12/21/1907 Newark CA		1933-34
Munger, George David, "Red"	1957	P	R	R	6-2	200	10/4/1918 Houston TX	7/23/1996 Houston TX	1943-44, 46-52, 56
Myer, Robert W., Jr.	1964	P	R	R	6-0	185	12/5/1942 San Antonio TX		None
Myers, Loren Lee, "Lonnie"	1953-55	P	R	R	5-11	180	10/11/1931 Everett WA		None
Nagy, Stephen, "Steve"	1951-54	P	L	L	5-10	170	5/28/1919 Franklin NJ		1947, 50
Neill, Thomas White, "Tommy"	1949	OF	L	R	6-2	200	11/7/1919 Hartselle AL	9/22/1980 Houston TX	1946-47
Newsome, Lamar Ashby, "Skeeter"	1948	SS, 2B, 3B	R	R	5-9	170	10/18/1910 Phenix City AL	8/31/1989 Columbus GA	1935-39, 41-47
Nicholas, Donald Leigh, "Don"	1958	OF	L	R	5-7	150	10/30/1930 Phoenix AZ		1952, 54
Niemiec, Alfred Joseph, "Al"	1940-42, 46	2B, 3B	R	R	5-11	158	5/18/1911 Meriden CT	10/29/1995 Kirkland WA	1934, 36
Niemiller, Frederick C., "Fred"	1945	C	R	R	6-0	175	1/24/1914 Rolla MO	12/1974	None
Nippert, Merlin Lee	1962-64	P	R	R	6-1	175	9/1/1938 Mangum OK		1962
Nokes, Joseph, "Joe"	1944	OF	L	R	5-11	150	2/7/1919		None
Norbert, Theodore Joseph, "Ted"	1945-46	OF	R	R	6-1	192	5/17/1908 Brooklyn NY	8/19/1991 San Juan, Puerto Rico	None
Novikoff, Louis Alexander, "Lou"	1946-48	OF	R	R	5-10	185	10/12/1915 Glendale AZ	9/30/1970 South Gate CA	1941-44, 46
Nusser, Alvin F., "Al"	1938	P			5-11	187	10/31/1909 Chicago IL	10/31/1998 Grenada Hills CA	None
Obregon, Francisco Jose	1960	SS	R	R	5-9	170	12/17/1936 Caracas, Venezuela		None
O'Brien, John Thomas, "Johnny"	1960	3B	R	R	5-9	170	12/11/1930 South Amboy NJ		1953, 55-59
O'Doul, Francis Joseph, "Lefty"	1957	MGR	L	L	6-0	180	3/4/1897 San Francisco CA	12/7/1969 San Francisco CA	1919-20, 22-23, 28-34
Oldham, John Hardin	1955, 58	P, 1B, OF	R	L	6-3	198	11/6/1932 Salinas CA		1956
O'Neill, John Francis, "Johnny"	1947-48	SS	R	R	5-9	160	4/19/1921 Shelbana KY	1/4/1993 Chicago IL	None
Oppliger, Russell L.	1949	P	R	R	6-1	160	8/25/1927 Chicago IL		None
Orphal, John Julius, "Johnny"	1945-47	P, OF	R	R	6-0	197	11/22/1917 Wapakoneta OH		None

Name	Years	Position	B	T	Ht	Wt	Birthdate	Birthplace	Death date	Death place	All-Star
Orteig, Raymond Joseph, "Ray"	1953-58	C	R	R	5-11	180	12/20/1921	Orchards WA	12/1993	Yakima WA	None
Ortiz, Louis Peter, "Lou"	1955	2B	R	R	6-3	195	5/14/1923	Albuquerque NM			None
Osborn, Donald Edwin, "Don"	1938	P	R	R	6-0	185	6/23/1908	Sandpoint ID	3/23/1979	Torrance CA	None
Osteen, Claude Wilson	1958-59	P	L	L	5-11	173	8/9/1939	Caney Spring TN			1957, 59-75
Palica, Alexander R., "Alex"	1945-46	P, PR	R	R	5-9	155	8/19/1926	Lomita CA			None
Palica, Ervin Martin, "Erv"	1960-62	P	R	R	6-1	180	2/9/1928	Lomita CA	5/29/1982	Huntington Beach CA	1947-51, 53-56
Parnell, Melvin Lloyd, "Mel"	1963	MGR	L	L	6-0	180	6/13/1922	New Orleans LA			1947-56
Pascual, Carlos Alberto	1953	P	R	R	5-6	165	3/13/1931	Havana, Cuba			1950
Passero, Joseph, "Joe"	1945	OF	L	L	5-7	150	1922				None
Patchett, Harold Robert, "Hal"	1945-46	OF	L	R	5-11	170	5/10/1909	Flint MI	3/31/1978	El Cajon CA	None
Pavlick, Peter, Jr.	1952	2B	R	R	5-11	180	1/16/1926	Bayonne NJ	9/5/1990	Bayonne NJ	None
Pearson, Isaac Overton, "Ike"	1946-47	P	R	R	6-1	180	3/1/1917	Grenada MS	3/17/1985	Sarasota FL	1939-42, 46, 48
Pedrazzini, Joseph Anthony	1962-64	1B	R	L	5-11	185	7/26/1935				None
Peek, Stephen George, "Steve"	1948	P	B	R	6-2	195	7/30/1914	Springfield MA	9/20/1991	Syracuse NY	1941
Penso, John N.	1944	2B, 3B	R	R	5-6	170	12/5/1916	Seattle WA			None
Pesky, John Michael, "Johnny"	1961-62	MGR	L	R	5-9	168	9/27/1919	Portland OR			1942, 46-54, 63-64, 80
Petrocelli, Americo Peter, "Rico"	1964	SS	R	R	6-0	185	6/27/1943	Brooklyn NY			1963, 65-76
Pettit, George William Paul, "Paul"	1959-60, 62	OF, 1B, P	L	L	6-2	195	11/29/1931	Los Angeles CA			1951, 53
Phipps, Jodie Sydney	1951	P	R	R	6-3	190	2/19/1919	Okay OK	11/29/1999	Oklahoma City OK	None
Pickrel, Clarence Douglas	1938-39	P	R	R	6-1	180	3/28/1911	Gretna VA	11/4/1983	Rocky Mount VA	1933-34
Pillette, Duane Xavier	1957-58	P	R	R	6-3	205	7/24/1922	Detroit MI			1949-56
Pinson, Vada Edward, Jr.	1958	OF	L	L	5-11	181	8/11/1938	Memphis TN	10/21/1995	Oakland CA	1958-75
Podbielan, Clarence Anthony, "Bud"	1956-57	P	R	R	6-1	170	3/6/1924	Curlew WA	10/26/1982	Syracuse NY	1949-55, 57, 59
Poland, Hugh Reid	1946	C	L	R	5-11	185	1/19/1913	Tompkinsville KY	3/29/1984	Guthrie KY	1943-44, 46-48

continued

Name, Nickname	Years with Rainiers	POS	B	T	HT	WT	Date and Place of Birth	Date and Place of Death	Years in Major Leagues
Popovich, John, Jr., "Jack"	1954	PR	R	R	5-11	180	10/28/1928 Kewanee IL		None
Posedel, William John, "Bill"	1947	P	R	R	5-11	175	8/2/1906 San Francisco CA	11/28/1989 Livermore CA	1938-41, 46
Prendergast, James Bartholomew, "Jim"	1938	P	L	L	6-1	208	8/23/1917 Brooklyn NY	8/23/1994 Amherst NY	1948
Priddy, Gerald Edward, "Jerry"	1954-55	INF, P, MGR	R	R	5-11	180	11/9/1919 Los Angeles CA	3/3/1980 N. Hollywood CA	1941-43, 46-53
Pulford, Burton Donald, "Burt"	1946	P	R	R	6-1	184	4/1/1916 Michigan	1/22/1963 Los Angeles Co. CA	None
Queen, Melvin Douglas, "Mel"	1960	P	L	R	6-1	197	3/26/1942 Johnson City NY		1966-72, 97
Rabe, Charles Henry, "Charlie"	1957-59	P	L	L	6-1	180	5/6/1932 Boyce TX		1957-58
Rackley, Marvin Eugene, "Marv"	1950-51	OF	L	L	5-10	170	7/25/1921 Seneca SC		1947-50
Radatz, Richard Raymond, "Dick"	1961	P	R	R	6-5	235	4/2/1937 Detroit MI	3/16/2005 Easton MA	1962-67, 69
Radunich, Nicholas, "Nick"	1939-40	P	R	R	6-1	180	5/18/1916 San Jose CA	10/6/1999 Monterey CA	None
Ramsey, William Thrace, "Bill"	1946-51	OF, 1B	R	R	6-0	175	10/20/1920 Osceola AR	1/4/2008 Memphis TN	1945
Rapp, Earl Wellington	1948	OF	L	R	6-2	185	5/20/1921 Corunna MI	2/13/1992 Swedesboro NJ	1949, 51-52
Regalado, Rudolph Valentino, "Rudy"	1959-60	1B, OF, 3B	R	R	6-1	185	5/21/1930 Los Angeles CA		1954-56
Reich, Herman Charles, "Herm"	1954	1B, OF	R	L	6-2	200	11/23/1917 Bell CA	10/22/2009 Fallbrook CA	1949
Reis, Thomas Edward, "Tommy"	1947-48	P	R	R	6-2	180	8/6/1914 Newport KY	11/6/2009 Ocala FL	1938
Renfro, Roy Clinton	1962	C	R	R	6-0	175	11/13/1940		None
Richards, Paul Rapier	1950	MGR	R	R	6-2	180	11/21/1908 Waxahachie TX	5/4/1986 Waxahachie TX	1932-35, 43-46, 51-61, 76
Richardson, Kenneth Franklin, "Ken"	1948	1B, 2B, 3B, OF	R	R	5-10	187	5/2/1915 Orleans IN	12/7/1987 Woodland Hills CA	1942, 46
Righetti, Leo Charles	1955-57	SS, 2B, 3B	R	R	6-0	170	3/3/1927 San Francisco CA	2/19/1998 San Jose CA	None
Rippelmeyer, Raymond Roy, "Ray"	1960	P	R	R	6-3	200	7/9/1933 Valmeyer IL		1962
Ripple, Charles Dawson, "Charlie"	1947	P	L	L	6-2	210	12/1/1920 Bolton NC	5/6/1979 Wilmington NC	1944-46
Ripple, James Albert, "Jimmy"	1944	OF	L	R	5-10	170	10/14/1909 Export PA	7/16/1959 Greensburg PA	1936-41, 43
Ritchie, Jay Seay	1961, 63-64	P	R	R	6-4	190	11/20/1936 Salisbury NC		1964-68

Name	Years	Pos	B	T	Ht	Wt	Born	Birthplace	Died	Death Place	Career
Rivera, Manuel Joseph, "Jim"	1951, 62-63	OF	L	L	6-0	196	7/22/1922	New York NY			1952-61
Roberts, Robert Lamar, "Bob"	1953-54	P	R	R	5-9	175	9/30/1928	Spokane WA			None
Robertson, Alfred James, "Jim"	1956	C	R	R	5-9	183	1/29/1928	Chicago IL			1954-55
Rocco, Michael Dominick, "Mickey"	1947	1B	L	L	5-11	188	3/2/1916	St. Paul MN	6/1/1997	St. Paul MN	1943-46
Rodin, Eric Chapman	1959	OF	R	R	6-2	215	2/5/1930	Orange NJ	1/4/1991	Somerville NJ	1954
Rolin, Samie Laverne, "Sammy"	1957	P	R	R	6-2	165	3/13/1938	Indio CA			None
Rucker, John Joel, "Johnny"	1947	OF	L	R	6-2	175	1/15/1917	Crabapple GA	8/7/1985	Moultrie GA	1940-41, 43-46
Rudolph, Frederick Donald, "Don"	1959-60	P	L	L	5-11	195	8/16/1931	Baltimore MD	9/12/1968	Granada Hills CA	1957-59, 62-64
Russo, Marius Ugo	1948	P	R	L	6-1	190	7/19/1914	Brooklyn NY	3/26/2005	Ft. Myers FL	1939-43, 46
Ryan, Cornelius Joseph, "Connie"	1958	MGR	R	R	5-11	175	2/27/1920	New Orleans LA	1/3/1996	Metairie LA	1942-44, 46-54, 75, 77
Ryan, Donald K., "Don"	1946	SS	L	R	5-10	182	4/16/1924	Seattle WA	7/16/1999	White Salmon WA	None
Salkeld, William Franklin, "Bill"	1950	C	L	R	5-10	190	3/8/1917	Pocatello ID	4/22/1967	Los Angeles CA	1945-50
Saltzman, Harold H., "Hal"	1947	P	R	R	6-1	185	5/3/1925	Portland OR			None
Sanders, Raymond Floyd, "Ray"	1948	1B	L	R	6-2	185	12/24/1916	Bonne Terre MO	10/28/1983	Washington MO	1942-46, 48-49
Savage, John Robert, "Bob"	1951	P	R	R	6-2	180	12/1/1921	Manchester NH			1942, 46-49
Savransky, Morris, "Moe"	1955	P	L	L	5-11	175	1/13/1929	Cleveland OH			1954
Scantlebury, Patricio Athelstan, "Pat"	1956	P	L	L	6-1	180	11/11/1917	Gatun, Panama	5/24/1991	Glen Ridge NJ	1956
Scarsella, Leslie George, "Les"	1941-42	1B	L	L	5-11	185	11/23/1913	Santa Cruz CA	12/17/1958	San Francisco CA	1935-37, 39-40
Schallock, Arthur Lawrence, "Art"	1956	P	L	L	5-9	160	4/25/1924	Mill Valley CA			1951-55
Schanz, Charles Murrell, "Charley"	1948-52	P	R	R	6-3	215	6/8/1919	Anacortes WA	5/28/1992	Sacramento CA	1944-47, 50
Scharein, George Albert	1947	3B, 2B, SS	R	R	6-1	174	11/21/1914	Decatur IL	12/23/1981	Decatur IL	1937-40
Schmees, George Edward	1953-55	OF, 1B	L	L	6-0	190	9/6/1924	Cincinnati OH	10/30/1998	San Jose CA	1952
Schmidt, Frederick Albert, "Freddy"	1950	P	R	R	6-1	185	2/9/1916	Hartford CT			1944, 46-47
Schmidt, Willard Raymond	1960	P	R	R	6-1	187	5/29/1928	Hays KS	3/22/2007	Newcastle OK	1952-53, 55-59
Schreiber, Theodore Henry, "Ted"	1961-62	2B	R	R	5-11	175	7/11/1938	Brooklyn NY			1963

continued

Name, Nickname	Years with Rainiers	POS	B	T	HT	WT	Date and Place of Birth	Date and Place of Death	Years in Major Leagues
Schult, Arthur William, "Art"	1955-56	OF	R	R	6-4	220	6/20/1928 Brooklyn NY		1953, 56-57, 59-60
Schuster, William Charles, "Bill"	1940-41, 50	3B, SS, 2B	R	R	5-9	164	8/4/1912 Buffalo NY	6/28/1987 El Monte CA	1937, 39, 43-45
Schwall, Donald Bernard, "Don"	1961	P	R	R	6-6	200	3/2/1936 Wilkes-Barre PA		1961-67
Scribner, Ira W.	1940-42, 46	P, 3B	R	R	5-10	178	5/12/1912 Friday Harbor WA	5/25/2004 Seattle WA	None
Segovia, Laurence, "Larry"	1957	PR	R	R	5-8	170	1/29/1932 Monterey Co. CA		None
Selway, Edward Benjamin, "Ed"	1939	P	R	R	6-3	190	5/12/1913 Washington PA	11/28/2002 Washington PA	None
Serventi, Marcello Lawrence, "Marcel"	1938	P	R	R	5-9	160	2/17/1916 Oakland CA	7/5/1941 Oakland CA	None
Sewell, James Luther, "Luke"	1956	MGR	R	R	5-9	160	1/5/1901 Titus AL	5/14/1987 Akron OH	1921-39, 41-46, 49-52
Shannon, Thomas Michael, "Mike"	1962	OF	R	R	6-3	195	7/15/1939 St. Louis MO		1962-70
Shartzer, Phillip Eugene	1958	SS	R	R	5-10	170	10/15/1935 Louisville KY		None
Sheely, Hollis Kimball, "Bud"	1950-51	C	L	R	6-1	200	11/26/1920 Spokane WA	10/17/1985 Sacramento CA	1951-53
Shepherd, William Lyman	1960	PH	L	R	6-6	195	7/1/1938		None
Sheridan, Neill Rawlins	1948-49	OF, 1B	R	R	6-1	195	11/20/1921 Sacramento CA		1948
Shetrone, Barry Stevan	1964	OF	L	R	6-2	190	7/6/1938 Baltimore MD	7/18/2001 Bowie MD	1959-63
Simmons, Thomas G., "Tom"	1940	P	R	R	6-2	200	1914 Camden IN		None
Singleton, Bert Elmer, "Elmer"	1955-56, 61-63	P	R	R	6-2	174	6/26/1918 Ogden UT	1/5/1996 Ogden UT	1945-48, 50, 57-59
Sinovic, Richard John, "Dick"	1950	OF	R	R	6-0	190	7/30/1925 Portland OR		None
Sisler, Richard Allan, "Dick"	1960	MGR	L	R	6-2	205	11/2/1920 St. Louis MO	11/20/1998 Nashville TN	1946-53, 64-65
Skeen, Archie Elwood	1962-63	C	L	R	6-0	195	7/27/1937		None
Skiff, William Franklin, "Bill"	1941-46	MGR	R	R	5-10	170	10/16/1895 New Rochelle NY	12/25/1976 Bronxville NY	1921, 26
Skizas, Louis Peter, "Lou"	1959-60	3B, OF	R	R	5-11	175	6/2/1932 Chicago IL		1956-59
Slack, William Henry	1961	P	L	R	5-10	175	5/3/1933 Sarnia, Ontario		None
Slider, Rachel Wayne, "Rac"	1962-64	SS, 2B	L	R	5-8	160	12/23/1933 Simms TX		None

Name	Years	Position	B	T	Ht	Wt	Born	Birthplace	Died	Death Place	MLB Years
Smith, Bobby Gene	1963	OF	R	R	5-11	185	5/28/1934	Hood River OR	4/11/1997	San Diego CA	1957-62, 65
Smith, Milton, "Milt"	1956	3B, 2B, SS	R	L	5-10	165	3/27/1929	Columbus GA			1955
Smith, Paul Leslie	1961-63	OF, 1B	L	L	5-8	165	3/19/1931	New Castle PA			1953, 57-58
Smith, Peter Luke, "Pete"	1962-63	P	R	R	6-2	190	3/19/1940	Natick MA			1962-63
Smith, Robert Gilchrist, "Bob"	1963-64	P	R	L	6-2	190	2/1/1931	Woodsville NH			1955, 57-59
Snyder, Donald A.	1943	PH	R	R	5-10	160	8/27/1924				None
Snyder, Robert Adney, Jr., "Bob"	1946-48	P	R	R	6-1	175	10/6/1918	Tacoma WA	9/25/1984	Lakewood CA	None
Soriano, Dewey	1939-42, 46, 50-51	P	R	R	6-3	200	2/8/1920	Prince Rupert, British Columbia	4/6/1998	Seattle WA	None
Spalding, Edward R., "Ed"	1946	P	R	R	6-5	215	7/20/1919	Santa Barbara CA	11/24/2000	Freeport ME	None
Spanswick, William Henry, "Bill"	1961-63	P	L	L	6-3	195	7/8/1938	Springfield MA			1964
Speece, Byron Franklin, "By"	1943-45	P	R	R	5-11	170	1/6/1897	West Baden IN	9/29/1974	Elgin OR	1924-26, 30
Spencer, George Elwood	1961-63	P	R	R	6-1	215	7/7/1926	Columbus OH			1950-55, 58, 60
Spindel, Harold Stewart, "Hal"	1938, 44	C, 1B	R	R	6-0	185	5/27/1913	Chandler OK	7/28/2002	San Clemente CA	1939, 45-46
Stagg, Robert G., "Bob"	1941-42, 46-47	C	L	R	5-11	185	6/13/1921	Spokane WA	5/8/2008	Seattle WA	None
Stallard, Evan Tracy, "Tracy"	1962	C	R	R	6-5	205	8/31/1937	Coeburn VA			1960-66
Stenhouse, David Rotchford, "Dave"	1959-60	P	R	R	6-0	195	9/12/1933	Westerly RI			1962-64
Stephens, Vernon Decatur, "Vern"	1955-56	3B, 1B, SS, OF	R	R	5-10	185	10/23/1920	McAlister NM	11/3/1968	Long Beach CA	1941-55
Stephenson, Jerry Joseph	1963-64	P	L	R	6-2	185	10/6/1943	Detroit MI	6/6/2010	Fullerton CA	1963, 65-70
Stickle, Ned F.	1939, 41-42, 46	SS, 2B, 3B	R	R	5-6	165	8/3/1917	Outlook WA	1/2/1961	Spokane WA	None
St. John, Thomas James	1958	OF	L	R	6-0	175	1933				None
Stockman, Bruce A.	1939	2B, 3B	L	R	5-11	175	2/7/1921	Los Angeles Co. CA	10/8/1964	San Francisco CA	None
Stotsky, Robert Donald	1962	OF	R	R	5-9	162	2/10/1938				None
Strange, Alan Cochrane	1938-39, 59	SS, MGR	R	R	5-9	162	11/7/1906	Philadelphia PA	6/27/1994	Seattle WA	1934-35, 40-42
Stumpf, Robert W., "Bob"	1946-48	C	R	R	6-2	210	8/12/1926	New York NY	12/15/2004		None

Name, Nickname	Years with Rainiers	POS	B	T	HT	WT	Date and Place of Birth	Date and Place of Death	Years in Major Leagues
Sturgeon, Robert Howard, "Bobby"	1949	SS, 2B	R	R	6-0	175	8/6/1919 Clinton IN	3/10/2007 San Dimas CA	1940-42, 46-48
Sturm, John Peter Joseph, "Johnny"	1947	1B	L	L	6-1	185	1/23/1916 St. Louis MO	10/8/2004 St. Louis MO	1941
Suchecki, James Joseph, "Jim"	1953-54	P	R	R	5-11	185	8/25/1926 Chicago IL	7/20/2000 Crofton MD	1950-52
Sueme, Harold J., "Hal"	1943-48	C, 1B	R	R	6-1	180	4/16/1909 St. Louis MO	4/20/2000 Sultan WA	None
Surkont, Matthew Constantine, "Max"	1958-59	P	R	R	6-0	205	6/16/1922 Central Falls RI	10/8/1986 Largo FL	1949-57
Sweeney, William Joseph, "Bill"	1952-53	MGR	R	R	5-11	180	12/29/1904 Cleveland OH	4/18/1957 San Diego CA	1928, 30-31
Swift, Robert Virgil, "Bob"	1955	C	R	R	5-11	180	3/6/1915 Salina KS	10/17/1966 Detroit MI	1940-53, 65-66
Tanner, Joseph N., "Joe"	1958	3B	R	R	6-0	175	11/16/1931 Laurel MS		None
Tappe, Theodore Nash, "Ted"	1957, 59	C, OF	L	R	6-3	185	2/2/1931 Seattle WA	2/13/2004 Wenatchee WA	1950-51, 55
Tate, John Haskell	1940	P	R	R	6-0	187	3/18/1916 Depot TX	4/28/1944 Keuntze TX	None
Taylor, Edward James, "Eddie"	1938-39	INF	R	R	5-6	160	11/17/1901 Chicago IL	1/30/1992 Chula Vista CA	1926
Taylor, Joseph Cephus, "Joe"	1956-57, 60	OF, C	R	R	6-1	185	3/2/1926 Chapman AL	3/18/1993 Pittsburgh PA	1954, 57-59
Theis, Joseph Michael	1962, 64	C	R	R	5-10	185	7/19/1936 Bloomington IL		None
Thom, William	1961-62	P	R	R	6-2	195	8/15/1937		None
Thomas, Leo Raymond	1952-54	3B	R	R	5-11	178	7/26/1923 Turlock CA	3/5/2001 Concord CA	1950, 52
Thomason, Dale Dean	1953	P	R	R	6-0	190	5/27/1930 Ewan WA	7/20/1987 Spokane Valley WA	None
Thurman, Robert Burns, "Bob"	1957, 59-60	OF, 1B	L	L	6-1	205	5/14/1917 Kellyville OK	10/31/1998 Wichita KS	1955-59
Thurston, Vance Lee	1947	P	R	R	5-11	175	2/16/1929 Long Beach CA		None
Tillman, John Robert, "Bob"	1961	C, 1B	R	R	6-4	205	3/24/1937 Nashville TN	6/23/2000 Gallatin TN	1962-70
Tincup, Frank	1943-44	P, OF	L	R	5-11	185	6/30/1919	10/1985 Wagoner OK	None
Tobin, Frank Edward	1941, 44	PH	R	R	6-1	185	7/10/1896 Sacramento CA	3/9/1976 Tacoma WA	None
Tobin, James Anthony, "Jim"	1946	P	R	R	6-0	185	12/27/1912 Oakland CA	5/19/1969 Oakland CA	1937-45
Tobin, John Patrick, "Johnny," "Jack"	1953-54	OF, 3B, C	L	R	6-0	165	1/8/1921 Oakland CA	1/18/1982 Oakland CA	1945
Toft, Martin	1961-62	OF, 3B	R	R	5-1	190	6/21/1936		None

Name	Years	Pos	B	T	Ht	Wt	Born	Birthplace	Died	Death place	MLB
Torgeson, Clifford Earl, "Earl"	1941-42, 46	1B, OF	L	L	6-3	180	1/1/1924	Snohomish WA	11/8/1990	Everett WA	1947-61
Tost, Louis Eugene, "Lou"	1946	P	L	L	6-0	175	6/1/1911	Cumberland WA	2/22/1967	Santa Clara CA	1942-43, 47
Tovar, Cesar Leonardo	1960	UTIL	R	R	5-9	155	7/3/1940	Caracas, Venezuela	7/14/1994	Caracas, Venezuela	1965-76
Tran, Leonard Allen, "Len"	1946, 52	3B, SS	R	R	5-8	185	2/23/1927	Seattle WA			None
Turpin, Harold, "Hal"	1938-45	P, OF	L	R	5-11	185	9/28/1903	Yoncalla OR	2/28/1997	Roseburg OR	None
Tuttle, William Robert, "Bill"	1963-64	OF, 3B	R	R	6-0	190	7/4/1929	Elwood IL	7/27/1998	Anoka MN	1952, 54-63
Umphlett, Thomas Mullen, "Tom"	1961-62	OF	L	R	6-2	180	5/12/1930	Scotland Neck NC			1953-55
Urquhart, Donald	1959	P	R	R	6-2	185	1931				None
Valentine, Harold Lewis, "Corky"	1956	P	R	R	6-1	203	1/4/1929	Troy OH	1/21/2005	Roswell GA	1954-55
Valo, Elmer William	1959	OF	L	R	5-11	190	3/5/1921	Ribnik, Czechoslovakia	7/19/1998	Palmerton PA	1940-43, 46-61
Van Fleet, Dwight Mernice, "Red"	1939	P	R	R	5-10	175	6/24/1907	Milton IA	3/3/1976	Ogallala NE	None
Vanni, Edo Joe	1938-41, 46-48, 50, 64	OF, MGR	L	L	5-8	175	4/2/1919	Black Diamond WA	4/30/2007	Bellevue WA	None
Veach, Theodore, "Ted"	1938	P	B	R	5-10	195	2/28/1905	Indianapolis IN	12/1971	Elmont NY	None
Verban, Emil Matthew	1951	2B	R	R	5-11	165	8/27/1915	Lincoln IL	6/8/1989	Quincy IL	1944-50
Verble, Eugene Kermit, "Gene"	1955	SS, 3B, 2B	R	R	5-10	163	6/29/1928	Concord NC			1951, 53
Vias, Manuel Joseph, "Manny"	1945	OF	R	R	5-6	160	1/19/1917	San Francisco CA	3/29/1991	Alameda CA	None
Vico, George Steve	1950-52	1B, OF, 3B	L	R	6-4	200	8/9/1923	San Fernando CA	1/13/1994	Redondo Beach CA	1948-49
Wade, Galeard Lee, "Gale"	1958-59	OF	L	R	6-1	185	1/20/1929	Hollister MO			1955-56
Waitman, Gerald Leon, "Gerry"	1945	2B, OF	R	R	5-9	185	7/12/1920	San Bernardino Co. CA	12/29/1990	San Bernardino Co. CA	None
Walker, William Henry, "Bill"	1939-40	P	R	L	6-0	175	10/7/1903	E. St. Louis IL	6/14/1966	E. St. Louis IL	1927-36
Wall, Murray Wesley	1960	P	R	R	6-3	185	9/19/1926	Dallas TX	10/8/1971	Lone Oak TX	1950, 57-59
Warren, Jack Carl	1948-50	C, OF	R	R	6-0	193	12/30/1921	Portland OR	9/6/2007	Portland OR	None
Watson, Emmett	1943	C	R	R	6-0	167	11/22/1918	Seattle WA	5/11/2001	Seattle WA	None

continued

Name, Nickname	Years with Rainiers	POS	B	T	HT	WT	Date and Place of Birth	Date and Place of Death	Years in Major Leagues
Watson, Richard Eugene	1955	SS	R	R	5-8	160	11/17/1934 Napa CA		None
Watson, Steven, "Steve"	1957	P	R	R	6-1	180	12/25/1937 Salt Lake City UT		None
Webber, Lester Elmer, "Les"	1938-41	P	R	R	6-0	185	5/6/1915 Kelseyville CA	11/13/1986 Santa Maria CA	1942-46, 48
Wellman, Robert Joseph, "Bob"	1954	OF	R	R	6-4	210	7/15/1925 Norwood OH	12/20/1994 Villa Hills KY	1948, 50
Wert, James Lawrence, "Jimmy"	1946	1B	L	L	6-2	185	2/22/1925 Yakima WA		None
Whipple, Jack Loren	1945	OF	R	R	6-0	175	6/17/1919 Los Angeles CA	6/7/1960 Portland OR	None
White, Joyner Clifford, "Jo Jo"	1939-42, 46-49	OF, MGR	L	R	5-11	165	6/1/1909 Red Oak GA	10/9/1986 Tacoma WA	1932-38, 43-44, 60
White, Samuel Charles, "Sammy"	1949	C	R	R	6-3	195	7/7/1928 Wenatchee WA	9/4/1991 Princeville HI	1951-59, 61-62
Widmar, Albert Joseph, "Al"	1952-55	P, 2B	R	R	6-3	185	3/20/1925 Cleveland OH	10/15/2005 Tulsa OK	1947-48, 50-52
Wieand, Franklin Delano Roosevelt, "Ted"	1958, 60	P	R	R	6-2	195	4/4/1933 Walnutport PA		1958, 60
Wight, William Robert, "Bill"	1959	P	L	L	6-1	180	4/12/1922 Rio Vista CA	5/17/2007 Mt. Shasta CA	1946-53, 55-58
Wilburn, John L.	1947	PR	R	R	6-2	192	8/15/1923 Spokane WA	2/21/1987 Los Angeles CA	None
Wilkie, Aldon Jay, "Lefty"	1940	P	L	L	5-11	175	10/30/1914 Zealandia, Saskatchewan	8/5/1992 Tualatin OR	1941-42, 46
Williams, Dewey Edgar	1950	C	R	R	6-0	160	2/5/1916 Durham NC	3/19/2000 Williston ND	1944-48
Williams, Marvin, "Marv"	1955	1B	R	R	6-0	195	2/12/1923 Houston TX	12/23/2000 Conroe TX	None
Williams, Robert Fulton, "Ace"	1946	P	R	L	6-2	174	3/18/1917 Montclair NJ	9/16/1999 Ft. Myers FL	1940, 46
Wills, Maurice Morning, "Maury"	1957	SS, 2B, 3B	B	R	5-11	170	10/2/1932 Washington DC		1959-72, 80-81
Wills, Theodore Carl, "Ted"	1961	P	L	L	6-2	200	2/9/1934 Fresno CA		1959-62, 65
Wilson, Arthur Lee, "Artie"	1952-54, 56	INF	L	R	5-10	162	10/28/1920 Springville AL		1951
Wilson, James Alger, "Jim"	1950	P	R	R	6-1	200	2/20/1922 San Diego CA	9/2/1986 Newport Beach CA	1945-46, 48-49, 51-58
Wilson, Robert Earl, "Earl"	1961	P	R	R	6-3	216	10/2/1934 Ponchatoula LA	4/23/2005 Southfield MI	1959-60, 62-70
Wilson, Robert James, "Red"	1952	C	R	R	6-0	200	3/7/1929 Milwaukee WI		1951-60

Name	Years	Position	Bats	Throws	Height	Weight	Birth Date	Birthplace	Death Date	Death Place	
Wincencik, Edward Joseph, "Ed"	1959	SS	R	R	5-9	165	4/16/1929	Chicago IL	6/13/1995	Spokane WA	1956-57
Windsor, George L.	1941	P	R	R	6-0	174	10/27/1915				None
Wtek, Nicholas Joseph, "Mickey"	1950	2B	R	R	5-10	170	12/19/1915	Luzerne PA	8/24/1990	Kingston PA	1940-43, 46-47, 49
Wolfe, Kenneth	1961-62	C	R	R	6-1	190	4/12/1938				None
Wood, Wilbur Forrester, Jr.	1963-64	P	R	L	6-0	180	10/22/1941	Cambridge MA			1961-65, 67-78
Yelovic, John G.	1943-44, 46-47	P	R	R	6-1	192	7/13/1913	Clarksburg WV	2/24/1994	San Pedro CA	None
York, Anthony Batton, "Tony"	1946-50	SS, 2B, 3B, OF	R	R	5-10	165	11/27/1912	Irene TX	4/18/1970	Hillsboro TX	1944
Zar, John Andrew	1942	P	R	R	6-3	205	11/25/1920	San Pedro CA	10/3/2008	Palm Springs CA	None
Zarilla, Allen Lee, "Al"	1954	OF	L	R	5-11	180	5/1/1919	Los Angeles CA	8/28/1996	Honolulu HI	1943-44, 46-53
Zernia, Harvey Elmer	1955-56	2B, 1B, 3B, OF	L	R	6-0	190	5/31/1926	Milwaukee WI	7/1/1980	Milwaukee WI	None
Zimmerman, Gerald Robert, "Jerry"	1960	C	R	R	6-2	185	9/21/1934	Omaha NE	9/9/1998	Neskowin OR	1961-68
Zoldak, Samuel Walter, "Sam"	1953	P	L	L	5-11	185	12/8/1918	Brooklyn NY	8/25/1966	New Hyde Park NY	1944-52
Zuvela, Jerry Mike	1955	OF	L	L	6-0	190	9/21/1928	San Pedro CA	7/28/1995	San Pedro CA	None

Bibliographical Essay

How do you write a book about the Seattle Rainiers, one of the nation's most successful and revered minor-league baseball franchises of any era, without leaving anything out? Fill out a lineup card using the *Seattle Post-Intelligencer*, Edo Vanni, and Dave Eskenazi as the first three batters in the order when pursuing historical resources. Sadly, only one of them is still around to see this book through. The newspaper ceased publishing after 146 years. Vanni died at the age of eighty-nine. Eskenazi, however, is reaching middle age, and his heart rate and breathing seem fine.

In gathering Rainiers information, there was no better place to start than the *Post-Intelligencer*, my place of employment for nearly thirty years until the newspaper ceased publishing in March 2009. One-time *Post-Intelligencer* sports editor and columnist and tireless civic promoter Royal Brougham, a person I met just once (it would have been twice had he not stood me up on an arranged interview for a college term paper), involved himself in the inner workings of this baseball team, and those of every other team in the city for that matter, in a way no other journalist could. He helped hire and fire people. He influenced public opinion. He personally arranged for Babe Ruth to visit Seattle on multiple occasions, with the newspaper footing expenses. You could count on Brougham's daily observations in print to be more insightful than those of the competition. Rainiers radio broadcaster Leo Lassen also served as the *Post-Intelligencer*'s baseball beat writer at all home games for several seasons, simultaneously offering audio and written reports. Emmett Watson, a former Rainiers catcher, high school teammate of Fred Hutchinson, and colleague of mine at the *Post-Intelligencer*, served as the newspaper's baseball beat writer before becoming a sports columnist. Watson, who was a superlative writer, always said he was going to write a Rainiers book, but he never did. The last person at the *Post-Intelligencer* to cover the Rainiers was Paul Rossi, who is also deceased. I sat next to him in the office for more than a decade, putting the paper out nightly and listening to his collection of Rainiers stories. And as if those connections weren't enough, Michele Turpin, the niece of pitcher Hal Turpin, was the *Post-Intelligencer* publisher's secretary. All I had to do to hear about this beloved baseball team was go to work.

Vanni, who played for the first Rainiers team and managed the last one, used to goad me to get this book done while he was still alive to read it. Sorry, Edo. He died in May 2007, nearly four full years before the manuscript was ready for a public unveiling. Vanni knew more about the team than anyone, and we conducted no fewer than a dozen interviews in person or on the phone. His basement was a veritable baseball Disneyland, filled with huge scrapbooks, musty uniforms hanging in a corner, autographs from baseball's biggest names, photos hanging on the wall, and all sorts of other memorabilia. His memory was a Rainiers treasure trove.

Eskenazi, a Seattle businessman and native son, knows more about the Rainiers than any other living person now. He doubles as a serious collector of all things related to Seattle's sporting past, with the Rainiers at the top of the list. He created a permanent Northwest baseball exhibition at the Mariners' Safeco Field and has provided exhibits all over the West Coast. Law enforcement missed out on a great detective in this guy, because he can find anything. Eskenazi handed over Rainiers-related letters, telegrams, office memos, fan mail, rare wartime periodicals, media guides, and a poem, stuff dating as far back as 1938, all for use in this book. Through his collecting activities and attendance at conventions and reunions, Eskenazi has met countless old Rainiers players, many of whom were long deceased by the time this book started to take form. Fortunately for me, he listened to their stories firsthand, and in some instances took notes when he spoke with them.

With all of those superior resources at hand, it wasn't hard for me, someone who views himself as an obsessive researcher of any matter that interests me, to leap into this world like an overeager skydiver. I interviewed upwards of 150 people for this book. Maury Wills called me from Dodgers Stadium as I was entering a car repair shop. I sat and talked with Elgin Baylor in his Los Angeles Clippers office for three hours, mostly going over his basketball career for a newspaper story, yet also touching on his Rainiers tryout, and he doesn't even like reporters. When I sat with Vanni in 2000 as he watched a Chicago White Sox–Seattle Mariners playoff game on TV, I hoped to get his take on the local big-league team for a newspaper story, but I also found myself reflexively taking notes whenever he mentioned the Rainiers, without knowing later I was going to write a book.

On weekdays I was accused of wearing out if not hoarding the aging and sometimes temperamental microfilm reader on the third floor of the *Post-Intelligencer*. On Saturdays, days off for everyone else at the paper, I would spend eight to ten hours alone in the office, reading about the Rainiers, reading about the corresponding Seattle historical milestones I needed to support the baseball story I wanted to tell, reading until my eyes could take no more.

One of the most incredible resource tools I encountered in my three decades as a sports journalist was an old newspaper archive online, offered and later discontinued by the Society for American Baseball Research. Thanks to the portal, I was able to read wartime issues of the *Los Angeles Times*, *New York Times*, *Washington Post*, *Chicago Tribune*, *Seattle Times*, and the *Post-Intelligencer* almost nightly for several months, which was especially useful when I was researching Babe Ruth's dalliance with the Rainiers' managerial job. All I had to do was punch in the key words and sit back for a glorious ride through history. I was never more surprised than when the dialogue between Rainiers team owner Emil Sick and Ruth popped up in a 1941 Associated Press story I found in the *Los Angeles Times*.

To familiarize myself with the rest of the Pacific Coast League and see what others had to say about the Rainiers in passing, I read Dick Dobbins's *The Grand Minor League* (Woodford Press, 1999), Rich Marazzi and Len Fiorito's *Baseball Players of the 1950s*

(McFarland, 2004), John Spaulding's *Pacific Coast League Stars* (Ag Press, 1994), Donald Wells's *Baseball's Western Front* (McFarland, 2004), Paul Zingg and Mark Medeiros's *Runs, Hits and an Era: The Pacific Coast League, 1903–58* (University of Illinois Press, 1994), and Gary Waddingham's *The Seattle Rainiers, 1938–1942* (Writers, 1987). For statistical research, Eskenazi provided me with Carlos Bauer's *The Coast League Cyclopedia: An Encyclopedia of the Old Pacific Coast League, 1903–57* (Baseball Press, 2003).

In identifying the Seattle milestones I wanted to use, I turned to James Warren's *King County and Its Queen City: Seattle* (Windsor, 1981), Murray Morgan's *Skid Road* (Ballentine, 1951), and one of the great Seattle contributions to the World Wide Web, HistoryLink.org (www.historylink.org).

One of the unexpected finds in my Rainiers research was Emil Sick's unpublished memoir, which was generously made available to me by his daughter Diana Ingman and has since been donated to the University of Washington. This memoir provided the next best thing to a face-to-face chat with the beer baron, although I encountered it four decades after his death. All the pertinent stuff was there about hirings and firings, plus the money earned and spent on important franchise decisions.

Chapter 1

For the book's opening, I used information gleaned from published accounts in the *Seattle Post-Intelligencer* and *Seattle Times* that described the unusual wave of multiple law-enforcement raids at Civic Stadium. This was front-page news in both papers, even used in a headline two inches tall in the *Post-Intelligencer*, and the story trickled into a couple of days of follow-up coverage. Lawsuits against the Seattle Indians were prominently reported in

326 | BIBLIOGRAPHICAL ESSAY

the local newspapers before and after the raids. I supplemented these reports with recollections from former Rainiers Rugger Ardizoia and Vanni, the latter a ballpark fixture as a clubhouse employee well before he became a player.

To pinpoint the earliest beginnings of professional baseball in Seattle, I referred to various *Post-Intelligencer* news accounts dating back to 1890. Former *Post-Intelligencer* and *Times* sportswriter Vince O'Keefe, now deceased, served as a good barometer on the topic when, in an interview with me, he touched on some of the city's most notable baseball travails, including the destruction of Dugdale Park, which he witnessed firsthand. My research of 1937 box scores revealed Ted Williams's rare lack of batting prowess while playing for San Diego at Seattle's Civic Stadium. Dan Dugdale's death and funeral were front-page news stories in both Seattle papers.

To introduce Emil Sick as Seattle's new baseball owner, I used *Post-Intelligencer* stories, Vanni's recollections, and Sick's memoir, the latter of which proved particularly helpful in explaining his interest in baseball and how he formed his relationship with New York Yankees owner Col. Jacob Ruppert, a fellow brewer.

Chapter 2

In sizing up Sick as Seattle's baseball savior, I obtained biographical information chiefly from interviews with his daughter Diana Ingman and grandson Sean Sheehan, who in particular offered a most honest portrayal of a sometimes overly demanding and hot-tempered man. Sick's memoirs were a rich source of information for both financial details and personal motivations, helping explain him and who he was. Sick, media savvy and enjoying his newfound spotlight, effectively used the *Post-Intelligencer* and *Times* to sell his baseball ideas.

The Rainiers' pursuit of Vanni and Hutchinson, and the players' ensuing contract negotiations, were spelled out in greatest detail by Vanni one afternoon at his kitchen table; segments of this information are confirmed in different Seattle newspaper accounts. Sick's memoir and Bob Karolevitz's biography *Torchy!* (Dakota Homestead, 1987) also offered signing specifics.

In setting the general scene for Rainiers games at Sicks' Stadium, I turned to several people, most notably Seattle baseball fans Addis and Leatrice Gutmann, whose parents each owned or shared season tickets and who considered the team an important part of their own courtship; Bob Molitor, who described in exacting detail his bus rides as a young kid with friends to the games; and Dan Evans, former governor of Washington, who recalled his earliest memories at the ballpark with family members.

Chapter 3

Hutchinson was an unforgettable character, which made it easy for his former high school teammates and opponents in interviews to weigh in with distinctive memories of the kid pitcher who captured the fascination of Seattle during the summer of 1938. Game accounts from the *Seattle Post-Intelligencer*, *Seattle Times*, *Los Angeles Times*, *San Francisco Examiner*, and *Portland Oregonian* provided basic, quoteless summaries of Hutchinson's outings. Vanni, as his roommate and only surviving Rainiers teammate at the time I was conducting research, and Eddie Carnett, an opponent who would later pitch for the Rainiers himself, added plenty of colorful detail.

Part of the myth surrounding Hutchinson for decades is the story of how he walked off the mound in the middle of a game in Seattle in order to retrieve a drink of water in the dugout and collect himself during a tough inning. This did happen, but in Portland, my research showed. Vanni supplied the brief banter that took place between the pitcher and manager Jack Lelivelt, and the motivation behind Hutchinson's unique time-out.

The *Post-Intelligencer* scored a news coup on September 11, 1938, when it published a story with Hutchinson's byline on top (plus accompanying tag "as told to Leo Lassen"). Hutch described his pitching likes and dislikes, and long-range dreams. Players rarely were quoted or interviewed in depth, if at all, by the Seattle press at that time.

A series of Western Union telegrams and letters from New York Yankees scout Joe Devine to various baseball executives that summed up Hutchinson's talents, the various offers made for the pitcher, and Devine's great frustration in failing to interest him or his father in a deal were supplied by Eskenazi. Hutchinson's rookie season with Detroit was well chronicled in Associated Press stories published in the *Post-Intelligencer*. Hutchinson's career big-league statistics were pulled from John Thorn, Pete Palmer, and Michael Gershman, *Total Baseball* (Total Sports, 2001).

The attendance figures for Rainiers games provided throughout the text (used in this chapter to establish a comparison with big-league teams in 1938) are from 1983 research conducted by Russ Dille, former Rainiers employee and SABR member.

Chapter 4

Rainiers player interviews with Charlie Metro, Van Fletcher, Carnett, Ardizoia, Buddy Hancken, and Vanni accounted for a majority of the information on Jo Jo White, Lelivelt, and the team's earliest championship seasons. *Post-Intelligencer* stories and Sick's memoir helped augment the portrayals.

Vanni, who was a know-it-all in the best sense of the word, if the connection hadn't been made by now, discussed White's salary with him and broke it down for me so I could include the story in this book. *Post-Intelligencer* accounts verified that White was paid more by the Rainiers than the Detroit Tigers.

Eskenazi's collection supplied the Rainiers media guides that provided the origins of White's nickname, the poem composed by fan Florence Charlesworth, and a letter that Lelivelt sent to the Tigers inquiring about White's post-trade mood.

Chapter 5

The *Seattle Post-Intelligencer* and *Times* provided detail in a surprisingly tempered fashion when reporting the Rainiers' pursuit of Ruth as manager and his rejection of the job. Associated Press reports in the *New York Times*, *Los Angeles Times*, *Chicago Tribune*, and *Washington Post* kept the story alive with quotes from others.

In interviews, Bob Stagg, Carnett, and Vanni, who would have played for Ruth had he come to Seattle, each weighed in on the possibility of the Yankees slugger taking the job. Stagg, a Rainiers catcher (now deceased), was interviewed at the Spring Hill Assisted Living Center in suburban north Seattle and made it clear he was not in favor of a Ruth candidacy; nor was Vanni, who had previously met Ruth. Carnett, however, was in favor of Ruth becoming his Seattle manager.

The *Post-Intelligencer* provided multiple stories and even full photo pages on the three occasions when Ruth visited Seattle, while the *Seattle Times* often had a single paragraph or nothing at all. The reason for the discrepancy: the *Post-Intelligencer*, which had paid for the visits, had exclusive rights and access to Ruth when he was in Seattle. For its part, the *Times* simply acted as if these events didn't happen. Correspondence between Ruth and Brougham, made available by the sports columnist's granddaughter Cathi Soriano, verifies the close relationship the two men enjoyed.

Chapter 6

With rationing in place during World War II, newspapers typically were a lot smaller, which meant that coverage of Rainiers games was far less extensive. The *Post-Intelligencer*, however, provided adequate news on war restrictions affecting the team, such as the changing of starting times and roster limitations. Interviews with eventual Rainiers TV broadcaster and bombardier builder Walt Milroy, plus with Vanni, Tran, Carnett, and Metro, helped flush out baseball details during the war. Eskenazi provided a *3 and 0 Umpire* newsletter that was published by the military and the Torchy Torrance letter asking a player about his wartime availability. Sick's memoir told of his war efforts, which included paying half the salaries of players who served in the armed forces, allowing the stadium to be used for military storage and ammunitions testing, and engaging in various business maneuverings.

Chapter 7

The Seattle newspapers never said a word about "Kewpie" Dick Barrett's lack of control—away from the mound—until the pitcher was arrested for shoplifting several years after his baseball career was over. Frank interviews with Ford "Moon" Mullen, Carnett, Ardizoia, Stagg, and Vanni, plus Rainiers broadcaster Rod Belcher, shed light on a man always in need of a drink and usually lugging around his own supply. The local papers preferred to glorify one of the franchise's most popular players until Brougham wrote of Barrett's fall from grace in a front-page story in the *Post-Intelligencer* on December 6, 1963, and implored readers to help rescue the now middle-aged man by making donations.

Eskenazi provided a Barrett profile written in a June 1943 issue of the *Diamond of PSI Upsilon*, a University of Illinois fraternity publication, one in which Barrett describes how his nickname was conceived. Eskenazi also supplied telegrams sent to Barrett from Pacific Coast League president Clarence Rowland and the *Post-Intelligencer*'s Brougham.

Chapter 8

The window to sources knowledgeable about the halfway point of the Rainiers story—which involved the introduction of TV to baseball, if not the general population, and the emergence of franchise icons Rogers Hornsby and Jim Rivera—would not be open indefinitely, although this didn't register with me at the time. For example, the first TV broadcaster to cover the baseball team was Bill O'Mara, and he died not long after I interviewed him about his pioneering efforts with that medium at the ballpark.

Hornsby was described in vivid detail as the unforgiving dictator that he was while delivering the 1951 pennant to Seattle by former Rainiers players Marv Grissom, Vern Kindsfather, and K Chorlton, each of whom also passed away shortly after submitting to interviews. Other information about Hornsby's tenure came from interviews with former players Jim Rivera,

Hal "Skinny" Brown, Art Del Duca, and Tran. Sick's memoir dealt extensively with Hornsby's managerial stint and bad temperament.

When reached in Indiana, Rivera was not inclined to address the well-documented misbehavior that had left him incarcerated more than once in other cities, but his former Rainiers teammates Earl Averill, Rocky Krsnich, Del Duca, and Grissom, plus one-time batboy Pat Patrick, offered telling details about this complicated man. Included in their stories was the disturbing report, confirmed several times, of the locker-room argument between Rivera and catcher Joe Montalvo in which Montalvo threatened his teammate with a knife.

Interviews with former Rainiers Hillis Layne and Artie Wilson provided insight on manager Paul Richards's brief stay, the comedic antics of Bill Schuster, and the eradication of the franchise's color line.

Chapter 9

This chapter was built around the triumphant return of Hutchinson to Seattle as a pennant-winning manager. Information preceding and encompassing Hutchinson's 1955 season with the Rainiers came from interviews with Tommy Byrne, Larry Jansen, Howie Judson, Lou Kretlow, John Oldham, Pat Patrick, Duane Pillette, Art Schult, and Bill Sears. Jansen, Kretlow, and Byrne since have died. Sick's memoir delved into Hutchinson's return at length, as did the Post-Intelligencer and Seattle Times.

Introduced on these pages was Sears, team publicist for the Rainiers and later the Seattle Pilots, and an invaluable resource for this book. He recreated past conversations with great certainty, including a talk he had with GM Dewey Soriano and manager Jerry Priddy about the initial reaction to softball pitcher Bob Fesler trying his hand at baseball.

Chapter 10

Love and war summed up this chapter. Patrick, the nosy Rainiers batboy and later president of multiple Seattle banks, first told me of the secret getaway apartment in the ballpark; Sears verified the existence of the love nest. So did a handful of sheepish players, though none could recall, or were willing to recall, any specifics about it.

I had to re-interview Judson and Schult after research uncovered their 1956 dugout fight. Neither man had mentioned the incident when originally contacted. Neither man was a big fan of manager Luke Sewell, whose dismissal likely was accelerated by their public squabble. Neither man had spoken to the other since the dustup. Eskenazi provided the rambling letter written by Sewell.

Broadcaster Jeff Heath's ballpark fight that sent his station manager tumbling down stairs was witnessed by Sears, other media members, and fans. The precise wording of Heath's on-air obscenity and apology was provided by several sources, foremost Dille, the local historian.

Chapter 11

A vivid character portrait of Lassen, the beloved Rainiers broadcaster, emerged in interviews with many of his radio and TV peers, a group that included Keith Jackson, O'Mara, Belcher, and Milroy. Rainiers players Johnny O'Brien, Gale Wade, and Vanni; Patrick the bat boy; and fan Addis Gutmann added Lassen details.

Eskenazi provided me with fan mail that came in the form of note cards (solicited by Lassen on air, the cards were mailed to him at the station and read as part of a pregame promotion), and a long letter Lassen wrote in response to one received from Rainiers fan Charles H. Freymueller Jr.

Viewing the critically acclaimed film *The Seattle Rainiers* (Crow and Sadis, 1999) gave me a chance to hear (and later describe) Lassen's melodic radio game broadcasts, and to understand why he was such a fan attraction.

Chapter 12

With Los Angeles and San Francisco getting ready to flee the Pacific Coast League and become big-league cities, Sick dealt more in depth with this subject than any other in the baseball section of his memoir, with his last entries describing how the league split up. What emerges in these pages is that Sick was prepared for the inevitable but was unwilling to let it happen without a struggle, demonstrating the determined businessman in him. Two decades of attendance totals showing the superiority of Sick's Rainiers over its two California rivals exiting the Pacific Coast League were supplied by the *Post-Intelligencer*.

Interviews with Rainiers players Dave Stenhouse, Eddie Basinski, Wills, Pillette, and Wade helped me to illustrate baseball's changing times. The letter in which Wills voiced his displeasure about being shipped from Seattle to Spokane appeared in the *Seattle Times*.

Patrick, the ever-observant batboy, was one of a handful of people allowed in the ballpark when it was locked down for Baylor's special tryout and passed along rare details.

In a lengthy interview, Ron Santo described the summers he

spent as a high school kid living near Sicks' Stadium; his stints as an all-purpose clubhouse attendant and groundskeeper for the Rainiers; his humiliating workout with the Reds; and his transformation into a top baseball prospect.

Chapter 13

I had never heard of Joe Taylor when I started researching this book. I wanted to write Taylor's biography when I got done. What a waste of big-league talent. In interviews players Dick Fitzgerald, O'Brien, Vanni, Wills, and Basinski, plus Metro as the rival Vancouver manager, each described him as a player with unlimited baseball ability and an alcoholic with no will-power whatsoever. O'Brien's account offered an insider's look at the difficulties involved in attempting to sober up Taylor. *Post-Intelligencer* and *Times* reports gave details of Taylor's unusual car accident.

In a revealing interview, former mayor Gordon Clinton explained his lack of political interest in bringing a big-league franchise to Seattle, perhaps the biggest reason the city didn't make the jump when Los Angeles and San Francisco were drawn to baseball's highest level. Interviews with Dave Mann, Stew MacDonald, Mel Parnell, Sal Durante, Larry Ellingsen, Rossi, Ingman, and Jackson helped me further examine the changing times in the Seattle baseball scene.

Chapter 14

Sears, the Rainiers' publicist, provided one of the more poignant moments during my research for this book when he recreated the conversation he had with Hutchinson shortly after the manager learned he had cancer. One got the distinct impression Sears had told that story nonstop since the chance meeting, so vivid was his recollection.

Dick Bee, the Rainiers' final general manager, described the final days of the franchise, as did Vanni and his players Rico Petrocelli, Jim Lonborg, and Averill. Sean Sheehan, Sick's grandson, supplied images of a hospitalized Sick and a decaying Sicks' Stadium.

Newspaper accounts and interviews described the deaths in chronological order of all of the Rainiers' leading characters. I personally attended Vanni's funeral, which provided a proper ending to the book.